The World of the Reformation

The World

of the Reformation

Hans J. Hillerbrand

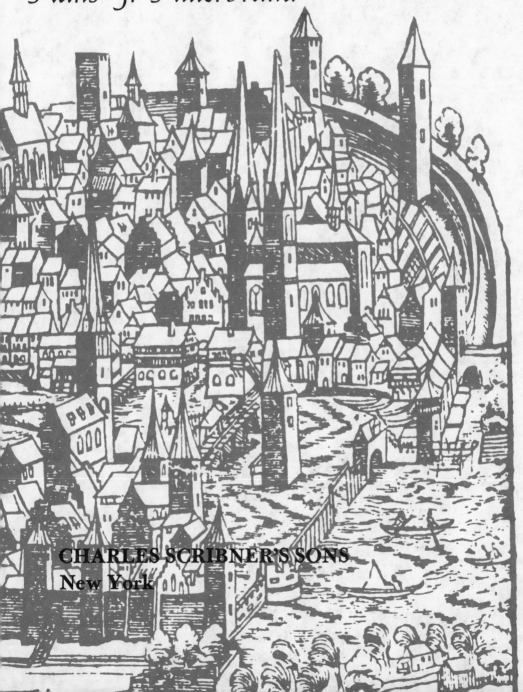

CHARLES SCRIBNER'S SONS
New York

To Wilhelm Pauck
mentor and friend

Contents

Contents

Preface

THIS ACCOUNT OF EUROPEAN SOCIETY IN THE
time of the Reformation of the sixteenth century attempts to do two
things: to sketch an outline of the factual course of events and to put
these events into a larger interpretative frame of reference. My
premises concerning the two objectives are simple and easily stated.
The Reformation was the foremost event engaging European society
in the first part of the sixteenth century. Moreover, I find myself
persuaded that, in its inception and initial thrust, it was a religious
phenomenon, and I must confess that I am inclined to see this
religious element not as an ideological ornamentation of prior socio-
political developments. Having said this, however, I add that in the
Reformation religion related immediately to society: religion and
society interacted by mutual influence. The priority of place is hard
to establish. A purely theological purview, therefore, is in my opinion
as inappropriate as the opposite approach that ignores the theological
and religious forces operative in society. The key word is interaction,
and it was an interaction in which the cause of religion was frequently
lost in the shuffle. I realize that I have dealt lightly with certain topics
and events, notably with political and diplomatic developments.
These *were* important, though I must admit that my attempt to
portray the Reformation as *the* cohesive phenomenon of the early
sixteenth century has relegated them to the background.

This volume has given me an opportunity to present a coherent
view of my understanding of the Reformation. Unable to improve on

my own earlier formulations, I have incorporated certain sections from my book *Christendom Divided*, which is now out of print. Conversations, both direct and indirect, with colleagues and friends have both deepened my understanding of the Reformation and made this a better book. I mention in particular Lewis Spitz, Erik Midelfort, Bernd Moeller, and Egil Grislis, the participants of the New York Reformation Seminar, and my students at The Graduate School and University Center of The City University of New York.

My research assistants Laura Fishman and Jason Berger have aided me at various stages of the preparation of the manuscript. My wife, Bonnie, and my children, Eric, Michael, and Stephan, have so manifested the splendid qualities of support of which most prefaces speak in the final sentence that I, too, must record my public appreciation.

New York   HANS J. HILLERBRAND
May 1973   *The City University of New York*

x

1 The Setting

IN THE FALL OF 1517, WHEN IT ALL BEGAN, nobody in Europe had ever heard of Martin Luther. The titans were Erasmus, Michelangelo, King Henry VIII, and Emperor Maximilian —rather than an unknown professor of theology at a third-rate university in academic "Siberia."

Within three years this was different. All of Europe was beginning to be embroiled in an intense controversy. A movement was beginning to sweep across Germany and, before long, the rest of Europe as well, precipitating one of the most serious crises European society had experienced. That movement, of course, was the Reformation; the "monks' squabble" turned into a revolution.

Before sketching its full course, a pause to analyze society in the early years of the sixteenth century is in order. The reasons are obvious: if society revealed any signs of fateful weaknesses or tensions, if there were telltale signs and symptoms, if the handwriting was on the wall, the task of explaining the upheaval is simplified.

No doubt, the historian of the Reformation is especially prone to paying homage to some form of historic determinism. A survey of early sixteenth century society suggests to him a variety of factors and forces,

1

all of which had the appearance of an irresistible, inevitable thrust for an upheaval. There would most likely have been a Reformation, in other words, even if Luther had died in the cradle. Most historians seem to agree that the cue to what happened after 1517 must be sought in the years before. They have pursued two different approaches, the one "two-cents plain," the other "two-cents fancy."

The one entails the argument that the lines between pre-Reformation society and the Reformation were plain and direct: for example, the immorality of the clergy or humanism created a situation that was as precarious as it was overt. People were consciously alienated, hostile, and dissatisfied; anyone could see that drastic changes were imminent.

The second approach is to see the causes of the religious upheaval not so much in overt matters as in certain fundamental characteristics of society at the time: the "crisis" of the early sixteenth century was structural, existing even though the surface may have been peaceful and tranquil; the worldly cleric, an exception; and ecclesiastical greed, not widespread. Externals notwithstanding, the balance of forces that formed a cohesive mantle over medieval society disappeared. Changing political, economic, and social conditions rendered the place of the medieval church increasingly meaningless and redundant. These developments took place, as often as not, underneath the surface and found few dramatic expressions. The influx of people into towns, for example, meant that a sizable number of men lived "uprooted," as it were, in a new social setting. Unrelated to the traditional guilds, they were particularly open to new ideas, and seemingly predestined to accept the Reformation.

The argument of these pages suggests a different understanding of events. While based hopefully on an adequate analysis of the sources, it presupposes a certain perspective with regard to the historical process itself. Most accounts of the Reformation subtly convey the notion that the state of affairs in the early sixteenth century was akin to an avalanche on its way down the mountain. History, however, rarely moves in so deterministic a fashion. At each particular point in time there are likely to be several options for the future, an openness that eschews determinism. A whole range of forces, all the way from the weather to personal temperament, acts upon the historical situation at a given time, and it is difficult to predict the outcome of events. The historian, who ought not to engage in writing history in the subjunctive, should never forget that numerous "ifs" are strewn, as it were, across the historical landscape, and that any of them might well have found realization and categorically influenced the course of events.

In addition to such general presuppositions having to do with the nature of the historical process, other considerations must be mentioned: the matter of geographic delimitation, for example. Study of the Reformation concerns the state of European society in the early sixteenth century. Geographically, should the purview be restricted to Germany where, after all, the controversy had its beginning; or should the scope be extended to all of Europe? The answer is not automatic. It is both difficult and precarious to categorize Europe as a whole, for in so doing one blithely overlooks the differences existing, for instance between Scotland and Italy, or between Spain and Sweden. Each of these countries, not to mention others, had its own particular propensity, and all generalizations must be modified by numerous exceptions. Especially if such bold slogans as "the impact of the Renaissance," the "rise of cities," the "decline of feudalism," or the "rise of nationalism," to mention but a few, are used, the complexity provided by different places and countries cannot be adequately evaluated.

There is justification for centering the discussion on Germany. The turbulence of the Reformation began there; indeed, it had its most dramatic phase there as well, so that one may make the point that German events constituted the beachhead, so to speak, that made the advances elsewhere in Europe possible. Broadly speaking, the fate of the European Reformation was decided in Germany.

Chronology is no less a problem. The "state of affairs" in 1517 means the sensitivity, outlook, and characteristics of the generation then living. Surely this suggests that evidence from the turn of the century can be included—if a static situation can be assumed from 1500 to 1517—but what about 1480, 1470, or even 1450? Can evidence from those years be included? Probably not; no matter how woeful and eloquent the lamentations at that time, by the turn of the century the situation could well have undergone a change.

An additional difficulty lies in the vagueness of the term "Reformation." Like all historical shorthand appellations, the term combines convenient accuracy with precarious simplification. While generally useful, the difficulties begin when more specificity is desired. "Reformation," after all, can mean many different things: a theological phenomenon, a religious mass movement, a demonstration of power politics, a legal issue. Each of these constitutes a possible definition; but, depending on which is preferred, different facets of the society before the outbreak of the controversy become important. In other words, if the Reformation had little to do with religion but very much with the fact that a few rulers hoped to enlarge the wealth (and power) of the state, then the state of theology on the eve of the Reformation becomes quite irrelevant. Conversely, if the Reformation was in its essence a theological confrontation, then the political facets

3

of pre-Reformation society become peripheral, less significant concerns. In short, when surveying the "setting" or "causes" of the Reformation, the historian must be guided by a clear idea of the movement's meaning.

To put it differently, the historian has two options. He can sketch a bird's-eye picture of European society at the turn of the century, pretending thereby that the Reformation never happened, and make an evaluation of the whole of societal life at a certain point in time. In so doing, a definition of "Reformation," precarious as that is, can be forgone, and society dealt with not in terms of "causes" or even "factors," but rather of the general framework within which the Reformation occurred. On the other hand, the historian may scrutinize those facts that, in his opinion, he can relate meaningfully to the subsequent Reformation. The problem with this is not only that there must be a prior definition of the Reformation, but also that such an approach—which looks with one eye on early sixteenth century society and with the other on the Reformation—tends to present a foreshortened picture of society, focusing only on those facets that became historically significant in terms of the Reformation, ignoring those that did not. This is a perspective cognizant of the outcome, quite ahistorical, of course, but appropriate for the understanding of the sweep of history.

The approach of this study is to seek a middle course. It will do more than select a few facets of pre-Reformation society but will do less than unfold a vast panorama in an attempt to re-create the "spirit" of European society in the early sixteenth century.

Society at that time and place seems to have been reasonably religious. This is a risky judgment, for it raises a rather tricky question, the definition of "religious." Is religiosity measured by indices of formal religious observance, by attendance at mass or reception of the sacraments, by acceptance of dogmatic propositions, or by explicit individual testimonials? Each of these possibilities provides a clue, a hint, a suggestion, but hardly more than that. The fact that some people were lukewarm toward receiving the Sacrament might well mean that they placed greater emphasis on the sermon, and thus were "religious." In addition, the profession of formal theological notions says little about the intensity of conviction. Inner conviction, faith, conscience, and the like are realities far easier claimed than possessed, more sweepingly conjectured than actually ascertained. They pertain to man's innermost being; he seldom wears his convictions on his sleeve, unless he wants to score a point.

There can be little doubt that in the early sixteenth century the subtle mysteries of the official dogma of the church were beyond most of the faithful. Indeed, one is inclined to suggest that theology was as far removed from them as is Einstein's relativity theory for most of us today. Ignorant of most doctrines, people reduced the Catholic faith to its lowest common denominator: a simple religion of rewards and punishments, mingled with vague ideas of God, Jesus, Mary, and the saints. Given the illiteracy of the time, the sophisticated theology of the church was bound to be haphazardly received. Whatever the intensity of the religious conviction of the people, it could not but be thwarted by a lack of familiarity with basic theological assertions.

At the same time, the details of ecclesiastical politics and maneuvering—such as the unsavory activities of the papacy in Rome in the latter part of the fifteenth century or the details of the arrangements for the sale of the special indulgence involving Albert of Hohenzollern that precipitated the Reformation—were beyond the knowledge, interest, and competence of most people. They knew little, if anything, of what was going on in high places, and a blatant instance of clerical immorality in the local setting weighed more heavily than the total of the financial and political involvement of the papacy.

Rome was far away, a fact which proved both blessing and curse. While such distance avoided the likelihood of intimate knowledge, the center of power and final authority appeared distant and removed, and was thus easily blamed for everything from the misdemeanor of the local cleric to the threat of Turkish invasion. Rumors and allegations came easily; facts were few. The disposition to charge local irritants or the imperfections of the universe to a distant "them" probably is a universal one in history; in the early sixteenth century "they" were "Rome."

Such, then, would seem to be the rough contours of religion in the early sixteenth century; it remains to fill in the specifics. There is no evidence to suggest that ecclesiastical conditions on the whole were either better or worse than at an earlier time. The main characteristic of the higher clergy seems to have been involvement in sundry secular pursuits. Since positions of ecclesiastical eminence entailed prestige, money, and frequently even power, the incumbents were often more concerned about such matters than about their spiritual functions. The secular preoccupation of the so-called Renaissance papacy is a matter of record, as are the various financial and political involvements of the episcopacy. In a speech in 1517, the Augsburg bishop Christoph von Stadion bewailed the preoccupation with luxury, attire, and food on the part of his episcopal colleagues. Other late fifteenth century chroniclers report similar weaknesses of the high dignitaries of the church, for example, their preoccupation with hunting, the arts, politics, or high finance. Perhaps this was the outgrowth of their uncommonly high income. Many of the church leaders, especially in

Germany, were also political rulers—the bishops of Würzburg, for example, were also dukes of Franconia—and the disposition to adapt to the life style of their worldly colleagues is understandable.

The lower clergy, the parish priests and the monks and nuns in the monasteries, were a different story. Financially, they were in a most lamentable state, their incomes hardly sufficient for even a modest livelihood. It is not surprising that some of them took to "moonlighting"—some priests actually operated taverns. Their educational background was unpretentious. Most of them never darkened the door of a university, though we must add that the scope of their responsibilities was rather restricted: their principal duties were to celebrate mass, which required nothing more than a rudimentary knowledge of Latin, and to hear confession. For those chores their background was probably sufficient. The literacy of the general populace, especially in rural areas, was also low, so the ill-trained priest fit harmoniously into the larger picture.

The stereotyped characterization of the lower clergy on the eve of the Reformation shows them as not only ignorant, but immoral as well. Volumes have been written about the widespread drunkenness, violations of clerical celibacy, and other assorted moral shortcomings. The noisy criticism of contemporaries depicted each parish house as a den of iniquity, each monastery as a house of ill fame. Such was, for example, the sentiment of the royal visitors to the English monasteries in 1535, who claimed this to be the sad story up and down the land. Specific instances of clerical misdemeanor were easily cited.

The statistical evidence suggests quite a different situation, however. The systematic interrogations of the clergy in the diocese of Lincoln, for example, revealed only an insignificant deviation from the accepted rules. While such evidence must be taken with the proverbial grain of salt, it is all that is available, other than a few scattered, melodramatic *causes célèbres*. The conclusion is that the criticism of contemporaries grossly exaggerated the actual facts. Moreover, as Erasmus illustrates, such criticism frequently came from men with an ax to grind. In all probability, most of the lower clergy, while not well educated and perhaps not even particularly spiritual, performed their tasks with reasonable conscientiousness. Sensitive souls were grieved by every single deviation from the ideals the church professed, but abuse and deviation, although they undoubtedly existed, were anything but widespread, and thus hardly a burning issue.

There is no evidence of any widespread alienation from the church in the decades before the Reformation. To be sure, there is the difficulty of attempting to measure such evasive categories as "spirituality" or "allegiance"; yet the evidence seems to suggest that no marked turnabout occurred in the decades before the Reformation. People were as observant in their Catholic faith as they had always been. A study of Flanders, for example, shows little change in the frequency of the reception of Communion in the course of the fifteenth century, while investigations of England and Germany suggest that bequests for religious causes continued at even a slightly increasing rate until the outbreak of the Reformation.

Some scholars have called attention to the various manifestations of lay religiosity, such as the Brethren of the Common Life in Holland and northwest Germany, the "confraternities of the Rosary," or the "oratories of the divine love," as cases in point. Indeed, the existence of these groups allows us to reconcile otherwise incompatible characteristics: the simultaneous presence of deep piety and ecclesiastical alienation. The argumentation is that people were spiritually inclined, but found their spirituality no longer met by the church and therefore sought (and formed) new structures. Such an argument would be persuasive if continuity could be shown between these pre-Reformation lay groups and the Reformation, in the sense that the former became proponents of the latter; unfortunately, the facts indicate otherwise.

Theologically, the scene was both restive and serene. In several respects the theological discussion elaborated upon assertions made by earlier theologians and, in the process, arrived at increasingly precarious positions. By the end of the fifteenth century the rich complexity of medieval theological discourse had given way to a rather one-sided emphasis on nominalist assertions. This scholastic system, traceable to William of Ockham, stressed the utter omnipotence of God whose commands derive from his will and not his being (if he were so to will, murder would be a good). By the same token, and in unmitigated paradox, theologians just before the Reformation stressed human freedom as the crucial category in theological reflection. Man was not a puppet, without freedom to choose; he was able to act morally, and so salvation was made contingent, to some extent, on his efforts. To be sure, divine grace constituted the primary factor, without which human effort was useless; but man's effort was seen as more important than it had been in previous theological discussion.

Inasmuch as freedom entails responsibility, this theological emphasis is understandable, though it upset the balance characteristic of most medieval theological reflection. Exemplified by Thomas Aquinas, medieval theologians had striven for a balance between God and man. This balance was disrupted, and the theologians moved farther from St. Augustine's view of God as pivotal and central.

A second ingredient in the theological scene must be noted: the discussion concerning the problem of authority in the church. In the course of the fifteenth century, conciliarism, the notion that a general council possessed greater authority than the pope, experienced both a spectacular victory and a devastating defeat, the former at the Council of Constance, where a council healed a schism in the church; the latter in 1460, when Pope Pius II condemned the idea. The issue was by no means dead, however, and by the early sixteenth century the question of the full range of power and authority attributed to the papal office was by no means clear.

Related was the problem of the source of religious authority. Needless to say, Scripture was viewed as containing revealed truth, and its authority was basic. But over the centuries another source of authority had emerged, at first by way of explanation and commentary of biblical truth: church tradition. How Scripture and such tradition were to be related was increasingly viewed in the fifteenth century as a pressing issue. Tradition was seen either as the explanation of scriptural truth, or as autonomous revelation in itself. Theologians provided no common answer, nor could they completely silence the nagging suspicion that Scripture and tradition might possibly be in disagreement.

If such were the focal points of theological dispute preceding the Reformation, there is no evidence of a state of acute tension or unresolved paradox. On the issue of human freedom with respect to salvation the pendulum had swung to one side, and sooner or later had to swing back, for in theology positions tend to move dialectically. Such an adjustment was hardly urgent, however, though it might possibly occur in a gray and distant future.

The Christian humanists, led by Erasmus of Rotterdam, raised other theological issues. Ostensibly loyal to the Catholic church, they contributed their share of criticism of alleged ecclesiastical abuses. The humanists' emphases, concerns, and complaints were many, but they all concurred in their distaste for the traditional methods of theology. The *Letters of Obscure Men* (1515) is a case in point: a biting, satirical attack upon the "obscurantist" scholastic theologians who pondered the number of angels that could dance on the head of a pin or who wondered about the moral implications of eating an egg on a meatless day when discovering, in the process of gulping—alas, too late!—that the chick had already hatched. In addition to their desire to be rid of hair-splitting theological sophistication (which entailed, concomitantly, the importance of moral precepts), they embraced a different method. The humanists preferred a free-flowing exposition to the scholastic method of aridly outlined questions and answers, with form and structure governed by content rather than preconceived categories. Moreover, they stressed the need to go "back to the sources," to

the writers of Christian antiquity, rather than dwell on the pronounce-
ments of the medieval scholastics. Erasmus edited the writings of
Jerome and Cyprian, while his French comrade in arms, Jacques
Lefèvre d'Étaples, preoccupied himself with the writings of St. Paul.

Much of this humanist emphasis was latent and implied rather
than explicit. There was no real clash; the prestigious academic
positions, after all, were occupied by scholastically oriented theologians. But the emphasis was present and, at the turn of the century,
was embraced by an increasing number of intellectuals and theologians. While medieval theology was never fully homogeneous, the
appearance of the Christian humanists added a novel element of
heterogeneity.

The crucial issue is whether there were underlying structural
tensions in the Catholic church on the eve of the Reformation, and
whether the church had lost its hold upon the people. In a way, this
seems to be the consensus of scholarship, Catholic historians arguing
that the overall theological emphasis before the outbreak of the
Reformation was so one-sided (and thus altogether "uncatholic") that
a reaction was inevitable. Other scholars have called attention to
contemporary evidence of disaffection and anticlericalism in the early
sixteenth century. In Germany, secular authorities compiled extensive
lists of grievances against the church. At the Diet of Worms (1521) the
list of these so-called *gravamina* included (with an arrogant repetitive-
ness) no less than 102 specific points, all the way from complaints
about the reservation of certain lawsuits to Rome to the exemption of
clerics from ordinary jurisdiction.

Even if the alleged charges of clerical abuse and corruption are
dismissed as sensation mongering, the fact remains that there were
sundry tensions between church and society. The church had accumu-
lated, over the centuries, a variety of legal and financial prerogatives.
Its clerics were exempt from general judicial procedure, as we have
already noted, and it was entitled to exact various legal fees. In the
beginning most of these prerogatives had a persuasive rationale, but
circumstances had changed. The prerogatives were increasingly felt as
a burden, an unnecessary one; it was not easy to perceive, for example,
the connection between the exemption of the clergy from taxation (in
view of its enormous wealth) and the eternal destiny of the believers'
souls. The tensions between church and society led to constant
attempts by secular authorities to curtail and restrict the place of the
church. The new breed of economic activists and political rulers could
only be frustrated by the restrictions that the formidable presence of
the church imposed. Of course, modifications were made as decades
passed, and by the early sixteenth century much that entrepreneurs
and rulers had wanted was achieved. Thus, interest up to 5 percent

9

was accepted in theory (and much higher interest in practice), while in town and country a great deal of control was exercised by political authorities over the external affairs of the church, a concomitant to the widespread process of governmental administrative consolidation.

Before speaking too easily of a "crisis," a disjointed society, or a time gone awry, it should be remembered that the notion of a golden age in the past, with which the present no longer conforms, is probably common to all generations. Sensitive men agonize over their own time and invoke the picture of a splendid past. This is particularly true in religion, where the real has a way of perpetually falling short of the ideal. The fifteenth and sixteenth centuries were no exception. The question pertinent here is whether a particularly striking sense of urgency existed in the early sixteenth century with respect to the problems, real or alleged, in the church. Antagonism and opposition to the church existed; it is not known whether such sentiment was more or less intense then than it had been fifty or a hundred years earlier.

In sum, then, the picture of the church on the eve of the Reformation was a mixture of tensions and tranquility. There were weaknesses, even abuses, in the church, but the people were, in all probability, as loyal to the church and as pious as they had always been. After all, even the immoral cleric is hardly an argument against the teaching of the church concerning the eternal salvation of one's soul.

With the proverbial insight of hindsight, the historian can detect "causes" or "factors" that subsequently gained significance in the Reformation. But such detection results from knowing the outcome of the story. Fundamentally, early sixteenth century society was in a state of equilibrium. This does not deny the existence of uneasiness, grievances, or even alienation—contemporaries, after all, did not completely manufacture their accusations—but merely places them in perspective.

Life was difficult and few men could enjoy the luxury of reflecting on matters beyond their comprehension and competence. The church continued to provide a solid foundation for their life and daily routine. It offered meaning with the notion of a life beyond; its ritual and splendor encompassed their lives. Of course, a heavy price was often exacted for all this: sundry fiscal obligations, legal curtailments, political impositions. To say, however, that the church had outlived its usefulness or no longer fulfilled its function would be to simplify a complex reality far beyond recognition.

2 The Prelude

Martin Luther

ON 17 JULY 1505, A YOUNG STUDENT KNOCKED at the door of the Augustinian monastery at Erfurt and asked to be admitted as a novice. Such commitment to monastic life occurred countless times in those days and was thus neither spectacular nor unusual. This particular case was noteworthy, for the student was Martin Luther, the man destined not only to become a great theologian but also to precipitate in Western Christendom the great schism we call the Reformation. Within the cloister walls that were to have separated him forever from the world, Luther pondered those thoughts that were to shake the very foundations of that world. His life began when it was to have ended.

Thus, at the beginning of the Reformation of the sixteenth century stands Martin Luther—not the condition of society or the church at the time, not even the state of theology, but this one man. To study the Reformation is like listening to a Wagnerian opera: exciting, tedious, long, involved, and full of pathos. Its leitmotiv is Martin Luther; the Reformation is unthinkable without him. To be sure, there were other factors at work, and the point must be made that but for them Luther would have died an early and ignominious death. His words, no

11

matter how profound, would have been written as on water. He was blessed with high qualities of intellect and charisma. But he was also born at a propitious time. This combination of character and circumstances elevated him to greatness.

He was born in 1483 at Eisleben on the eastern slope of the Harz Mountains in central Germany, the son of a hard-working middle class entrepreneur who was determined to give him the benefits of his newly acquired prosperity. Hans appears in his recollections as a stern and opinionated character, but if the details of the relationship between father and son intimate future significance, they are also quite enigmatic. The evidence available has prompted Erik Erikson, a psychoanalyst, to see the father as a major factor in Martin Luther's personal as well as theological development, suggesting that he pictured God in the same way he saw his father, that his theological problems were, in other words, an extension of his personal ones. This thesis has been widely hailed, though the exuberance of the reviews has generally been in inverse relationship to the reviewer's competence in the field of Reformation studies. The experts, in other words, have been uniformly unpersuaded.

More can be said, however. Surely it must be possible to combine the (healthy) skepticism of the layman for purely psychoanalytic terms such as "genital," "anal," and "oral" with the acknowledgment of some authentic insight into the formation of Martin Luther. It is necessary to understand a great man's childhood and youth, and creative energies are often forged out of the crucible of childhood tensions and stresses. Such exploration indicates that the "young man Luther" lived with a tension. It seems equally clear that he was able to resolve it, and Erikson's suggestion that there was a connection between Luther's paternal and religious problem surely is a viable conjecture.

At this very point a caveat is in order. If Martin Luther's formation is thus understood a bit better, the temptation is to insist that this is the key to the Reformation, the possibility notwithstanding that a similar situation might apply to John Calvin or even Henry VIII. After all, whatever the influence of Hans Luther, there were other events of more formidable historical importance along the way: Charles V and his peripatetic dynastic concern, Frederick the Wise and his protection, the feud between Spain and France, and the dilatory distribution of power in Germany, to name but a few. Martin Luther's personality happened to mesh with these factors; it is a moot question if a different personality encountering the same factors (or the same personality encountering different factors) would have produced a different course of events than the actual one. Conversance with the psychological formation of great men can help us to understand, but hardly to explain. The historian, in short, does well to eschew any monistic interpretive scheme and to adopt a stance that embraces multiple causes.

Luther's childhood and youth seem to have been routine enough for a time when life was as Brueghel's canvases depict it: earthy, hard, exuberant, each day a new struggle of joy and sorrow. Luther's few recollections from his childhood take us into a strange world of credulity. He reports, for example, that a woman at Eisenach gave birth to a mouse and that he never heard any exposition of the Lord's Prayer and the Ten Commandments; otherwise the comments are without worthwhile substance.

In 1501 "Martinus Luther ex Mansfeld" matriculated at the University of Erfurt. He pursued the customary course of study in the liberal arts, and received, probably in 1503, the baccalaureate and in 1505, the master's degree. That summer, in line with his father's wish, he began the study of law, proudly clutching his copy of the *Corpus juris,* the standard text of the law, which his father had bought for him. Less than three months later, however, he entered the monastery. The explanations vary. It is possible that the decision was impulsive, though in later years Luther himself observed that he had entered the monastery in order to obtain "my salvation." But even if we acknowledge that spiritual anxieties prompted Luther's decision, we can allow for catalytic events: the death of a close friend, an injury that might have been fatal, or the realization that his legal studies were an erroneous vocational choice. In his own mind, however, one incident stood out as decisive: the experience of a thunderstorm near Stotternheim that mortally terrified him and brought about his vow to become a monk.

In the fall of 1506 Luther made his monastic profession and for the next twenty years or so he was an Augustinian monk, an unusual one if his own recollection may serve as a trustworthy guide. With scrupulous determination he sought to find the resolution of his spiritual problem. "If ever a monk came to heaven through monkery, it should have been I," he observed on one occasion, and added, "In the monastery I lost both the salvation of my soul and the health of my body." He was overwhelmed with the realization of his sinfulness; he brooded endlessly whether he had done enough penance, prayer, and fasting to be acceptable to God, and always concluded that he had not. If Luther was perturbed because he had committed sins, perhaps of a sexual sort, evidence is completely lacking, and indeed points in the opposite direction: Luther's nagging problem was that despite his proper demeanor he still thought himself unacceptable to God.

At last he found the answer. The sinner is justified before God not by his moral behavior but by something else. He must acknowledge his self-centered sinfulness; thereby he "justifies" God who has called him a sinner and he can claim the forgiveness that God has offered to sinners. Justification takes place by faith, because the sinner appropriates by faith the divine promise of forgiveness as it is found in the Gospel, and also because it is contrary to outward experience: outwardly man remains a sinner, but God has already accepted him. "I felt as though I had been born again and entered the gates of paradise," Luther reported later in life. The key scriptural passage was Rom. 1:17, "For in it the righteousness of God is revealed through faith for faith; as it is written, 'He who through faith is righteous shall live.'" Luther concluded that God's righteousness, as revealed in the Gospels, does not give man what he deserves, but freely offers him forgiveness. As far as he was concerned, his discovery was new, dramatically new, "contrary to the opinion of all the doctors."

Alongside Luther's spiritual pilgrimage took place the more or less routine career of a brilliant monk. He was ordained to the priesthood in 1507, and afterward began formal theological studies, first at Erfurt, then at the recently founded University of Wittenberg. In the fall of 1512 he received the doctorate in theology at Wittenberg and assumed the professorship in biblical studies. Professor Luther was "a man of middle stature," reported a student, "with a voice that combined sharpness in the enunciation of syllables and words and softness in tone. He spoke neither too quickly nor too slowly, but at an even pace, without hesitation and very clearly, and in such fitting order that every part flowed naturally out of what went before."

During the next few years Luther lectured on various biblical books. Though some of his lectures are extant only in the form of student notes (which must be used with caution), they are important evidence of an interesting move from the traditional exegetical scheme of the medieval expositors to a stress of the literal meaning of the text. A collection of ninety-seven theses "against scholastic theology" of September 1517 constituted a public manifesto of his new theological perspective.

An innocuous event suddenly catapulted the unknown professor into the public limelight. Infuriated by certain claims made in the sale of indulgences by the Dominican friar Johann Tetzel, Luther drafted a set of ninety-five theses dealing with the topic of indulgences and planned an academic disputation on the matter. On 31 October he sent a copy of his theses, together with a covering letter, to Archbishop Albert of Mainz, asking him to stop Tetzel's preaching.

The theses had been moderate (certainly in comparison with those of September), calling only for a reinterpretation of a practice that had not as yet been doctrinally defined by the church. What Luther did not know was that he had reached into a hornet's nest: Tetzel was part of an elaborate financial and political scheme that involved the Curia, Archbishop Albert, the banking house of the Fuggers, and even the next German emperor. Luther could not possibly have chosen a more inopportune occasion to express a theological concern. At stake was the jubilee indulgence for the reconstruction of St. Peter's in Rome. It was a worthwhile purpose, though its sale was anything but a success. Virtually all territories in north Germany had prohibited the sale, and one suspects that this indulgence would have fallen into the nescience of history had there not been an unexpected turn of events.

In 1514 Albert of Hohenzollern, twenty-four years old, was elected archbishop of Mainz, after having already been elected the previous year archbishop of Magdeburg and administrator of Halberstadt. Such accumulation of ecclesiastical offices, especially by someone not yet the prescribed age for the episcopacy, violated a provision of Canon Law. After lengthy negotiations with the Curia, Albert agreed to pay a sum to procure a papal dispensation. To make the payment attractive the Curia proposed that the jubilee indulgence should be sold in north Germany with half of the proceeds accruing to Albert and the other half to the Curia. This was a financial transaction of major proportions, and the young archbishop may well have had sleepless nights, though anticipation of the income from his new ecclesiastical benefice, his politically influential stature (as archbishop of Mainz he was also a German elector), and the realization that countless indulgence buyers would assume the major share of his debt must have soothed him.

Luther, of course, knew only about the practical side of the matter: the reports of the activities of Johann Tetzel, the chief salesman of the indulgence in north Germany. When Luther obtained a copy of the *Instructio summaria*, the instructions for the indulgence, he was shocked by its mercenary spirit. His reflection on the place of indulgences in the church resulted in the drafting of the Ninety-five Theses.

Written in Latin, clothed in proper academic form, intricate in theological argumentation, the theses were not intended as a clarion call for an ecclesiastical revolution; they were merely the basis for an academic discussion. "This I presented for debate and did by no means put into emphatic affirmations," he wrote a few months later. Only occasionally were the words those of a man in anger: "Those preach man-made doctrine who assert that, as soon as the coin rings in the coffer, the soul departs from purgatory"; or, "to say that the crucifix erected with the papal coat of arms can do as much as the cross of Christ is blasphemy."

A staunch partisan of Luther wrote many years later that the Ninety-five Theses spread throughout Germany within weeks "as if

angels from heaven themselves had been their messengers." One must
be skeptical about the accuracy of this statement, both because of its
metaphysical implications and its breathless chronology. Luther's
fame (or notoriety) was long in coming. When the year turned, Luther
was still widely unknown and awareness of his theses was restricted to
a small circle of officials and scholars. Their spread was a slow process;
only during the early months of 1518 did they become known to a
wider public.

They also became quite notorious, for upon learning of them
Tetzel launched a vehement, if superficial, counterattack, in which he
asserted that souls were freed more quickly from purgatory than the
falling of a coin (in payment of an indulgence) in the coffer; after all,
the coin required time to fall! By the spring of 1518 a theological
controversy was in the making. Luther contributed to the debate with
his immensely successful *Sermon on Indulgence and Grace*, his first tract in
German, and also published his *Heidelberg Theses*, written for a
disputation in connection with a meeting of the German congregations of the Augustinian order at Heidelberg.

Luther's foremost antagonist proved to be Johann Eck, who was
always ready for a theological fight. Three years younger than Luther,
Eck was a brilliant and widely known scholar. He had jotted down a
few *obelisci*, comments on the Ninety-five Theses, and circulated them
among friends. When Luther saw them, he composed an aggressive
reply, labeled *asterisci*, in which homely comparisons with the animal
kingdom made their entrance into Reformation polemics. Then
Andreas Carlstadt, Luther's senior colleague at Wittenberg, exuberantly joined the controversy. During Luther's Heidelberg sojourn, he
had compiled 379 theses, which he subsequently enlarged to 405, an
exhausting and exhaustive delineation of the new Wittenberg theology. Eck responded with theses of his own, and Carlstadt, unwilling to
let his opponent have the last word, published another set of theses in
late summer. One round of controversy followed another, and with
each round the tone became more bitter and vehement.

Alongside the theological controversy was a second development,
feeble at first, but of incisive and tragic significance in the end: the
official ecclesiastical proceedings against Luther undertaken in Rome.
The controversy at the beginning was not a matter of theological
opinion only, but also an affair of state. There was an ominous
awareness on the part of all that every work was placed on a golden
scale, so to speak, in Rome in order to enforce orthodoxy and suppress
heresy. The first step in this connection had come with surprising
speed. In the middle of December 1517, Archbishop Albert reported
the matter to Rome, asking for the commencement of the *processus
inhibitorus*, the first step in heresy proceedings, against Luther.

In the spring of 1518, proceedings began. A Curial theologian, Sylvester Mazzolini Prierias, was assigned the task of investigating the theological aspects of the case. He hastily composed a treatise, angrily informing his readers that it had kept him from the more serious task of continuing a commentary on St. Thomas Aquinas. Entitled *Against the Presumptuous Theses of Martin Luther Concerning the Power of the Pope*, the treatise smacked of superficiality and was characterized by the studied boredom of a renowned scholar taking on a fledgling from the provinces. It was basically a defense of authority, but it failed to distinguish between normative dogma, where church authority had to be accepted, and theological opinions, where freedom of discussion was permissible.

Early in August 1518 Luther was commanded to appear in Rome as a reputed heretic, and toward the end of that month the head of the Saxon province of the Augustinian order and Cardinal Thomas de Vio, known as Cajetan, the papal legate in Germany, were instructed to have Luther apprehended as a notorious heretic. Pope Leo X wrote Elector Frederick of Saxony to be mindful of the faith of his fathers and to turn the "son of iniquity" over to the ecclesiastical authorities. The wheels of ecclesiastical machinery had moved swiftly and with determination. The case of Martin Luther, Augustinian monk and professor of theology, writer of bold theological theses—possibly a heretic—was about to be closed.

At this juncture extraneous considerations impinged upon the course of theological and ecclesiastical events. A German diet was in session in Augsburg. Emperor Maximilian I was preoccupied with the question of his succession, but the most important matter before the German Estates was the financing of a military campaign against the Turks. The papacy was greatly interested in this venture and its concern was underscored by the presence of Cardinal Cajetan as papal legate. The estates were reluctant to shoulder the necessary tax. They agreed that such a campaign was an honorable matter and a Christian responsibility, but insisted that the mood among the people did not allow for levying a new tax. They called attention to the widespread complaint about money already contributed to various worthy causes and, for good measure, added a long list of grievances against Rome that should be alleviated, such as the appointment of foreigners to ecclesiastical posts in Germany.

This was the setting for the next phase of Luther's case. He had appealed to his elector to secure a hearing in Germany, and the active interest of Elector Frederick caused the matter to take a different turn. Frederick supported Luther's request and received Cajetan's concession that Luther be examined at Augsburg.

The Catholic church was represented there by Cardinal Cajetan.

17

One of his early biographers related his mother's dream that St. Thomas Aquinas himself taught her son and carried him to heaven. Such pious anticipation may have guided the childhood and youth of her son, who could soon boast of a brilliant ecclesiastical and theological career. He was general of the Dominican order and one of the most learned men of the Curia. Indeed, his nine-volume commentary on St. Thomas's *Summa Theologica* continues to this day as an impressive exposition of the magnum opus of the Angelic Doctor. Cajetan's legatine assignment to Germany was to influence the German Estates to a vigorous suppression of the Hussites and a war against the Turks, while keeping a watchful eye on the paramount political issue in Germany: the question of the succession of the ailing Emperor Maximilian whose demise was imminent. Elector Frederick's request to have Luther examined in Augsburg was bound to fall on fertile ground: as German elector, Frederick occupied an important role, and the church, vitally interested in the new emperor, could hardly afford to slight him.

Luther and Cajetan met three times at Augsburg. Their meetings ranged through the whole diapason of politeness, subtle argumentation, theological discussion, and explosive anger. Neither was impressed by the other. Cajetan thought Luther an obstinate and uncouth monk, with "ominous eyes and wondrous fantasies in his head," who did not revoke because of fear of personal shame rather than because of his conviction. Luther, on the other hand, held that Cajetan "possibly might be a famous Thomist, but he is an evasive, obscure, and unintelligible theologian and Christian."

At the end of their third meeting Cajetan dismissed Luther with the exasperated comment that he need not return unless he was ready to recant. Luther thereupon appealed to "a not-well-informed pope so that he be better informed," explaining that ill health, poverty, and the threat of sword and poison made his journey to Rome impossible. He volunteered not to write anything against Scripture, the Fathers, and Canon Law, and then fled from Augsburg. There was good reason for his nervousness. Papal instructions of the end of August had empowered Cajetan to have Luther apprehended and sent to Rome. Back in Wittenberg, Luther published an account of his conversation with Cajetan and drew up an appeal to a general council. Then he settled back into academic routine to await the future with his belongings packed, ready to flee Wittenberg at a moment's notice.

At this point Karl von Miltitz, a young Saxon nobleman and papal chamberlain, appeared. He had been entrusted with the delivery of the Golden Rose, a papal decoration, and special indulgences for the Wittenberg Castle church to Elector Frederick. He was not officially involved in the controversy; nevertheless, he tried to resolve it. His efforts failed, and compared with the increasingly complex interweaving of ecclesiastic and political scheming, this one-man tour de force possessed only peripheral significance. Yet von Miltitz was one of the few men who had a realistic notion of how the controversy might be resolved. His plan was to impose silence on both sides and reduce the matter to a purely academic controversy.

After his meeting with von Miltitz at Altenburg early in January 1519, Luther wrote the pope a letter in which his deep religious concern, his awareness of the problems and anxieties caused by his teaching, and his desire to find an acceptable solution found graphic expression. Luther declared himself willing to be silent, if his opponents were silent, and to write a treatise exhorting everyone to honor the church. Clearly, Luther was not a revolutionary, and at Altenburg he gave evidence that he would respond to conciliatory gestures. Still, the agreement came to naught, and in the annals of Reformation history the encounter with von Miltitz is only a fleeting and even comic interlude in the swiftly moving course of events.

A disputation between Eck, Carlstadt, and Luther took place at Leipzig in June 1519. A high mass and academic convocation formally opened the debate on 27 June. For those who delighted in the splendor of academic festivities, the day must have been memorable. An academician delivered an oration, a two-hour exercise that pompously belabored the obvious. He covered the range of history as well as of religion, and spoke of the great debates of the past and of the need for truth and modesty. Duke George of Saxony expressed surprise that theologians were so godless as to need such exhortations. The debate itself began inauspiciously. Carlstadt, who had insisted upon debating first, cut a poor figure beside the eloquent and flamboyant Eck, who cited his authorities, several at one time, from memory (whether accurately or inaccurately proved to be a contested question), whereas Carlstadt had to look up his citations, causing tedious delays. Both Eck and Carlstadt succeeded in obtaining minor concessions from one another, but on the whole the interchange, though profound, was listless. During Luther's encounter with Eck the discussion shifted to the question of papal supremacy, and Eck at once charged Luther with Hussite heresy. This sent chills up and down the spines of those who heard it, for the University at Leipzig had been founded by German emigrants leaving Prague in opposition to Hussitism. Luther issued an emphatic denial, adding he did not care about what Hus had or had not taught. Later in the debate, however, he remarked that not all of Hus's views had been heretical; some had been Christian, such as his assertion that there is one holy Christian church.

Again and again Eck accused Luther of being a Hussite, with

Luther each time asking Eck to tell him what was wrong with the statement that there is one holy Christian church. In exasperation, Luther finally said that the condemnation of some statements of Hus at Constance showed that councils, too, can be in error. Upon hearing Luther's words, Duke George burst out "I'll be damned!" and walked out of the room; he, for one, recognized the implications of Luther's words.

The two men debated for several days about assorted theological topics. To everybody's relief, one suspects, the debate was concluded on 15 July. The universities at Erfurt and Paris had been asked to render a decision—the debate had been an academic affair, a scholarly exchange. But word about it spread even in the vernacular, so that instead of remaining an esoteric affair among professionals the Leipzig disputation became a widely known event that symbolized Luther's defiant rejection of ecclesiastical authority. In actual fact, however, Luther had tempered his rejection of councils with a crucial qualification—"in matters not[!] *de fide*"—but it was lost in the shuffle.

All this time, the theological controversy had been overshadowed by political developments. Emperor Maximilian had died, not unexpectedly, in January 1519, and the powerful in Europe began to involve themselves in the election of his successor. Formally the election lay in the hands of the seven German electors, but in reality it was the *cause célèbre* of European politics during the first six months of 1519. Four candidates were mentioned at one time or another: Henry VIII, Frederick of Saxony, Francis I, and Charles I; but only the latter two were serious contenders. The most obvious candidate was Charles, a young man eighteen years old who had never been in Germany and could not speak German. As grandson of Maximilian he possessed a nominal claim, and indeed his grandfather had almost succeeded in formalizing his succession before his death. Charles ruled Spain and the Hapsburg territories—the Netherlands, Burgundy, and Austria—and the imperial crown seemed to be a means of consolidating these geographically heterogeneous possessions. The other serious candidate, Francis I of France, was bound to enter the race if for no other reason than to keep the prize from Charles who, as German emperor, threatened to control lands along virtually all of the French border.

German nationalism, antipathy toward the French, and warm memories of Emperor Maximilian became important elements as the election approached. But in the end, it became a financial transaction with the prize going to the higher bidder. The sums expended by Charles and Francis staggered the imagination: the Spaniard's figures were more impressive and, in the end, persuasive.

Charles's election was unanimous. An election agreement specified the relationship between the emperor and the territorial rulers: imperial offices were to be occupied only by Germans; the German language was to be used exclusively in official matters; all diets were to be held in Germany; no foreign soldiers were to be brought to Germany; no one should be outlawed without a hearing. A *Reichsregiment*, imperial regiment, was to be established to administer imperial affairs during the emperor's absence from Germany, though the exact nature of this institution was left to subsequent agreement. The German people hailed the new emperor enthusiastically. Poems, sermons, and odes sang his virtues. It was like a spring morning, with signs of budding and flourishing everywhere; the German people looked forward eagerly to Charles's rule. Luther remarked in his *Open Letter to the Christian Nobility* that "God has given us a young, noble blood to be our head and thereby awakened many hearts to great and good hopes." Soon these "great and good hopes" vanished.

The Wild Boar in the Vineyard

IN THE FALL OF 1519 THE ECCLESIASTICAL proceedings against Luther, slowed down by the imperial election, received new stimulus. Johann Eck had sent pessimistic prophecies about the spread of Luther's ideas to Rome. His gloomy picture incited action.

In February 1520, a papal commission hastily condemned several of Luther's teachings whereupon some members of the Curia counseled more extensive deliberations. Consequently, another commission, comprised of the heads of several monastic orders, was appointed. The commission rendered the surprisingly mild verdict that some of Luther's propositions were erroneous and a few were heretical; they were mainly "scandalous and offensive to pious ears." Then Johann Eck appeared in Rome and poured oil on the fire. "It was appropriate that I came to Rome at this time," he wrote a friend, "for no one else was sufficiently familiar with Luther's errors." He made sure that such ignorance was promptly dispelled. New deliberations resulted in the papal bull *Exsurge Domine*, promulgated on 15 June 1520, which rejected forty-one propositions culled from Luther's writings. This bull is known as are few items in Reformation history, notably for the picturesque, if biblical, flavor of the language: Luther was "the wild boar which has invaded the Lord's vineyard"; Christ, St. Peter, St. Paul, the apostles, the saints, indeed the entire church, were to arise and defend their cause against his onslaught. The bull described

21

Luther's past history, called his forty-one condemned propositions "heretical, offensive, erroneous, objectionable to pious ears, misleading to simple minds, and contrary to Catholic teaching," and bewailed his stubborn refusal to recant. Like all heretics, Luther scoffed at the scriptural interpretation of the church and substituted views of his own. He was given sixty days during which to recant; otherwise he and his supporters were to be declared heretics.

Exsurge Domine is a dubious summary of Luther's teaching. It is true that most of the forty-one condemned sentences can be found in Luther's writings, but a curious procedure characterizes the quotations. Thus, the bull compressed into a single sentence what Luther wrote at different places on a given page. In one instance Luther merely cited the opinion of others, and in another he only expressed his hope about a general council. If Luther's teaching were extant only in the form provided by the bull, we would be sorely misled. Some of the condemned propositions dealt with peripheral points, such as, "The spiritual and temporal rulers would be well advised to do away with begging," or "The burning of heretics is against the Holy Spirit." There were also outright contradictions. At one place the bull stated that all of Luther's writings were to be burned; at another, only those containing any of the forty-one condemned errors. In short, the bull seemed to give little evidence of a willingness to take Luther seriously. Those familiar with his writings (above all, of course, Luther himself) were bound to observe that they had been neither seriously considered nor fully understood. Far from clarifying the situation, the bull intensified the uncertainty, and many people became obsessed with the notion that Luther had not been fairly treated. Ever more loudly the demand was made that Luther should receive a "real" hearing.

On 3 January the bull *Decet Romanum pontificem* was promulgated. Since Luther had not recanted his erroneous views, he was excommunicated. The church had spoken. The next step was to seek the cooperation of the secular authorities to execute the ecclesiastical verdict, but once again alien considerations encroached upon the case. Emperor Charles V asserted that he would gladly give his life for the church, but recognized that the resolution of the matter depended on more than his sentiment. His election agreement had stipulated that no one should be outlawed without a proper hearing. Many thought that Luther had not received such a hearing. Those who yearned for ecclesiastical reform felt that Luther's plea, despite its vehemence, deserved more careful consideration than it had been afforded. The German nationalists resented the Curial condemnation as foreign intrusion, while some territorial rulers saw unilateral imperial action against Luther as a fateful step in the direction of increased imperial autocracy. In short, for a variety of reasons people in Germany were unhappy with the resolution of Luther's case. The suggestions of what to do varied. One proposal was that he should receive a hearing, though the details, the form of such a hearing and who should conduct it, were nebulous. Increasingly the recommendation gained acceptance that Luther should appear before the forthcoming German Diet.

The papal nuncio Aleander emphatically insisted that a condemned heretic could not receive a hearing and that a mandate against Luther should be issued at once. The emperor shared Aleander's sentiment for prompt action, but for diplomatic reasons he explored alternate means that would achieve the same end. The emperor's chancellor Gattinara urged him repeatedly not to issue a mandate against Luther without prior consultation of the German Estates. The realization that the emperor needed the estates for future support influenced Gattinara. In February the estates refused to pass a bill suppressing Luther's writings and demanded, in view of the restlessness of the common people, that Luther should be cited before the diet "to the benefit and advantage of the entire German nation, the Holy Roman Empire, our Christian faith, and all Estates." At this juncture Charles recognized that the sentiment prevailing among the estates made Luther's citation the only practicable option. Though some had bitterly opposed it, in the end everybody gained by it. The emperor conformed to the stipulation of his election agreement; Elector Frederick demonstrated his continued interest in his professor; the territorial rulers asserted their autonomy; and the humanists and others desiring reform of the church could assure themselves that the church had not had the final word. Even Aleander must have recognized that Luther's coming was in the ecclesiastical interest: his revocation might resolve the whole controversy, whereas his condemnation by the diet, in case he did not revoke, would put the blame on the Germans rather than on the Curia.

Luther's journey to Worms turned into a march of triumph. Wherever he paused along his route he was feted at banquets and toasted with wine. He was warned that he would be burned to ashes, as had been done with Hus at Constance. "We will come to Worms," retorted Luther, "in spite of all the gates of hell," a phrase which he afterward changed into the more picturesque statement "even if there were as many devils to spring upon me as there are tiles on the roofs."

On 17 April 1521, shortly after four o'clock in the afternoon, came the confrontation: the monk and the emperor, the dissenter and the ruler of the empire. Seeing Luther escorted into the hall, Charles remarked that this man would never turn him into a heretic. Luther was told that he had been cited for two reasons: to acknowledge the books placed on a table as his own and to repudiate their content.

Luther acknowledged himself as the author of the books, but "in a very soft voice" requested time to ponder his answer to the second question. This caused consternation, but after a brief consultation Luther was given twenty-four hours, after which he was to state his answer.

On the following day he appeared once more before the dignitaries of the empire. It was late afternoon, darkness engulfed the room, and the wavering light of the torches added to the dramatic mood. Luther had overcome his timidity of the previous day. His writings fell into three groups, he stated. Some dealt with faith and morals, some with papal tyranny, some were written against literary opponents. At times he had been vehement in tone, more vehement than became a Christian; for this he apologized. But revoke? If he were convinced by scriptural texts he would do so and be the first to burn his own books. He was told that his answer had not been clear enough. Luther's response has made history: "Since your majesty and your lords demand a simple answer, I shall give one without horns and teeth. Unless I am convinced by the testimony of Scripture and evident reasoning I am convinced by the Sacred Scripture I have cited—for I believe neither solely the pope nor the councils, for it is evident that they have erred often and contradict one another. My conscience is captured by the Word of God. Thus I cannot and will not revoke, since to act against one's conscience is neither safe nor honest." The official retorted that Luther should forget about his conscience; he could never prove that councils had erred. Luther insisted that he could, but at this point the emperor interjected that enough had been said, and Luther was escorted from the hall. Aleander reported to Rome that Luther, when leaving, raised his arms "as is the custom of German soldiers when they rejoice over a good hit."

The following day Charles asked a group of territorial rulers for their opinion in the matter. When they expressed the need for further reflection, he told them that he for one did not need to ponder his position. His ancestors, he said, had been faithful sons of the Catholic church and had bequeathed their faith to him. A single monk had set his own opinion above the consensus taken by the church for more than 1,000 years. "I am therefore determined to use all my dominions, possessions, and friends, my body and blood, my life and soul to settle this matter." This principle was to guide Charles's German policies until the day of his abdication thirty-five years later; it proved to be his destiny. Indeed, when speaking to the members of the Spanish *consejo real* and *consejo de estade* a few years later, Charles remarked that while future historians would note the outbreak of the Lutheran heresy during his reign, they would also acknowledge that it was

24

"extinguished through my help and eagerness." Charles abhorred heresy, and at Worms set out to suppress it.

When Charles demanded the concurrence of the estates, he found them reluctant. They suggested that further conversations be held with Luther since he had not been told his specific errors. Luther had expressed his willingness to be shown his errors and this should be done. The emperor agreed. In subsequent negotiations Luther was told that he was dividing the Christian church; that pious men had read the Gospel before him and had not broken with the church; that, by not revoking, the good that he had written would also be condemned. But Luther insisted that his scriptural interpretation was correct and declared that he could accept a decision of a general council only if it agreed with the Word of God. Obviously, the situation was hopeless. When Luther was finally asked, in exasperation, how the matter was to be resolved, he responded with the elusive scriptural passage: "If it is a work of men, it will perish; is it from God, ye will not quench it." On his way back to Wittenberg Luther was captured by Frederick's orders and secretively taken to Wartburg Castle, where he was to spend ten months.

Frederick's action had come in time. On 8 May the emperor ordered an edict against Luther, drawn up by Aleander several days earlier, to be put into proper legal form. Four days later he was ready to sign, with pen in hand, when he decided to take counsel once more with the estates in order to gain their approval. The diet had adjourned and many of the rulers had departed from Worms; yet this bit of unfinished business remained. Finally, on 25 May, Elector Joachim of Brandenburg assured the emperor of the consent of the estates, whereupon Charles signed the edict of 8 May. It enumerated Luther's errors in line with *Exsurge Domine*. Luther and his supporters were declared political outlaws, and his books were to be burned. This edict proved to be an ambiguous matter (rather like the bull *Exsurge Domine*), for doubts about its legality were raised at once. Indeed, this dubious legality may well have constituted a major factor in its practical insignificance in the subsequent course of events. The edict was issued after the adjournment of the diet and the phrase "with the unanimous counsel and will of the electors, rulers, and estates" was plainly inaccurate. Most of the rulers, such as Frederick of Saxony, had left Worms by the middle of May. The authority of the emperor stood behind the document, nothing more. Before Luther came to Worms the estates had assured the emperor that he could act if Luther did not revoke; this was an important consideration for him, and, indeed, his justification for what appeared to be unilateral action. But what Charles had conveniently overlooked was that during the

25

negotiations in May the estates had clearly reversed their earlier sentiment. It was an open question if Charles had the authority to proceed unilaterally. Moreover, since the signature of the imperial chancellor, Albert of Mainz, was lacking, the edict was of dubious legality if taken as imperial law. If, on the other hand, the edict were considered an imperial mandate, its applicability was definitely restricted. In short, a fateful uncertainty prevailed.

With the edict the curtain fell on what should have been the final act of the drama of Martin Luther. Surely, most of his contemporaries thought this was the end; but it was not, and from the vantage point of subsequent events the reason is not difficult to discern. None of Luther's opponents recognized the vitality and explosive exuberance of his teaching. Nor did they sense that the situation called for new solutions. They all tried—Charles, Gattinara, Aleander, and the others—but they all failed to sense the profundity of the hour.

3 The Beginning

The Reformation: A Matter of Definition

THE HISTORIAN, WHO SUPPOSEDLY KNOWS everything—well, almost everything—so much better than contemporaries did, generally compresses the complex course of events that commenced in 1517 and terminated around the middle of the century into the single appellation "Reformation." In doing so, he follows a lengthy historical precedent, for the label has its own historical vindication: that is the way many people in the sixteenth century experienced the events and many people in subsequent generations described them.

There are problems with the term "Reformation," its usefulness as a historical shorthand notwithstanding. These have to do with the complexity of events. It is tempting to view events too closely from the perspective of the eventual outcome—to see the beginnings in terms of the ending, drawing a consistent course from the beginning to the end. Such a view runs the risk of ignoring the open-ended dynamic of the several stages along the way (especially of the situation before the outbreak of the controversy) and of insisting that the character of events at any stage was such as to allow the same label of "Reformation." Differentiation surely must be made. It might be well that for reasons of chronology we do not speak of a "single" Reformation but rather distinguish various aspects. A precise definition of the Reformation entails a chronological schematization that recognizes that events in 1517 had a different character from those of twenty, or even ten, years later. At the beginning was a controversy surrounding a single man, Martin Luther, a squabble among monks, the theological hairsplitting of the sort that had made the theologians experts in determining the number of angels on the head of the pin. This controversy quickly attained notoriety. The reasons had to do with neither the seriousness of the debated issue nor even with the desolate state of the time, but rather with elements of personal jealousy and jurisdictional disputes.

At the time of Luther's formal censure by church and state, the character of events underwent a change. The Luther affair increasingly became a broadly based movement for spiritual edification and reform. No longer did it concern merely one individual. Supporters appeared, men and women who had read Luther's pamphlets, heard his message, and somehow or other came under its sway. Others, who had their own pet peeves and grievances, felt that the time had come to express them and stepped forward to do so.

A movement appeared, vague, undefined, heterogeneous, and unstructured. Its composition was as elusive as its program. Concerned about religious matters, it was not devoid of economic and political notions, as the freewheeling pamphleteering of Ulrich von Hutten or Eberlin von Günzburg suggests. The religious aspirations were many, though they, too, were vague and inchoate. While to echo Luther's cause was to support a man who was both a declared heretic and political outlaw, people seemed able to reconcile their endorsement with allegiance to the Catholic church.

Contemporaries spoke of the adherents of the movement as "Martinians" or "Lutherans." In its character, it was a revival phenomenon. Even as it lacked clear theological assertions it possessed no organizational structure or cohesiveness. Pamphleteers and spokesmen propounded a vague vision of a new gospel. In various towns ministers proclaimed such notions, Zwingli in Zurich, Andreas Osiander in Nuremberg, Rhegius in Augsburg. They were convinced that they had discovered the true gospel.

The new proclamation encountered coolness and hostility from the ecclesiastical and political authorities. Tensions arose, confrontations occurred, mandates were passed, and persecution commenced. Such events took place both on the local level, and on the larger scale of the empire, where diet upon diet sought to resolve the twin issues of ecclesiastical reform and Martin Luther.

At this point in the course of events, two new elements appeared.

One was the awareness that some of the new theological and religious propositions required practical changes and alterations. If monastic vows were unbiblical, something had to be done about the institution of monasticism, the ubiquitous monasteries and nunneries in town and country. If the theological basis of the mass was called into question, its celebration had to be discontinued, or at least modified. This awareness of practical consequences precipitated disagreement about the strategy to be followed: whether the necessary changes were few or comprehensive, whether they should be undertaken immediately or some time in the future.

The second element was the increasing theological sophistication among the "Lutherans." In actual fact, of course, their homogeneity during the controversy had been more ideal than real; they were muddled by generalizations. As time passed the divergence of positions became more evident. Disagreements arose over the theological ramifications of the "Lutheran" movement and dominated the scene.

Different partisans of Luther's cause, in other words, had different ideas of the nature of the new faith. Their disagreements were intense, an indication of the depth of emotional and existential engagement. Indeed, the clash among the various "reforming" factions became as vehement as that between the reformers and Catholics. The Reformation became a house divided. A loss of inner strength and resilience was the consequence. When, in the years after 1525, the great decisions affecting the future of the Reformation movement were made in the councils of state, Luther and Zwingli were preoccupied with their bitter feud over the interpretation of the Lord's Supper.

The outward manifestation of these disagreements and feuds was the emergence of several theological-ecclesiastical factions for which old labels no longer sufficed; new ones became necessary. As a result, the term "Lutheran" underwent change and refinement; it became specific, exclusive, detailed. Moreover, new labels appeared, such as "Zwinglian," "Anabaptist," and "Calvinist." Opposition to Rome no longer sufficed as a mark of distinction. The hallmark of each group became the uniqueness vis-à-vis the other Protestant groupings. Thus, a fourth and final phase in the pattern of the Reformation consisted in the formation of new ecclesiastical bodies. This was both a theological and organizational event—theological because it involved a clearer understanding of the doctrines involved, organizational because it meant the formation of new ecclesiastical structures. Internal clarification and consolidation of the change were necessary. This was where the government authorities—the lawyers, city councils, rulers, counselors—came in. Their concurrence afforded the new faith its structural consolidation, sometimes for religious, sometimes for nonreligious, reasons.

Alongside this chronological scheme must be placed another important way of ordering the complex reality labeled "Reformation." In a way, it is implied in the chronological scheme, though it possesses its own separate viability. We should distinguish between three different facets of the "Reformation": the "spiritual" (or "religious"), the "theological," and the "political." These three Reformations flowed into each other as hues in a watercolor; yet they may be distinguished.

The "spiritual" Reformation deserves priority of time and significance. That was what the early controversy was all about: a concern to have religion taken seriously. This was Luther's plea which was echoed a thousandfold by his contemporaries. The early reformers propounded a spirituality, proposals for a manner of Christian living. They expressed concern for the devotional life, prayer, and worship. At issue in the numerous pamphlets was not the "doing" of good works but religion.

The "theological" Reformation, in turn, is the one so well known and customarily elaborated. It entailed the sophisticated and creative reformulation of the propositional truths of the Christian religion, the notions concerning man and God, sin and redemption. Luther propounded them in his academic lectures and theological treatises—his tract on the *Babylonian Captivity of the Church*, for example, or his *Bondage of the Will*, or his several tracts on Communion. John Calvin labored endlessly, so it seemed, over his *Institutes of the Christian Religion*, an architectonic work of impressive grandeur. Richard Hooker, the Anglican divine, wrote his *Laws of Ecclesiastical Polity*, of similarly majestic sweep. More works of a similar sort could be added; all of them had in common that they analyzed theological issues and offered answers. The battlefield was dominated by the professionals; the language they used was Latin, the argumentation, technical. The common people (whose role in the course of events is enigmatic) probably could not have cared less.

Finally, there was the "political" Reformation: the involvement of religion, either as spirituality, theological system, or ecclesiastical institution, in the machinations of power politics. Even a cursory glance at events in the sixteenth century suggests that frequently the sacred was but a means toward a profane end, even as, quite conversely, the profane was often utilized in order to achieve the sacred. Religion and politics went hand in hand. A subsequent chapter will fully discuss exactly how this occurred. At this juncture we merely note that the cause of religion became inextricably tied to politics. The institutionalization of the Reformation, of which we spoke in connection with the chronological scheme of events, would have been impossible without it.

The Reformation, in short, was a coat of many colors. It took many forms, many meanings, many expressions. It meant different things at different times and to different people. It was simple as well as complex, pure as well as adulterated. In such ability to absorb such diversity of roles and meanings may well lie the secret of its historical success—defined rather modestly as its establishment as an institution and an idea that lasted beyond its own time.

The Message

THE NEWS OF LUTHER'S DISAPPEARANCE SPREAD quickly. Only a few knew what had actually happened, and most people thought of foul play—that Luther had been arrested, perhaps even killed. The artist Albrecht Dürer penned some stirring lines in his diary upon learning of Luther's disappearance. "O God," he wrote, "if Luther is dead, who will henceforth proclaim to us the holy Gospel?"

Emperor Charles observed many years later that it had been a major mistake of his rule to have honored Luther's safe conduct. There is persuasive logic in this reflection: had Luther been apprehended and punished as a heretic, the storm might have yet proved to be a tempest in a teapot. But Charles's comment suggests that even in retrospect he failed to understand what had happened. For all practical purposes it seemed indeed as though Luther were dead. But the issue was not, as Charles assumed, a single monk with heretical ideas, but a phenomenon of increasingly widespread dimensions. Thus, neither the honoring of the safe conduct, nor even Elector Frederick's decision to "kidnap" Luther, was the decisive factor. What did save the Lutheran cause was the increasing enthusiasm for Luther's message. In the months following the diet the *affaire* Luther became the German Reformation. Everywhere people began to take up Luther's slogans and to echo his sentiments. From the pulpits in Saxony, Nuremberg, Augsburg, Ulm, Strassburg, the Netherlands, and East Frisia came the new proclamation and from the pews, a response.

In his *Sermon on Good Works* Luther wrote that he had been accused of "writing only small tracts and German sermons" and retorted, "I am not ashamed that I preached and wrote in German for the unlearned laity—even though I can also do it the other way—for I do believe that if we had heretofore been more concerned about this, Christendom would show more improvement than it does from the

31

high and mighty books and questions typical of the academicians of the universities."

In so writing Luther put forward a definite program for ecclesiastical change that consisted of a direct appeal to the common man in order to alter the ecclesiastical state of Christendom. He himself made the beginning with his *Sermon on Indulgence and Grace* of 1518, which saw no less than twenty-three reprints during the first three years of the controversy. Most of Luther's subsequent tracts, especially those in German, enjoyed a similar popularity. Ten, fifteen, and even twenty reprints of a tract were not at all unusual. In all, one million copies of Luther's tracts may well have been in circulation by 1524.

Between 1518 and 1522 the character of publications in Germany underwent a far-reaching change. The earlier preponderance of secular writings, from astrological prognoses to current events pamphlets, disappeared and religion became the most important subject. The papal nuncio Aleander reported in 1521 that "daily there is a veritable downpour of Lutheran tracts in German and Latin . . . nothing is sold here except the tracts of Luther." He may have overdramatized the issue, but the quantitative evidence clearly demonstrates the impact. Luther's own impressive literary production, now found in no less than 100 volumes of the so-called Weimar edition of his works, was only a part. The other reformers were equally prolific, though not always equally profound. The writings of Philipp Melanchthon, Martin Bucer, and Heinrich Bullinger, to mention but a few, fill several volumes, and one reason for the lack of scholarly editions of the minor reformers is surely that they simply wrote too much. Carlstadt wrote more than fifty tracts, and the edition of Kaspar Schwenkfeld's works comprises nineteen formidable volumes. Such quantity was more the rule than the exception.

In addition there were the even lesser known proponents of Luther's cause, men who had neither the brilliance nor the creativity to become figures of lasting significance. Still, they wrote prolifically on behalf of the Lutheran gospel. Mere numbers reveal how dramatically the quantity of religious publications increased in Germany. In 1517 there were less than twenty; in 1522, approximately a hundred, excluding those of Erasmus and Luther. While one must treat such figures with caution (the size of individual editions, for example, is variable), the basic conclusion seems inevitable. There was great interest in "Lutheran" writings, and not only educated people, but the common people as well, read them extensively.

One of the most significant factors in the spread of the Lutheran gospel was thus a technological development that on the surface had nothing to do with the controversy: the invention of movable type.

32

Without it, the extensive dissemination of religious literature would simply have been impossible, and Luther's movement would have been deprived of its single most effective means of communication and propaganda. Even contemporaries saw the significance, principally Luther himself: he wrote that printing was a divine gift for the spreading of the gospel. John Foxe, the chronicler of the English Reformation, introduced his account of events with a detailed commentary on the invention of printing. As far as he was concerned, it was the *sine qua non* of the success of the Reformation: "To restore the church again by doctrine and learning, it pleased God to open to man the art of printing."

At the same time, publications changed their format. Whereas before the Reformation they had been weighty and voluminous, religious tracts were soon published in pamphlet form: eight, sixteen, perhaps thirty-two pages in length, convenient to use, decorated with woodcuts, low in price, and, most importantly, in the vernacular.

The use of the vernacular to propound religious ideas had no precedent. With rare exceptions the religious and theological literature before the Reformation was in Latin, as were the writings of the humanists, such as *Praise of Folly*, the tract *Julius a coelo exclusus*, and the *Epistolae obscurum virorum*. The medium of the humanists was Latin, the language of the learned. In using it they were concerned about more than the revival of an elegant and versatile language: they expressed a program of reformatory renewal. The appeal for change was addressed to the educated circles and the elite in the hope of influencing them and, through them, society at large. Luther and the reformers, on the other hand, chose to speak to the common people and to persuade them directly. The reformers' publishing effort was a large-scale attempt to confront the common man with the challenges of religion, as Luther had argued in his *Letter to the Christian Nobility*, in which he had written that the laity should help in the reform of the church. The reformers were concerned about the common people— about the artisans and the burghers in the towns, about the peasants in the country. Erasmus had waxed lyrical about his desire to have the peasant recite the words of Sacred Writ behind his plough, but he himself always wrote in Latin. Theretofore neglected and considered incompetent to deal with religious issues, the common man found himself in a different role. He was wooed and exposed to fervent appeals to embrace the new teaching. Nothing is more symptomatic of this temper than the dramatically new position occupied by the lowliest of the lowly, the peasant. Some Lutheran tracts addressed themselves directly to the peasant, depicting him as a wise and perceptive observer of the religious controversy. The tract *Karsthans*, first published in 1521 and reprinted no less than nine times, made a simple peasant the judge of a theological disagreement between Luther and his Catholic opponent, Thomas Murner.

Luther's own *A Simple Way to Pray, Written for a Friend* illustrates his concern for the propagation of the gospel message among the common folk; the "friend" was Luther's barber. Few theologians in Christian history have bothered to expound the Christian faith to their barber or grocer or neighbor. Luther did so, and with flair and feeling. "A competent and conscientious barber must keep this thoughts, mind, and eyes completely on his scissors and the customer's hair. Nor must he forget what he is about—if he talks too much, thinks of other matters, or looks at something else, he is likely to cut his customer's mouth or nose, perhaps even his throat. Anything, if it is to be done well, must be done with complete attention. . . . How much more does prayer call for a single-minded and sole attention, if it is to be good and proper?" These words reveal something of the secret of the appeal of the Reformation.

Luther's linguistic flair, his gift of style, his ability to state a complicated argument simply and succinctly, combining substance with elegance, proved a crucial element in the force of his message. He could on occasion be boring, grind on endlessly, or belabor the obvious, but in general his writings breathe an electrifying spirit. That he was a genius with language can be seen in this description of the burdens (and blessings) of marriage: "The clever harlot, namely natural reason, comes along, looks at marriage, turns up her nose, and says: 'Why should I rock the baby, wash his diapers, change his bed, smell his odor, heal his diaper rash, and do all sorts of such things? It is better to remain single and live a quiet and carefree life.' . . . But what does the Christian faith say? A father opens his eyes, looks at all these lowly, distasteful chores—and knows that they are adorned with divine approval as with precious gold and silver. God, and all his angels, will rejoice, not because diapers are changed, but because it is done in faith."

The tracts sought to accomplish two purposes: to expound, in simple terms, the new understanding of the Christian gospel, and to respond to possible objections from Catholic proponents. This latter purpose explains the widespread popularity of the dialogue, which made it possible to voice certain objections (in as vulnerable a form as possible) to the new teaching, and then to dismiss them with a skillful combination of logic, biblical references, and rhetoric. Today's reader will find these dialogues a bit stilted and less than fully convincing, especially since their outcome is all too obvious from the very first, rather like a minister's sermon on sin. But the sixteenth century man, unaccustomed to reading anything in his own language, found it all both exciting and persuasive.

The dialogue seemed not only to provide for literary flair, but also for a subtle kind of argumentation in that the demurrers of the Catholics were presented, but then eloquently dismissed. These dialogues, which took place between an endless variety of participants, moved all too obviously in the direction of the conversion of those who opposed the Lutheran cause. Such was the case, for example, in the *Dialogue between a Father and His Son* (1523), in which, rather in keeping with the youthful orientation of the Reformation as a whole, the son converts his father to the "true faith."

A variety of other literary forms were used: sermons, open letters, poems. There were also satires, such as *Satan's Declaration of War against Luther*, and parodies, such as an account of Luther's appearance at Worms clad in the form of the Gospel narratives of Jesus's passion.

Another genre of pamphlets purported to speak in the voice of Jesus. N. Hermann's *Mandate of Jesus Christ*, for example, was Jesus's own appeal on behalf of the new interpretation of the Gospels. It was reprinted no less than twelve times in the 1520s (twenty-two times in all in the sixteenth century): "I painted and depicted your foe, who his helpers are, with whom he might fight, wolves in sheep's clothing—ecclesiastical, pious, and work-righteous men, Pharisees, scribes, prelates, cardinals, bishops, officials, canons, deans, abbots, monks, popes: all tempters."

The visual arts also played an important role, from the time the first crude woodcut of Luther made its appearance on the title page of a published sermon of 1519 to Lucas Cranach's drastic, if vulgar, cartoons depicting the "abomination" of the papacy in the 1530s. Luther himself naturally was a favorite object of such artistic endeavors. He was variously depicted with the demeanor of Hercules, or with saintly halo, or in knight's armor; his opponents were transformed into replicas of the lower animal kingdom. The most popular of these pictorial propaganda efforts, the *Passion of Christ and Antichrist*, depicted in parallel woodcuts the contrast between the simplicity of Christ and the splendor of the papacy: Christ washing his disciples' feet, the pope having his feet kissed; Christ wearing a crown of thorns, the pope wearing the tiara.

The enormous quantity makes any generalization about the content of Lutheran tracts difficult, though it is obvious that they were not "Lutheran" in the modern sense of the word. But neither was Luther. His German publications during the first years of the controversy by no means portray the "entire" Luther, as modern scholarship might reconstruct him. There is astoundingly little writing on justification. The overwhelming quantity of Luther's literary pronouncements (his sermons, his exposition of various psalms, his tracts on confession, marital life, and temporal government) propound his religious views, but in very simple form. The "entire" Luther was not known to contemporaries, for his letters, his academic lectures (especially the unpublished early ones), and even his Latin works were hidden in the solitude of Wittenberg, and were known only to a few. Some key themes were sounded and could be heard repeatedly with the simplicity of a Gregorian plainsong: the insistence on the scriptural basis of the Christian faith; the notion that the Bible rather than ecclesiastical tradition must form the ground for religious truth; repudiation of "human traditions," including not only the official pronouncements of the church but also the opinions of scholastic theologians. He insisted on the centrality of faith, the assertion that salvation was not by works, but by faith; not by striving, but by grace. He rejected the complex medieval understanding of the Christian faith in favor of a "simple" faith; indeed, simplicity may well be said to have been Luther's key slogan. Reform was simplification. The restoration of the gospel to its uncorrupted state was to be accomplished by removing the welter of "traditions."

The message of the Gospels, then, was simple; it concerned the life of faith and trust, not of externals and ritual. True religion allowed for no real distinction between clergy and laity, for the superiority of the clerical profession over the lay vocation. The message was easily comprehensible and, moreover, meaningful to all those who for whatever reason had grown discontented and restless with the church and who felt, without ever voicing overt criticism, that true religion must be different. There are numerous testimonials of men and women who acknowledged that the new religious movement had effected a kind of conversion in them. Albrecht Dürer, for example, wrote that Luther "had delivered him from terrible distress," while Thomas Müntzer called him "a lamp of the friends of God."

Luther's message was a call for a deepened spirituality, for truly internal religion in contrast to mere external observance. To be sure, there were theological ramifications (or presuppositions) involved, but one should not confuse the peripheral with the essential. The insistence on explicit theological particularities, even the formulation of new theological systems, came only in subsequent years. The disposition to emphasize the existence and divergence of theological positions was a characteristic of a later phase of the Reformation.

This observation is supported by noting those of Luther's tracts that were most frequently reprinted and thus gave evidence of their popular appeal: *Concerning the Proper Preparation for Dying*; *The Lord's Prayer Expounded for Simple Laymen*; *A Meditation on Christ's Passion*;

Comfort When Facing Grave Temptations; *A Sermon on the Worthy Reception of the Sacrament.* These titles convey the thrust of Luther's concern: the intensification of spirituality, with a minimum of theological discourse. As far as the first phase of the Reformation is concerned, theological differences could be either accentuated or ignored; the course of events shows that both happened.

If so defined, the reform movement in Germany during the early 1520s loses some (though not all) of its uniqueness and can be placed in the larger setting of "evangelical reform" of the late Middle Ages, associated with such names as Erasmus and Lefèvre. Whatever the theological uniqueness of Luther and the Reformation, during the early phase it was hidden underneath more explicit currents.

The Response

WHATEVER MAY BE UNCERTAIN ABOUT LUther's proclamation, there can be little doubt that it called forth a widespread response. One may question the religious sincerity of those who embraced Luther's cause; that people did embrace it, however, cannot be contested. Luther became a reformer and his personal religion became a historical movement because his contemporaries responded to his message.

The question of whether the Lutheran movement was a popular phenomenon must be answered, though put at once into its proper setting. While it is important for understanding the inner momentum of the movement, the matter of the popular dimension says little, if anything, about the reasons for its historical success or failure. The Reformation neither failed nor succeeded in specific situations because it boasted a certain number or percentage of adherents and partisans.

An affirmative response was no easy thing. It meant the repudiation of the church and of one's religious heritage; such happened, not in isolated instances, but thousands of times. Monks who had vowed obedience to the pope became his mortal enemies. Nuns who had pledged themselves to lives of celibacy entered matrimony. Priests who had thought the mass the very heart of the faith denounced it as the abomination of abominations. To do this required courage and the change could hardly have been made in lighthearted fashion. Those who embraced Luther's cause set out to live their religious lives in a strikingly new way.

The nature of this change of loyalties was dramatic. This must not obscure, however, the fact that for a while the whole controversy could be thought to pertain to peripheral matters only, so that the acceptance of this new message did not entail comprehensive repudiation of the Catholic church. Unless this is kept in mind, the course of events between 1521 and 1541 loses its inner rationale; that is, we fail to understand the repeated assertions of contemporaries that the disagreements pertained only to marginal concerns. The situation in the early years of the Reformation was characterized by a certain ambiguity—a repudiation of traditional religious norms that was both courageous and defiant, the insistence that no fundamental issues were at stake. The explanation probably lies in the fact that great importance was attributed to the individual's reorientation, while the implications of such reorientation for ultimate loyalty to the Catholic church were minimized.

The number of Luther's partisans was legion. In 1521 Aleander remarked that nine-tenths of the German people had rallied around Luther and two years later Ferdinand of Austria reported that "Luther's teaching is so firmly embedded in the Empire that among a thousand persons not a single one is completely untouched; it could be hardly worse." While both comments (as well as many others that might be cited) make up in exuberance what they lack in hard facts, they express the atmosphere at the time.

There are additional means to gauge Luther's impact. The free imperial cities in Germany provide persuasive evidence of the popularity of the new message. In most of these cities a measure of democracy prevailed that gave the burghers a voice in the conduct of civic business. Popular agitation was thus bound to find relatively easy expression in the cities, in contrast to the territories where the ruler made all the difference. The acceptance of the Protestant faith in the Swiss cities was delayed where there was little popular participation in municipal affairs. Zurich, with a contingent of artisans on its city council, moved with ease, whereas Berne and Basel, where patrician families dominated the council, required almost a decade to make the change.

The city councils were the retarding forces, while agitation for change came from the burghers and the guilds. Had the issue been one of greater control of ecclesiastical affairs by the secular authorities, the councils would have been anxious to repudiate the ecclesiastical status quo. The fact is that they did not and, on the contrary, strove to thwart the propagation of the new faith. The Protestant cause was initially advocated by those who seemed to derive no obvious political advantage from any change. But to reject one erroneous interpretation must not lead to replacing it with another precarious half-truth. If those who had all along battled with the Catholic church over legal prerogatives did not stand in the forefront of seeking change, the fact remains that those who did advocate change clearly had political goals as well. They were antiestablishment oriented, with respect to politics no less than religion. They were not only concerned with true religion; they wanted political changes in their communities as well.

Why did the people respond positively to the Lutheran proclamation? The possible answers vary. One may cite nonreligious factors: economic greed for wealth of the church and resentment over its legal prerogatives; desire to control all affairs in a given commonwealth, including those of the church. It is noteworthy that at some places the demand for discontinuation of payments to the church and for "evangelical" ministers was made in the same breath as that for greater popular participation in governmental affairs. On the other hand, one may insist on the preeminence of religious concerns and suggest that people found the new faith a persuasive interpretation of biblical religion. The evidence is ambiguous, and the historian will never know what went on in the minds of people in the third decade of the sixteenth century.

In all probability there was no single factor. One must differentiate between the situations prevailing at different times and in different places. In the 1530s, when Protestantism in Germany had attained political strength, political prudence may have made the acceptance of the new faith an understandable decision. In the early 1520s, however, the situation was different: both ecclesiastical and political authorities had condemned Luther and his followers. The emperor had left no doubt about his intention to suppress heresy in the realm. To support Luther meant to support heresy, and heresy had never prevailed. No matter how many hundreds of pamphlets hailed Luther's cause, he was still a heretic against whom the universal church had rendered its verdict.

The historian knows that in the end Luther and the other major reformers died peacefully in bed, and that acceptance of the new faith, far from inescapably entailing loss of property or life, could be economically profitable as well as politically prudent. But all this could not be known in 1523 or 1524, when the prospects seemed rather grim for anyone accepting the new faith. If, in the face of such difficulties, many were willing to do so, genuine religious enthusiasm must have been present.

Support of Luther, or what we have called the embracing of the new faith, did not mean categorical rejection of the Catholic church or a deliberate attempt at a parting of the ways. It was support for, rather than against, something—for deepened spirituality, for example, or a more courageous faith. It was merely a challenge to the church to honor the legitimacy of this concern. Even where individual sentiment jelled into collective agitation for ecclesiastical change, the underlying assumptions were not different. As a rule, the foremost demand of the proponents of the new faith was for "evangelical" preachers. The goal was not to repudiate the church, nor to break away from it, but to make changes within.

The question of possible patterns of "conversion" or "loyalty" remains. It would be splendid if the matter of becoming (or not becoming) a supporter of Luther followed a discernible pattern, so that all people in the cities (or in the country), in the north (or in the south), with education (or without), with wealth (or without) became Lutheran. No such pattern exists or, if it does, it is obscure. A few comments, however, may be made. One pertains to the humanists, from whose ranks had initially come Luther's most ardent supporters. Indeed all of the minor reformers were Erasmian humanists; there can be little doubt that the humanist circle provided the reservoir from which the reform movement drew its adherents. They had wanted the correction of ecclesiastical abuse and a reformed religion. They employed their pens to precipitate it, and at first they gave their vigorous support to Luther. But soon they abhorred Luther's theological reformulation as too radical and too tumultuous. None expressed this sentiment better than Erasmus when he wrote in 1527 "the reformers should have not heedlessly wrecked anything without having something better ready to put in its place. As it is, those who have abandoned the Hours do not pray at all. Those who have put off pharisaical clothing are worse in other matters than they were before. Those who disdain the episcopal regulations do not obey the commandments of God." In the end, humanists could be found on both sides of the issues of the Reformation.

If a goodly number of the humanists remained cool toward Luther and his cause, the universities and the established theologians did even more. The academic community generally remained closed to the new faith. Wittenberg was an exception; at most other universities the reaction of the academicians was uniformly negative. At Leipzig, a phalanx of theologians opposed Luther; at Erfurt, Luther's own alma mater, he had a few supporters, but the eminent members of the faculty did not make his cause their own. Cologne, Ingolstadt, Heidelberg, Freiberg, Tübingen, and Frankfurt likewise remained Catholic.

If the university community showed itself immune to the challenge of the Reformation, the clergy proved a different picture. While the higher clergy generally remained faithful to the Catholic church, the lower clergy joined the Protestant ranks in large numbers. Indeed, the men who first carried the new gospel to success had formerly been Catholic priests and monks. They were the foot soldiers of the Reformation and without them no lasting achievement would have been possible. The persuasiveness of the printed word alone would never have sufficed to effect a socialization of the new faith. They were the "little Luthers" who exposed their congregations to the new proclamation and restructured ecclesiastical life in their communities.

Finally, the common characteristic of the advocates of the new theology was youth. Luther was thirty-four at the outbreak of the controversy, and Huldreich Zwingli just a few months younger; Melanchthon was twenty. Other reformers were equally young: Wenzeslas Link was born in 1483; Friedrich Myconius, in 1491; Jacob Strauss, in 1485; Andreas Osiander, in 1498; Johann Brenz, in 1499; Johann Oecolampadius, in 1482; Martin Bucer, in 1491; Wolfgang Capito, in 1478; Bugenhagen, in 1495; Urban Rhegius, in 1489; Thomas Müntzer, in 1490. Virtually all were young men in their 20s and 30s when the controversy broke out, a fact that helps to explain the vitality of the new faith. The Reformation was a movement of youth.

4 The Confrontation

PROMINENT IN THAT COMPLEX OF FORCES called the Reformation was the clash between the protagonists of two divergent positions. It was a conflict between conservatives and liberals, between those who were convinced that the way of the past was the right one and those who were persuaded that a new way of looking at things was the best. The issues were complex, and the sites of the controversy differed, but examination of the divergence of those who looked forward and those who looked backward offers the best description of the nature of events.

According to the scholarly consensus, this confrontation is evidence for irreconcilable differences between sides. A profound gap is said to have separated the two, and the eventual outcome of the matter, the tearing asunder of the Body Christian, was the inevitable consequence. To be sure, theological as well as ecclesiastical differences existed; they were extensive, and they were real. There was also a host of other factors, nontheological in character but equally important and equally crucial in the unfolding course of events. The Reformation was not merely a testimonial to the persuasiveness of ideas; rather, ideas became flesh in human beings. Their various characteristics, emotions, and polemics had a great deal to do with the course of the Reformation.

Although the controversy started, in a way, as a theological matter, the full grasp of which required not only interest but also sophisticated competence, it ceased almost at once to be solely this. The real arena of the contest became neither the lecture hall nor the study of the academic theologian, but the marketplace, the tavern, the street corner, wherever the common people gathered; the controversy thus involved the laity. This was the result of a deliberate effort on the part of the reformers: the controversy broadened because they engaged in an effort to make it do so. They were determined to take their understanding of the Christian faith to the people and argue their case not merely with their fellow theologians but with common folk as well.

If the reformers simplified the language of religious discourse, they simplified its content as well. In place of the cumbersome system of traditional religion, they offered a dramatically new version of the gospel whose hallmark was simplicity. Thus, the complex web of charitable responsibilities toward one's neighbor—notions that, whatever their theological persuasiveness, had become rigid over the years—was replaced with the notion that only "faith" was necessary as a guide, a faith "active in love."

The simplification of the reformers brought about the easing and even repudiation of many requirements that the church had placed upon the faithful. The medieval practice of religion had been rigid and difficult; the Reformation proclamation simplified it greatly. In his tract *Christian Liberty*, for example, Luther suggested that external practice did not produce Christian righteousness, and then went on to say: "It will not harm the soul if the body is clad in secular dress, if a man dwells in an unconsecrated place, or eats and drinks as other men do, or does not pray aloud or neglects to do certain other things; after all, hypocrites can do all that."

Its simplicity made the message persuasive. This is paradoxical, for the attraction of medieval religion had been its clearly defined and regulated form: men knew what to do, specifically and in detail, in order to attain eternal salvation. The new proclamation, on the other hand, was simple, yet it was also abstract, vague, and uncertain. Faith, as a substitute for clearly prescribed external routine, surely may appear as a less desirable alternative.

The reformers' intention was to enunciate a more rigorous understanding of the Christian faith; the demands of freedom were to take the place of the ease of rigid prescriptions. People must have found the Christian religion simpler in its tenets and easier in its requirements, however. Jakob Burckhardt, the nineteenth century historian, saw this as the common sense explanation for the change of loyalties: "The Reformation must have had an enormous attraction for all those who enjoy not having to do something any longer."

Precisely because the gospel was so simple, it could be understood by the "simple-minded," by the artisan in his shop and by the peasant behind the plow. Erasmus had waxed eloquent about the common man's use of the Scriptures, yet he never wrote in the vernacular. The reformers, however, combined word and deed.

The reformers' proclamation thus introduced an element of egalitarianism into the religious scene. It found expression in a variety of related efforts and practices: the translation of the Bible into the vernacular, for example, or the introduction in 1525 of vernacular hymnals, such as that of the Rostock reformer Joachim Slüter, who noted in the preface that he wanted artisans to understand Scripture.

The approach seemed to imply an anti-intellectual stance. The reformers asserted that those who should know about the authentic understanding of the Christian faith—the clergy, the professors of theology, the learned ones—did not know about it. Their learning had removed them from the truth; it was given to the simple folk to understand the true meaning of faith.

Both church and university had failed to teach the true gospel. "In spiritual matters," Luther remarked, "a child, servant, woman, or layman may as well have the grace of God as an older person, be he even pope or a doctor." His words seemed indicative of an antiauthoritarian sentiment. They were an indictment of the traditional differentiation between the learned and the ignorant. Formal education was not necessary to understand the gospel: "Universities are indeed the ultimate in the synagogue of Satan, in which the rule belongs to those Epicurean swine, the sophistic theologians." While Luther's picturesque language echoed classical antiquity, his sentiments (as well as his antecedents) were plain, a reiteration of the medieval underground of mysticism, which afforded little prominence to learning, even as at the beginning of the sixteenth century many humanists stayed consciously aloof from the academic establishment.

The reformers were not, however, anti-intellectual; they could spin out sophisticated and even scholastic argumentation as well as any of their scholastic peers. But in their controversy with the theological "establishment" antiauthoritarian notions certainly were present. They utilized a new vocabulary. They expressed theology differently, in different categories, in different terms. There could be little dialogue between the two sides, since each one cited its own authorities.

The protagonists, moreover, were adamant in their insistence on the validity of their own positions. The assertion that they, and they alone, possessed the true insight was a foremost characteristic of the entire controversy. Indeed, such insistence occasionally extended into the past as well, as evidenced by Martin Luther's comment that "until this present time no one has known what the gospel is."

Foes were denounced as false teachers and prophets. The polemical literature of the Reformation suggests that the protagonists often were as much concerned with exhibiting their ability to coin new epithets as they were with vindicating their own theological position. The vehement and often abusive denunciation of the opponents seemed to be an elementary credential for anyone engaging in the polemic. Inevitably, this attitude sharpened the controversy, for at stake was not merely an issue on which men in good conscience might properly differ, but a single position, authenticated by a strikingly obvious truth. The unwillingness of the opponents to yield merely precipitated antagonism.

This vehemence finds its explanation in the assumption, aggressively held by each protagonist, that his own position was right, self-evident, and persuasive. Those unwilling to accept it demonstrated their stubbornness and lack of good will. Luther exploded in anger when told, on one occasion, that Charles V persecuted the Protestants because his conscience compelled him to do so. Since Charles was in error, Luther insisted, he could not claim his conscience.

Moreover, the early years of the Reformation were characterized by utter confusion. The identification of the real issue (or issues) of the controversy seemed exasperatingly difficult—whether pertaining to practical abuse or theological error; whether the theological disagreement pertained to the problem of justification, the church, the sacraments, or authority. This imprecision made for a kind of free-for-all situation which eventually was bound to benefit the reformers.

Part of the difficulty lay in the diversity among those who took up Luther's cause in the early years of the Reformation. It extended the support far beyond what might have been the case had everyone clearly understood Luther's teaching. Anyone with a pet peeve could come forward as the self-appointed spokesman for his own cause, even if it were vaguely related to Luther's. There were many strange bedfellows in his camp in the first years of the Reformation. Men with a variety of grievances, positions, and orientations gathered around Luther, who himself did nothing to clarify the situation.

These "supporters" must not be chided for having manipulated Luther's cause to fit their own. The insight of subsequent generations of historians as to the pivotal issue does not obscure the evident confusion on the part of contemporaries. They were bound to interpret

Luther in their own way, if for no other reason than the limited scope of his publications. Many of the pamphlet writers in the early 1520s seemed quite unaware of profound differences between Luther and the Roman church.

In any case, diversity produced strength. Because different kinds of people flocked to Luther's side for different reasons, the movement was larger and more formidable than it might have been had everyone clearly understood its theological *raison d'être*. Thus, it was found in numerous places, among the clergy no less than among the humanists, among the artisans in the towns no less than among governmental councillors. The diversity also explains why it was so difficult to suppress the movement when the decision to do so was made.

The common ground for the host of "supporters" in the early years of the Reformation was their opposition to things Roman, though even in this respect diversity prevailed as to what exactly was offensive in the established religion—the political involvement of the church, its financial greed, sagging spirituality, or erroneous theology.

The language of the controversy frequently had an abusive quality. Invariably, coarseness, uncouthness, vulgarity, even obscenity, appeared. Comparisons (uncomplimentary, of course) with the lower animal kingdom abounded. Sylvester Prierias's very first pronouncement, *Against the Presumptuous Theses of Martin Luther*, introduced this literary convention into the polemic with his bit of wisdom to Luther: "I fear your father may have been a dog." Andreas Carlstadt entitled a broadside against Eck *Against the Utterly Stupid Ass and Arrogant "Mini-Doctor" Eck*. John Calvin compared the Council of Trent to a "diseased whore" and the council fathers to "horned beasts" with "stinking mussels."

Luther is often cited as the example par excellence of this coarse and vulgar polemic; when it came to the poignant epithet or the derisive denunciation, his ability was second to none. Since he wore his heart on his sleeve (and talked incessantly), the proof texts are easily found; for example: "Who has ever heard more blasphemous, poisonous, satanical, heretical, tyrannical, and stupid words than those pouring out of [Hieronymus] Emser's poisonous hell-jaws?" Or: "The Louvainists must be crass pigs of Epicurus and absolute atheists, who without fear tell such wanton and blasphemous lies in the sight of God and men."

Luther's Catholic counterparts were not exactly paragons of literary naïveté. Emser entitled his reply to Luther *To the Ox at Wittenberg*, and Eck remarked that Luther was a "lying prophet, whose father is the devil," a "poisonous spider," "ass," and "bastard." Even the usually gentle Thomas More, writing about the origin of Luther's

46

teaching, remarked, "All that they had collected from any place whatever, railings, brawlings, scurrilous scoffs, wantonness, obscenities, dirt, filth, muck, shit, all this sewage they stuff into the most foul sewer of Luther's breast. All this he vomited up through that foul mouth into that railer's book of his, like devoured dung." In short, the use of abusive and vulgar epithets was not exclusive to one side (or one man); abuse and vulgarity were no respecters of ecclesiastical labels. The gentle and sensitive spirits were the exceptions on both sides.

This vocabulary, the very use of which attests to the intensity of the controversy, evoked reactions of anger, despair, and frustration. That both sides stooped so low would indicate that both experienced the same emotions. Catholics despaired that a heretical movement, formally condemned by the church, continued to raise its head and propagate its ideas. The reformers were infuriated, since what to them was the clear teaching of the Gospels was not accepted. If we add the whole range of emotions concerning academic rivalries, dismay of senior scholars over the insolence of the young (and vice versa), indeed, if we bear in mind that the controversy was after all over man's eternal destiny, the intensity of the situation becomes understandable.

All this suggests that there was a confrontation of temperaments. It came to the fore in the fall of 1518, during Luther's meeting with Cardinal Cajetan. Of course, there also were differences of a theological sort between the two men; but something else happened during those fateful days, and the subsequent comments made by the two men indicate that they themselves were aware of it: there was a clash of temperaments between the cultured, logical, restrained cardinal and the impulsive, explosive, emotional professor. Cajetan was offended; Luther's subsequent apology for his immodest, sharp, and irreverent demeanor was evidence of a belated awareness of the emotional significance of what had passed.

The advocates of reform had an annoying tendency to simplify matters—indeed, to oversimplify them. They made blanket generalizations and sweeping assertions. Their pronouncements were categorical; they knew of no qualifications or exceptions. To them the matter was simple: their own teaching was found in Scripture and in the writings of the church fathers, while their opponents based their views on erroneous, man-made traditions. Thus, the reformers claimed that the Catholic church did not approve of the Scriptures and did not want them placed in the hands of the common people. They maintained that all priests were ignorant; all monasteries, dens of iniquity; all members of the hierarchy, power hungry and greedy. Interspersed with such freewheeling charges were touching confessions of earlier personal ignorance—Luther's comment, for example, that he had never seen a Bible in his youth, or Müntzer's insistence that he had diligently sought instruction in the true Christian faith.

It was a moving story, and there was a kernel of truth in the assertions. But, while it may have been truth that the reformers spoke, it surely was not the whole truth, and those who were loyal to the Roman church could not help but wring their hands in dismay over such blatant simplification and generalization. No respectable medieval theologian had ever taught that salvation could be attained by good works, nor had the Catholic church ever rejected the Scriptures.

The defenders of the Catholic church required some time to understand the new rules of the game, and this delay tended to weaken their case. Jacob Latomus, a theologian from Louvain, was one of the first to catch on. He wrote a tract against Luther entitled *Ratio ex sacris literis et veteribus tractatoribus* (1521), in which he argued the Catholic case concerning sin and grace not only on the ground of tradition but also on that of the Bible. This tract must have caused Luther some consternation, but he regained his theological (or hermeneutic) equilibrium by announcing that there was a true and a false way of interpreting Scripture, and that Latomus, indeed all Catholics, interpreted the Scriptures the false way.

In any case, the reformers had the catchier slogans and the more persuasive phrases. Their stress on the "Word of God" and on "faith" may have been theologically ambiguous, but their slogans were simple. The stereotyped references to the "Word of God" as authoritative norm were surely more impressive than the complicated citations of scholastic theologians.

The reformers were bound to have the upper hand in the confrontation. This is not to suggest that they were destined to be successful, that they advanced the more persuasive arguments, nor that they propounded the truth. Rather, they possessed a strategic advantage that was difficult to counter, and were able to determine the course of the controversy. The defenders of the Catholic church had no choice but to follow the lead. The Catholics could never be sure where the next polemical attack would occur, nor what issue would be raised by the next pamphlet or the next reformer.

In addition, the reformers painted an impressive picture of the Christian religion in their writings, talking splendidly about true commitment, faith, and devotion, quite unperturbed about how these lofty notions would work out in practice. Their Catholic opponents had the liability of being firmly tied to existing conditions. The reformers were eager, perhaps naïve, in their conviction that they had discovered the authentic meaning of the Gospels. It was not until their own forms of ecclesiastical life had emerged that their antagonists, both to the left and to the right, Protestant radicals or Catholic conservatives, could also do what they themselves had done: namely, level charges of a variety of practical shortcomings and insist that not even the tree of the Reformation brought forth good fruit.

The reformers profited by anticlericalism and the various ecclesiastical grievances. Luther himself did so in a dramatic way in his *Open Letter to the Christian Nobility*, which at certain points simply reiterated the traditional German grievances against Rome. The denunciation of practical abuses, far removed from subtle theological considerations, was a tool used in the polemic of the early Reformation.

Such were the accusations; the actual facts made little difference. The credulous took the accusations at face value, even though in reality the picture may have been, and indeed was, quite different. In terms of its dynamics, a rumor is as powerful as a fact. Men in the early sixteenth century were willing to accept the truth of the sundry charges against the church and its clergy. The picture of the monastery as a den of iniquity, of the priest as a lewd man about town, or of the bishop as a greedy manipulator was found to be within the realm of possibility. People wanted to believe the charges, and believe them they did; the countless devout, conscientious, sincere clerics were overlooked.

The Catholics were the tragic figures in the story. Those loyal to the Catholic church discovered that they were called upon to defend not only its teachings, but its practices as well; and that was a difficult task. Indeed, it was virtually impossible, for the whole range of prevailing ecclesiastical practices and doctrines could not possibly be defended. The Catholic protagonists had to realize that they were trapped on both sides. Both the sweeping assertion that there was nothing wrong with the church and the acknowledgment that certain aspects of the life of the church needed reform were bound to add fuel to the attack of the reformers, the one because it conflicted too blatantly with reality; the other, because it dramatized the need for reform.

The former attitude characterized, for example, Tetzel's initial response to Luther's Ninety-five Theses. In effect, he argued that any practice of the church was vindicated by its existence. Whatever practice existed, in other words, was right. His unsophisticated theme was taken up by Sylvester Prierias, who similarly argued that any challenge of existing ecclesiastical practices was tantamount to heresy. But this attitude was as unsatisfactory as the other, recognition by sensitive Catholics of the need for reform. Duke George of Saxony observed, "It is not completely untrue what he [Luther] has written nor unnecessary to be brought to the light of day"; Pope Adrian VI acknowledged ecclesiastical shortcomings in 1522.

49

In this exasperating situation, the Catholic polemicists moved into a direction that was catastrophic, even though it was understandable. Increasingly, they defended every ecclesiastical practice and every theological affirmation challenged by the reformers. When, in the early Reformation, the reformers asserted the need for a vernacular worship service, J. Clichtoveus responded that vernacular readings would be occasions for grave error. The result was that, as often as not, one-sided positions were taken to be normative for the Catholics.

Also, the writings of the Catholic theologians seemed to attempt to outdo one another with ever lengthier and more detailed lists of the "theological" shortcomings of their opponents, while the Protestant divines, less given to such flights of quantitative fancy, argued ever more vehemently that justification by faith was the very heart of the Gospels, from which no syllable could be detracted.

Johannes Cochlaeus was the first of the Catholic quantitative experts. His *Articuli CCCCC Martini Lutheri ex sermonibus eius* (1525) covered no less than 500 articles in which, as far as he was concerned, Luther was in error. Five years later, Johann Eck, never willing to be outdone, presented a list of 404 articles, culled from the writings of the reformers, and Berthold Pistinger's *Tewtsche Theologie* (1528) required as many as 100 chapters to explain the theological differences between the two sides.

Many Catholics had an attitude of boredom (as in the case of Sylvester Prierias) or viewed the matter as a routine theological controversy (as in the case of Johann Eck). In either instance, the result was that Luther's religious intent was not afforded serious consideration. The Catholic polemicists tended to search for specific sentences and phrases in their opponents' writings that might be erroneous or heretical, showing little interest in their overall intent, thereby further accentuating the differences.

Ironically, some Catholic polemicists were in effect formidable propagators of the new gospel in spite of themselves. Johann Eck and Johannes Cochlaeus probably did more to spread the Lutheran cause than many of Luther's own partisans: their own views notwithstanding, they wrote so lengthily about Luther and denounced him so emphatically, that some people surely decided to check for themselves. Catholic writers probably precipitated, albeit inadvertently, a good deal of the support for Luther. This was true not only in Germany, but also in other European countries. In England, for example, the theologians learned of the Lutheran "conflagration" before word of it had filtered down to the people. Their elaborate attacks upon the new teaching promptly familiarized a great many Englishmen with the issues. Henry VIII's elaborate defense and Thomas More's sophisticated pronouncement probably contributed more to acquaint Englishmen with Martin Luther than did Luther's own writings or those of his English partisans. More's work included large portions of Luther's tracts, even as John Fisher's *Confutatio* printed verbatim Luther's defense against his censure. The counterattack produced curiosity; vehement indictments created widespread publicity; and categorical denunciations evoked empathy.

The best strategy might have been to acknowledge that the church had spoken and the verdict had been rendered; Luther and his followers, after all, were stubborn heretics. Such a treatment—contemptuous (or "benign") silence—might have worked. As matters turned out, the arena became crowded with self-appointed (and second-rate) spokesmen for the Catholic faith. The vehemence of their defenses or attacks helped bring about (as far as Catholics were concerned) a disastrous course of events.

5 The Division

MARTIN LUTHER DOMINATED THE REFORMA-
tion for several important years and nothing illustrates this centrality
better than the label "Martinian" or "Lutheran" ascribed to all those
who took up Luther's cause or expressed a yearning for ecclesiastical
reform. Their own respective positions mattered little.

Then it became evident that there did indeed exist a good deal of
diversity among those who had taken up Luther's banner—the
characteristic of the third phase of the Reformation described earlier.
Most of this had little bearing on the larger events, being but the
private opinions of theologians, uttered from the pulpit and printed in
pamphlets, in the sixteenth century prompting an occasional raised
eyebrow, in our own day exciting the fancies of dissertation writers. Of
the many reformers few, if any, agreed completely with Luther. Most
of them had their own particular slant and interpretation.

No period in the history of the Christian church has been exempt
from such activity; at no time did the theologians ever agree
completely with one another. The theological scene during the
Reformation was not different in this regard, though most of the

diversity is important primarily for the understanding of individual theologians rather than of the Reformation as a whole.

Some of the divisions were important, however, since theological difference led to sociological differentiation. The exposition of different theological positions meant in several instances the emergence of distinct Protestant factions. The seriousness of the differences hopefully proves the key to the matter: lesser differences were resolved (or ignored) and bigger ones led to division.

The fact is that extraneous considerations also entered the picture. In some instances geographic factors played a role in the unfolding of different ecclesiastical bodies. Moreover, the temperament of the protagonists, the timing of the controversy, political elements—these, and others, were at times as influential as outright theological differences. In other words, there was an accidental quality to what we might call the "theological consolidation" of the Reformation.

Huldreich Zwingli

THE ZURICH REFORMER HULDREICH ZWINGLI IS a good case in point. His proclamation agreed with that of Luther, yet it possessed its own distinct emphases. Zwingli's monument at Zurich depicts him with Bible and sword, as a man of the Word and of deed. More than pious patriotism of Zurich burghers fashioned this monument: Zwingli was as much a Swiss patriot as he was a Christian theologian. Thus his program of reform was informed by elements alien to that of Luther. For Zwingli, "reform" meant not only reform of theology and the church, but also of society in light of the gospel.

Huldreich Zwingli was born in 1484 at Wildhaus, then as now a small village amid impressive mountains on the eastern edge of Switzerland. His first biographer suggested that the reformer's birthplace possessed theological significance: the nearness of heaven, he wrote, made God a profound reality. One need not pay homage to such geographic determinism to acknowledge that Zwingli's appreciation of nature, his reserved character, and his rustic language betray the setting in which he grew to manhood, in the sight of the grandeur of the mountains, where man and nature appear to exist in unbroken continuity. After studies at Vienna and Basel he received the baccalaureate degree in 1504, and two years later he concluded his studies in the liberal arts with the master's degree.

In 1506 Zwingli became minister to Glarus, where he was to spend ten years pursuing his various ministerial responsibilities in the village and several outlying hamlets. But instead of falling prey to what Shakespeare a century later was to call the "insolence of office" in the small village, he applied himself to serious intellectual pursuits. He attained a solid competence in classical studies and became conversant with theological scholarship. In this the Christian humanism of Erasmus was his guiding light.

In 1516 Zwingli moved to Einsiedeln and two years later to Zurich, where he was appointed *Leutpriester*, people's priest, a prestigious post that offered opportunities for scholarly studies and a welcome proximity to humanist friends. Zurich had some 6,000 inhabitants; it was prosperous and politically influential among Swiss cities. In line with a constitutional agreement of 1498, government lay in the hands of a Large Council, the "Two Hundred," and a Small Council, with fifty members. Power was wielded by the Large Council, which dealt with foreign affairs and basic policy; the Small Council supervised domestic administrative matters. Membership on the two councils was by election.

Zwingli began his ministerial responsibilities with some startling homiletic innovations, but before their impact was felt, the indulgences controversy began to overshadow everything else. In December 1518 Luther's name made its first appearance in Zwingli's correspondence. Zwingli sought to obtain his writings; he praised them, and furthered their colportage. A "new Elias" had been given to the world, he exclaimed exuberantly, and later he wrote that Saul (Erasmus) had slain a thousand, but David (Luther), ten thousand. Yet, when asked about Luther's influence on his religious thinking, Zwingli denied it. "I do not want to be called Lutheran," he wrote in 1522, "for I did not learn the teachings of Christ from Luther, but from the Word of God."

Political considerations oriented to some extent Zwingli's expression of aloofness from Luther. The Edict of Worms had declared Luther's followers outlaws; for Zwingli to acknowledge himself as Luther's disciple would have meant a threat to his own work. His disavowal was an act of understandable prudence. But more was involved. Zwingli was convinced that he had proclaimed the gospel before he had ever heard of Luther. His accuracy hinges on his meaning of "gospel." When he used it to describe his thought, he gave it a connotation that it later did not possess. His "gospel" was that of Erasmus; later this element persisted, but a new strain was added: the Pauline notion of law and grace. Christ was first the great exemplar, the giver of the Sermon on the Mount. Later came Zwingli's emphasis on Christ as redeemer and liberator from the Law. Luther was the guide along the way. The Wittenberg reformer was the catalyst, confirming here and suggesting there, but never overpowering.

54

Zwingli saw it this way when he wrote that Luther "propelled me to eagerness."

Zwingli could argue the independence of his religious insight all the more forcefully since an intensely personal experience in 1519 wove his life and thought into one indivisible pattern. In August 1519 the plague struck Zurich. Zwingli contracted the dreadful disease and for weeks wrestled with death, until slow recovery restored his health. From the experience came a personal religious document, the *Pestlied*, or *Hymn of Pestilence*. Zwingli, in facing the reality of death, became persuaded of the reality of God; personal experience had merged with theological insight.

Four factors, then, converged to lift the unknown *Leutpriester* of Zurich to historical prominence: Erasmus, increasing theological maturity, Luther, and a personal experience. Not all of these may have been of equal importance, but all were present.

The Reformation in Zurich

AT THE BEGINNING OF THE ECCLESIASTICAL transformation in Zurich were two pork sausages eaten in 1522 during Lent by several eager partisans of Luther's cause, who thereby violated the rule of the church. The harmless culinary feat became an *affaire d'état*, particularly when an extensive investigation revealed additional instances of violation of the fast. Zwingli's proclamation, or perhaps Luther's, had borne its fruit. The apology of the culprits pointed to a basic consideration: "We must keep all our lives and our doings in accord with the Gospel," one of them wrote, "or else we are not Christians."

Shortly thereafter Zwingli published a sermon entitled *Concerning Choice and Liberty of Food*, the first public statement of his theological position. The theme was the relationship between faith and works, between inward piety and outward prescription; its motif was that of the freedom of the Christian man: the Christian does not stand under the law, but above it. Genuine morality does not stem from external observations, but from free and joyful commitment.

The city council decided that a theological disputation should solve the contested issues. If the church at large did not convene a council, then the Christian congregation of Zurich was at liberty to proceed on its own, to ponder the issues, and come to its proper conclusions. Such a claim to ecclesiastical and theological independence was revolutionary.

In preparation for the disputation Zwingli compiled a list of propositions, sixty-seven in number, delineating his understanding of the needed reform of the church. These Sixty-seven Conclusions covered the full range of religion and morality, ceremonies and faith. Two basic assertions set the tone: the centrality and self-sufficiency of the Scriptures; the centrality of Christ and the need for the proclamation of his gospel. "Those who assert that the gospel is nothing without the confirmation of the church are in error and blaspheme God." The main part of the treatise contained reflections about the papal office, ecclesiastical practices, church property, clerical celibacy, and monasticism.

The disputation took place on 29 January 1523. More than 600 persons were present, though few of them were defenders of the old faith. After a somewhat listless morning the city council announced that "Master Huldreich Zwingli should continue, as heretofore, to proclaim the Holy Gospel and the Sacred Scriptures." The same exhortation was given to the clergy of Zurich.

Several minor changes then took place. Monks and nuns were allowed to leave the monasteries: The endowments of the Minster church were to be used for charitable purposes. By and large, however, ecclesiastical life continued unchanged. The mass was observed in its traditional form, as was most of the ritual, and statues and pictures of the saints remained in the churches. Since some considered both mass and statues particularly offensive, restlessness beset the city. In one church the "eternal light" was torn down by some fanatics "while everyone was at supper" and in another a painting of Jesus disappeared. A crucifix wound up in a ditch outside one of the city gates. Toward the end of September the city council appointed a committee to examine the lingering religious problems. This committee suggested a second disputation.

If the January disputation had been a lame and uninspiring affair, this second gathering, held in October, was a lively meeting of minds. In January the controversy had been between the proponents of the old and of the new faith; this time it was among the followers of the new faith. There was a bitter dispute, not over whether images and the mass should be abolished, but rather when. The conclusion was to proceed cautiously. The images must first be taken down from the hearts of man; then the external removal would come without turmoil in its own time. As Zwingli expressed it, "the people must first of all be instructed with the Word of God that neither vestments nor singing is a proper part of the Mass. If presently anyone would celebrate Mass without vestments uproar will result." By the middle of December the absence of changes revived the earlier restlessness. The city council announced that at Whitsuntide "the matter should be taken up again and brought to a conclusion agreeable to God and his holy word." Political prudence prompted the delay. The disputation had evoked repercussions among those Swiss cantons loyal to the Catholic church and the Zurich council did not want to add fuel to the fire.

On Whitsuntide in 1524, the Zurich council ordered that the images be removed from the churches "so that all would turn completely from idols to the living and true God." For two weeks workmen were busy. When they were done, the Gothic magnificence of richly ornamented shrines had been transformed into the cool austerity of simple worship houses. The walls were white, the windows clear, the view unobstructed. Precious works of art, priceless objects of religious devotion, had disappeared under the chisel, the hammer, and the paintbrush. Treasures of art were gone forever.

The abolition of the mass took longer. Not until the spring of 1525 did the city council rule that the mass should be discontinued and "the remembrance of the institution and the table of God as practiced by the Apostles" observed instead. For ears accustomed to the chanting of the mass and for eyes used to its ritualistic splendor, the Communion service, then introduced, was a radical innovation. It was simple. After the sermon Zwingli took a place behind a table "covered with a clean linen cloth." Wooden bowls and goblets contained the bread and wine, which were carried by helpers to the congregation. The liturgy was in the vernacular. Although it followed the traditional pattern, there were changes: one of the Scripture lessons was read by one of the lay helpers, and the Gloria and the Credo were recited antiphonally by minister and congregation. The mystery of the mass had become the simple communal gathering of a congregation commemorating Christ's death.

The course of events in Zurich was hardly spectacular—no flaming oratory, no dramatic encounter, no heroic deeds. What took place there between 1522 and 1525 was to recur in countless places throughout Germany: the proclamation of ideas that were vaguely "Lutheran" and thus at odds with the Catholic church; the agitation for certain changes in ecclesiastical practice; the intervention of governmental authority, first with the call for a mediation between the old faith and the new, then with the statutory introduction of ecclesiastical change. Thereby the fabric of the one church was torn and a rival form of Christianity established itself against the church represented by the pope.

The question of the ultimate rationale in the minds of those who demanded ecclesiastical change was whether or not they wanted to break permanently with the Catholic church and seek to go their own way. Some of the changes were marginal (the closing of the monasteries or the removal of images); others were more crucial, such as the discontinuance of the mass. But always the conviction on the part of the reformers that they were propounding the true gospel and that this true gospel would be victorious—not in the sense of a defeat of the Catholic church but rather in the acceptance by this church of the true gospel—was what mattered. Their boundless enthusiasm may have prompted the reformers to be naïve about the future.

The Emergence of Radical Movements of Reform

THE EMERGENCE OF RADICAL MOVEMENTS OF reform has been interpreted as either triumph or defeat. If interpretations of the radical Reformation thus differ, the facts are simple: in most centers of the Reformation, a new kind of reformer appeared, consisting of men who had been under the sway of Luther's or Zwingli's teaching and had been their disciples. They had grown dissatisfied. They began to question, to denounce, to "out-Luther" Luther and to "out-Zwingli" Zwingli, and eventually go their own ways. Although their impact upon the contemporary scene was modest and does not compare with that of Luther or Calvin, they should be neither ignored nor caricatured, a fate that has been theirs ever since the sixteenth century. In some ways, some of these radicals were heralds of the modern age, advancing principles that, though fiercely disputed in their own time, have become the common possession of society. They insisted on religious freedom and tolerance, for example, claiming that government should not interfere with religion; others argued that most theological disagreements pertained only to secondary matters and could therefore be disregarded.

Doubtless the new movements received their impetus from the Reformation, since those who subsequently turned radical flirted with the Lutheran or Zwinglian programs of reform before they grew dissatisfied with their own way. The Reformation provided the initial religious stimulus. Nonetheless, the Reformation hardly suffices as full explanation for the emergence of Protestant radicalism. There were other factors, such as humanism, especially of the Erasmian variety, the mysticism of Johannes Tauler, Thomas a Kempis, and the *German Theology*, as well as the enigmatic underground of medieval apocalyptic and philosophical speculation, about which it is easier to offer plausible conjectures than hard facts. Nor must we overlook the import of the Bible, which these radicals read in the vernacular and with a disarming freshness and from which they may well have received some of their insights.

58

In contrast to the other ecclesiastical groupings in the sixteenth century, these dissenters did not obtain the support of governmental authority, which, at most places was grimly determined to crush all deviating religious sentiment. The story of the radical reformers is the story of an underground movement suppressed with countless mandates, ordinances, and edicts. The radicals were the outcasts of a society that, having closed its ranks against them, offered them neither the opportunity to worship nor the status of citizenship. Theirs was the story of persecution. Michael Servetus, the Spanish Antitrinitarian radical, was burned by Catholics in desire and by Protestants in reality. Such a spectacular demise symbolizes the fact that there was no place for the radical in the sixteenth century.

The radicals were a company of martyrs. All religious groupings in the sixteenth century supplied the stake and the executioner's block, the Calvinists no less than the Lutherans, and the Catholics no less than the English Protestants. The radicals, however, provided martyrs in larger numbers, though the precise number is a matter of conjecture. The several martyrologies written at the time sought to provide devotional inspirations rather than exact statistical information. A total of some 4,000 victims appears as a likely estimate for the century.

The radicals were martyr-minded. Persecution, martyrdom, and even death were, for them, not accidental misfortunes but the very essence of the Christian confession. Christ himself had walked the way of suffering and death, and he beckoned his disciples to come and follow him. Often the radicals did not know subtle points of theological argumentation or the answers of biblical interpretation. When they were interrogated, they were pathetically ill-equipped to match the sophisticated theological wits of their opponents. Still, they were persuaded that they had been called to follow in Jesus's steps, to do as he had commanded them to do, to suffer, and to die. They quoted Jesus's words that the "disciple is not above his master, nor the servant above his lord," and held that the disciple was called upon to be like his master in his rejection, suffering, and death. Martyrdom was a test of obedience, and they would not shrink from it. They were on a pilgrimage and looked beyond the flames of the stake and the executioner's sword to the promised land.

One of the most moving documents came from a Dutch Anabaptist woman who wrote to her infant daughter:

> I have borne you under my heart with great sorrow for nine months, and given birth to you here in prison, in great pain. They have taken you from me. Here I lie, expecting death every morning. . . .
> I pray you, that wherever you live when you are grown up, and begin

to have understanding, you conduct yourself well and honestly, so that no one need have cause to complain of you. And always be faithful, taking good heed not to wrong any one . . . and run not in the street as other bad children do. Take up a book, and learn to seek there that which concerns your salvation. . . .

So I must also leave you here, my dearest lamb. The Lord that created and made you now takes me from you in His Holy will. I must now pass through the narrow way which the prophets and martyrs of Christ passed through, the many thousands who put off the mortal clothing, who died here for Christ, and now wait under the altar till their number shall be fulfilled. Your dear father is one of them and I am on the point of following him, for I, too, am delivered up to death. . . .

The fear of the authorities that the radicals were conspiring to overthrow the established order clearly was behind some of the severity of the persecution. Though doctrinal deviation in itself entailed grave legal consequences, torture and other measures of suppression were often used in an effort to unmask a political "conspiracy." Most of the radicals were peaceful. When they talked about the upheaval of society, theirs was more the naïve speculation of men heavy with the mysterious language of Holy Writ than the manifesto of committed revolutionaries. But there were also a few exceptions, men who, carried away by their fancies and aspirations to alter society instantly, justified the suspicion of the authorities. Moreover, in one sense the accusation of the disruption of law and order was correct: the radicals rejected the identity of the political and religious community that was universally accepted by Protestants and Catholics alike. They argued that church and state were different, and that to be a citizen of a commonwealth did not mean automatic identification with an ecclesiastical community.

Although the number of the radicals was quite small, their theological concerns were legion. In some instances this meant the outright splintering into separate groups, in others a baffling constellation of affinities. It is easier by far to determine what the radicals opposed than what they advocated. They opposed both the Reformation and the Catholic church, hurling charges of compromise against the former and of perversion against the latter; they wanted a reformation of the Reformation. As one of them remarked, "Luther broke the pope's pitcher, but kept the pieces in his hand." The radicals, in turn, were resolved to drop the pieces.

The radicals do not seem to have possessed a common vision of what constituted the Christian religion. Current nomenclature speaks of the "radical reformation," suggesting that the radicals ventured to go to the very "root" of the Christian faith for its restoration. This is delicate language, for the major reformers claimed to do the same, only defining "root" differently than did the radicals. The label thus begs the question. Another suggestion speaks of the Reformation's "left wing," a term taken from political parlance, and stresses the radicals' disavowal of governmental interference in religious affairs. Both suggestions contain accurate insights. A purview of the full spectrum of Protestant dissent in the Reformation, however, suggests a somewhat more general characteristic. The common denominator of all radicals was their insistence that the Reformation, too, had to be reformed. The reformers had not gone far enough; they left unquestioned what should have been challenged, and affirmed what should have been rejected. The specific criticisms differed from radical to radical. The Antitrinitarians were concerned about the ancient Christological dogma, whereas the Anabaptists and Spiritualists stressed what may be called "practical Christianity." The scriptural statement "by their fruit ye shall know them" served as their motto. Their recurrent theme was that the Christian profession had to manifest itself in the daily walk of life.

The radical movement raises the same fundamental question as the Reformation at large: whether it was an ideological phenomenon in which religious ideas only formed the veneer for more basic social or economic concerns. The movement, after all, seems to have recruited its adherents primarily from the lower classes of people, from the peasants and artisans, so as to suggest a socioeconomic homogeneity of striking simplicity.

The evidence, however, is far from conclusive. Indeed, upon detailed analysis it points to a bewildering situation suggesting that no easily ascertainable economic or social common denominator exists. While lacking extensive involvement of the upper classes, the movement possessed far more heterogeneity than appears at first glance—if not in social class then certainly in economic standing. This conclusion is underscored by the numerically insignificant dimension of the Anabaptist movement. The Anabaptists never comprised more than a small fraction of society; precisely that smallness renders impossible any definite socioeconomic identification of its adherents.

Anabaptism

ANABAPTISM BEGAN IN ZURICH IN JANUARY 1525 with the administration of believer's baptism. Its ideological beginnings, however, are shrouded in darkness. Some of those who became Anabaptists had been influenced by Erasmus, and the impact of

Carlstadt and Müntzer, two early maverick reformers, cannot be discounted. Nor must we overlook the obvious, the influence of Luther, Zwingli, and the Bible. A complex of influences molded the Anabaptist theological temper.

Initially, there was a growing impatience with the slowness of ecclesiastical reform in Zurich. In 1524 the dissatisfied gravitated toward one another, talked theology and reform, and attained theological sophistication. Eventually the break with Zwingli was over baptism, but there was an issue of more fundamental importance: the nature of Christian commitment. To be a Christian meant a voluntary and deliberate decision, which expressed itself in reception of adult baptism and separation from the "ungodly."

The ostensible split came in January 1525 with the administration of believer's baptism by a small group led by Conrad Grebel and Felix Mantz. This act constituted a flagrant violation of the mandates of the Zurich city council. The circumstances were highly unusual: a living room was the sanctuary, and a kitchen ladle was used for pouring the baptismal waters. Within two weeks, more than thirty people had been so baptized. The authorities promptly interfered and the Anabaptists were arrested. Since most of them recanted, they were soon released; the few who did not were expelled from Zurich territory.

From the outset there was present in the Anabaptist movement a centrifugal tendency that prompted its spread throughout central Europe. Expulsion from Zurich left some Anabaptists with no alternative but to move elsewhere, where they continued to proclaim their message. The Anabaptists perceived the difference between their own view of the gospel and that propounded by others in categorical terms. Theirs alone was the true gospel; the world was in darkness. Therefore men everywhere had to be called to follow Christ and to signify their commitment with the reception of adult baptism. Even if the Anabaptists had experienced no persecution in Zurich, they would have taken their message to other places. That there was persecution made the carrying out of the principle expedient as well as necessary. Obvious factors influenced the geographic direction of the expansion. The Anabaptist message could be communicated only in German-speaking areas. Moreover, it was easier to follow the well-established roads to the north than to move eastward across the mountain ranges into Austria. Their missionaries enjoyed an initial period of toleration. By the time the authorities moved to suppressive action, the Anabaptist evangelists had formed the nucleus of a congregation. Persecution forced this congregation underground and made further expansion virtually impossible.

Some people were ready for the Anabaptist message. They were the spiritually sensitive ones, those dissatisfied with the course of the ecclesiastical transformation and religiously aroused by the Lutheran proclamation but bewildered by its increasing theological sophistication. The Anabaptist message seemed to supply their need by combining the message of the Reformation with something new: the insistence that the believer must bring forth the fruit of his commitment.

Its expansion was unsystematic, sporadic, haphazard, and theologically unsophisticated. With few exceptions, the Anabaptist missionary was theologically illiterate. To be sure, there were sophisticated men such as Balthasar Hubmaier, Hans Denck, and Hans Hut, but most Anabaptist evangelists were simple men whose religious enthusiasm had to compensate for the lack of theological training. The consequences were inescapable. The Anabaptist message was reduced to its essentials. Subtle points of theological argumentation had to be ignored, but this proved to be its strength.

Once a nucleus of believers had been formed, the missionary who had introduced the message moved on and the new congregation was on its own. It would study the Bible and read the few Anabaptist pamphlets that were available. By and large its contacts were limited; the congregation was like an island in an ocean, part of a universal brotherhood, yet basically living its own life. The proclamation of the reformers initially encountered the same difficulty, for the exposition of Luther's theology by thousands of well-meaning clerics, all of whom had been Catholic priests, was bound to lead to diversity and problems. The pulpits in Lutheran territories hardly propounded uniform Lutheran doctrine. Yet the Reformation had the advantage of the dissemination of its ideas by the printed page and a formal ecclesiastical structure; Anabaptism generally did not.

Little is known about the success of this Anabaptist evangelistic effort. A network of Anabaptist congregations throughout Austria and south Germany was established and a relatively small number of Anabaptists can be identified through court records. The evidence available suggests that Anabaptism was never a mass movement. Moreover, the expansion was a mixed blessing. Anabaptism ceased to be the homogeneous phenomenon that it had been at its inception. The larger the movement, the greater its doctrinal diversity and the greater also the need for theological clarification. Such clarification occurred in three places in 1527: at Nikolsburg in Moravia, at Augsburg in south Germany, and at Schleitheim on the Swiss-German border. In all three cases the sources are enigmatic.

Anabaptism was an underground movement. It had no organizational structure, but consisted of more or less autonomous congregations scattered throughout central Europe. It possessed no generally binding confessional statements. In a way, the situation of Anabaptism was similar to that of Protestantism in France or Scotland during the struggle for official recognition, though Protestants in those countries received support from abroad, notably from Geneva, and they were numerically large enough to establish early organizational structures and confessional standards.

The absence of organizational structures in Anabaptism had two consequences. First, one can hardly write the history of Anabaptism as a "movement." With the exception of its Hutterite branch, which did possess organization (and confessional norms), there is an open-ended complexity about Anabaptist history that makes it difficult to do more than expound the thought of the eminent leaders. A second consequence was the perpetuation of theological strife among factions.

Anabaptism was a network of loosely knit congregations. There was no formal training for the leaders. Occasionally a figure of charismatic qualities would appear and through organizational ability or theological exposition make his mark. Since the theological contribution often took the form of clandestinely printed tracts, it is not surprising that historical nescience has frequently obscured it. The south German Anabaptist Pilgram Marpeck is a good case in point. Virtually unknown to historians until the beginning of the twentieth century, the discovery of his extensive literary production established him as the most prolific Anabaptist writer in the first half of the sixteenth century.

The spread of Anabaptism from its Swiss cradle into south Germany was paralleled by a northward expansion into central Germany and the Low Countries. A south German furrier and lay preacher played the crucial role: Melchior Hofmann, at once a quiet man ready to suffer for his conviction and a brooding dreamer who became increasingly preoccupied with the evasive arithmetic and imagery of Scripture. He was obsessed with what he called the "figure," the meaning of the allegorical and figurative parts of Scripture. After several years as a traveling evangelist, Hofmann extended his activities to Holland in 1531. Persecution set in promptly. The prisons were filled, the fires kindled around the stakes, and the executioner's ax sharpened. In itself this turn of events was not particularly noteworthy; it was but a painful repetition of widespread practice. Important in this particular instance, however, was the reaction of Hofmann, who interpreted the outbreak of persecution as the obvious sign of the last days. He announced that all baptism of believers (the external cause of the persecution) should be suspended for two years.

Hofmann himself became his own pathetic victim. A man told him that he would be in prison for half a year before God would call him.

This prediction proved to be of crucial importance, for Hofmann's biblical arithmetic had led him to see 1533 as the time of the Second Coming. He hurried to Strassburg, the "New Jerusalem," to fulfill the prophecy. Upon his arrival he was arrested, but he rejoiced over this turn of events. "And he praised God that the hour had come and he lifted his hat from his head . . . raised his fingers to heaven, swearing to the living God that he would take no other food or drink than water and bread." The first part of the prophecy had come true.

Münster was the next chapter in the history of Anabaptism. In this city in northwest Germany the Anabaptists succeeded where they had failed elsewhere: they attained political control and proceeded to establish their New Jerusalem. A strange one it was, at least for outsiders, characterized not only by adult baptism, but also by polygamy and communism. Contemporaries considered it the abomination of abominations, the proof that all Anabaptists were evil, immoral, and heretical. It mattered little that there were significant differences between the Anabaptists in Münster and those elsewhere. The common affirmation of adult baptism obscured these differences for both the authorities and the reformers.

At the beginning stood a relatively harmless transformation of ecclesiastical life in Münster along Anabaptist lines. Like many cities in the early years of the Reformation, Münster had passed through a period of ecclesiastical tension. The agitation of Bernhard Rothmann, a former priest, brought about ecclesiastical change, and in February 1533 Münster became Protestant. Since many cities in Germany were then taking the same step, the course of events in Münster was not unusual. But Rothmann increasingly favored more drastic change, and he was able to pull the city along with him. In May 1533 he publicly denounced infant baptism. The news of this development spread abroad and prompted many Anabaptists to flock to Münster.

In January 1534 two followers of Jan Matthijs arrived in Münster and proclaimed that believer's baptism should be administered. Rothmann and many others—a contemporary spoke of more than 1,400 people—were baptized. This baptism and the other changes in Münster made a deep impact upon Anabaptists in the north. Believer's baptism had been suspended upon Melchior Hofmann's exhortation that the end was imminent. Hofmann himself lay in a Strassburg prison, impatiently awaiting the Great Day. The dramatic change at Münster seemed to be the vindication of Hofmann's prophetic views. Persecution had ceased, the elect were unmolested, and the city had changed its face to conform to the vision of the New Jerusalem. Jan Matthijs's exhortation that believer's baptism could be administered again ushered in an atmosphere of spiritual exuberance. Matthijs arrived in Münster soon thereafter, and his presence denoted the occasion for extensive change. Elections to the city council brought an Anabaptist majority. All who were unwilling to be baptized had to leave the city.

When the last of these emigrants had disappeared outside the city walls, Münster had become their "New Jerusalem," for the "ungodly" had been driven away and only the "elect" remained. On the face of things, Münster was Anabaptist, but a deviation from Anabaptist principles had taken place. The notion of the church as a minority within society was replaced by the assertion of the identity of church and society. The *corpus christianum* was reestablished.

The rulers of the surrounding territories, however, were unwilling to accept the change in the city, and a siege commenced. Jan Matthijs was killed in battle, but the loss of the prophet created only a temporary vacuum, since his place was taken by another Dutchman, Jan van Leyden. A tailor by trade, with a keen awareness of political reality and an extraordinary sense of spiritual vocation, Leyden was convinced that God had called him to rule over his elect at Münster and throughout the world. He was the third David, whose pretentious emblem was a globe with the inscription "king of righteousness over all."

Leyden introduced communism in Münster. The precarious economic situation created by the siege was undoubtedly a major factor in this step, but there was also the determination to follow the biblical precedent of the Book of Acts. Polygamy was introduced, again against the backdrop of practical necessity and theological insight. Women outnumbered men in Münster, and since in those days single women were legally helpless, a way had to be found to deal with their problem. The claim to biblical precedent was supported by reference to the patriarchs of the Old Testament, who demonstrated that polygamy was evidently practiced without divine disapproval.

Early in 1535 the besieging forces succeeded in taking the city and restoring the rule of the legitimate authorities. The three Anabaptist leaders were put into iron cages and hanged from the steeple of the largest church. Afterward, persecution of dissenting religious sentiment intensified (though not everywhere with equal measure), for the fear of the authorities that the Anabaptists were political revolutionaries in disguise had received melodramatic justification.

The result of the Münster episode was to make Anabaptism even more inner directed, eschewing any attempt to impose their ways upon society. Quietism became the hallmark of the movement, which sought to survive persistent oppression and persecution. In some places, notably Austria, ruthless persecution succeeded in crushing the movement. In others, such as Poland and Moravia, a tolerant atmosphere allowed the Anabaptist groups to live a peaceable existence, until the thrust of the Catholic Counter-Reformation created new and pressing problems. In Holland and Germany the situation was more ambivalent, although the organizational genius and spiritual qualities of Menno Simons, a former Dutch priest, allowed the Anabaptist movement to emphasize the principles of peaceful and moral Christianity. Soon called "Mennonites," the Anabaptists of the Reformation survived into the seventeenth century.

Protestant Spiritualism

THE PROTESTANT SPECTRUM IN THE SIXTEENTH century included a group of radicals for whom the label "Spiritualists" has become accepted nomenclature. These radicals neither got excited about adult baptism, or infant baptism, for that matter, nor did they take the Trinitarian dogma as the apex of theological perversion; therefore they have been distinguished from both Anabaptists and Antitrinitarians. In contrast to all other religious groups in the sixteenth century, however, they made no real attempt to alter the prevailing ecclesiastical status quo. They criticized the existing forms of religion, but they never decided to form a new church. They were individualists; thus, they are without history. They are outsiders, forgotten men, who live only in the pages of their writings. Most of them conformed to the expected external routine of their respective communities. Only a few were emboldened to testify to their conviction, in a way almost by default. These few are the sole evidence we have of their kind, though there must have been many who thought like them, but who lacked the courage or the determination to make themselves known.

"In the beginning was the Word": this biblical dictum was the motto of the Spiritualists. Theirs was a unique definition of the "Word": they did not refer to the outer word, the Bible, which they considered an obscure and enigmatic book, where one part disagreed with the other and interpretation stood against interpretation. As a matter of fact, they delighted in collecting scriptural passages that, as they claimed, contradicted one another. Their "Word" was God's direct communication to man. Scripture was only the external witness and record of this. This basic insight prompted the Spiritualists to label all empirical manifestations of religion as peripheral and insignificant. They preferred the living voice of God to the dead record of Scripture. They considered spiritual baptism more important than the baptism of water at whatever age, and the spiritual partaking of Christ more meaningful than the eating of bread and the drinking of wine. Outer form was rejected in favor of inner spirituality. The Bible and ceremonies, the sacraments and the church, creeds, and ecclesiastical polity were unimportant, for they were externals. Such emphasis meant the rejection of a great deal of traditional dogma, or, at any rate, a reversal of priorities, so that the doctrines that were not outrightly questioned were relegated to a place of insignificance.

Sebastian Franck, a soapmaker, printer, historian, and theologian, deserves primacy. His versatility may be considered characteristic, for the Spiritualists were laymen, jacks-of-all-trades, and amateur theologians of boundless exuberance and endurance. Franck traversed the full spectrum of religious options in the early sixteenth century, beginning as a Catholic, becoming Lutheran, then Anabaptist, and finally deciding it best to walk his own way. "I do not want to be a papist," he wrote, "I do not want to be a Lutheran, I do not want to be an Anabaptist." His reason was that he found fault with all. His was a brief life and, considering the turbulence of the time, a tranquil one; but beneath the tranquillity lay revolutionary thoughts that altered the Christian religion beyond recognition. Franck saw Christianity as another expression of man's universal religion, to use language made popular by English Deist Matthew Tindal 200 years later, "a republication of the religion of nature." Accordingly, religious insight was valid regardless of where it was found, within or without the Christian church, within or without the Christian tradition. The great events of the Bible were seen as timeless symbols of God's dealings with man. Eternal truth expresses itself in historical form, Franck argued, and only the former is important. "The histories of Adam and Christ are not Adam and Christ," he remarked, and added, "The external Adam and Christ are but the expression of the inward, indwelling Adam and Christ."

Another Spiritualist, Sebastian Castellio, made compassion a theological principle. He paid for it with a life of personal hardship, an early death, and nearly universal repudiation by his contemporaries, but he acquired a place in history. He expressed his compassion for the Antitrinitarian Michael Servetus in an eloquent repudiation of governmental suppression of deviate religious opinion entitled *De haereticis, an sint persequendi* ("If Heretics Are to Be Persecuted?"), published in 1553, in response to Servetus's execution in Geneva. This book was neither an emotional appeal nor a tightly knit argument; rather it was a simple anthology of statements of famous theologians, from Augustine and Jerome to Erasmus and Luther, on the treatment of heretics. Its single theme, repeated with many variations, was that the noblest minds of Christendom through the centuries had been against the persecution of heretics. Persecution was wrong because it contradicted the principles of Christ. Besides, the definition of "heretic" was not easy: "If you are reputed in one town a true believer, you will be reputed in the next town as a heretic. Accordingly, if anyone wants to live today, he must have as many confessions of faith and religions as there are towns and sects, just as a traveler has to change his money from one day to the next." Although Castellio's motivation was the simple virtue of compassion, horror over the pain and anguish of a fellow human being, he also adhered to the dichotomy of "external" and "internal" that Franck proposed. He assumed that differences over the interpretation of certain doctrines did not touch on the essence of the Christian faith; therefore, such differences should be disregarded. The practice of virtue and a moral life were of greater importance than agreement over the proper interpretation, for example, of the Trinity. In short, Castellio's religion was undogmatic, latitudinarian, and practical, a strange departure from the norms so universally observed in the sixteenth century.

Sebastian Franck and Sebastian Castellio are examples of what must have been a much larger number of their contemporaries, men who had neither the capacity nor the interest to concern themselves with intricate theological questions, who felt that the competing ecclesiastical factions differed only over subtle points of doctrine, and who were persuaded that in the final analysis one of these factions was as good as the other.

The Antitrinitarian Dissent

A THIRD AND FINAL EXPRESSION OF RADICAL reform was found among those men, known as "Antitrinitarians," who attacked the Trinitarian dogma. Like the Anabaptists and the Spiritualists, they were heirs of the late medieval tradition as well as of the Reformation. Antitrinitarian soteriology was not Catholic, though it was a far cry from what may be called the Protestant consensus. Interestingly, the early representatives of Antitrinitarianism appear to have nurtured their radicalism while yet in the bosom of the Catholic church. To trace the phenomenon exclusively to the Protestant Reformation does not explain a complex situation. That the Reformation exerted a powerful stimulus cannot be doubted, however, both by its questioning of many traditional notions and by insisting on the primacy of the Scriptures as source for Christian theology. Once many theological points had become exposed to biting criticism, it was not surprising that the Trinitarian dogma should be similarly attacked.

The Antitrinitarians may be classified with both the Anabaptists and the Spiritualists, not only because they exhibited certain theological similarities, such as the repudiation of infant baptism, but also because they shared the characteristic attitude of denouncing the old church and the new as equally perverted and divorced from scriptural truth. Yet there were differences, the principal one being that virtually all Anabaptists and Spiritualists were orthodox Trinitarians. The Anabaptists viewed the person of Christ in traditional terms, and although the Spiritualists wrote rather obscurely—one almost feels that at times they themselves did not understand their beliefs—their essential orthodoxy also is certain. Moreover, the Anabaptist and the Spiritualist concern was primarily religious rather than theological; their watchwords were "commitment," "obedience," and "new walk of life." The Antitrinitarians were concerned about theology.

The epic of sixteenth century Antitrinitarianism began with solitary individuals. Decades later came the relatively unmolested establishment of Antitrinitarian congregations in eastern Europe. The story was halted, at least temporarily, with the virtual extinction of these congregations in the first half of the seventeenth century. Since Antitrinitarianism was basically a theological phenomenon, it had a lively theological history, from the repudiation of the orthodox Trinitarian dogma to the painful groping for positive alternatives, which often led to assertions of tritheism or the like that were more complicated than the repudiated doctrine. Indeed, the Antitrinitarians did not advance any essential argument that had not already appeared in the great Christological debates of the early church. That they were called "new Arians" was an apt expression of their connection with the past. Their ideas were hardly novel; they had been considered in the doctrinal controversies of the early church and had been found wanting.

Michael Servetus, a Spanish humanist, physician, geographer, and lay theologian, began the movement. As with so many other Reformation figures, we know little about his childhood and youth; history had not yet made him prominent. His first piece of writing shows him conversant with the biblical languages as well as theology, an indication that his schooling must have been thorough and extensive. In the fall of 1530, when he was barely twenty, he moved to Basel and there began to nettle the reformer Johann Oecolampadius with bothersome questions concerning the Trinity. During the six months he spent at Basel, Servetus worked on a tract dealing with his Trinitarian views. Early in 1531, he succeeded in securing a printer for his manuscript, which he entitled *De Trinitatis erroribus* ("Errors of the Trinity"). Servetus's position was Sabellian modalism: Father,

Son, and Holy Spirit were seen as the three "modes" or "dispositions" of God. Jesus was divine, indeed the Son of God, but not in the orthodox sense. The following year Servetus published a second treatise, entitled *Dialogorum de Trinitate libri duo* ("Dialogues Concerning the Trinity"), which, despite a number of minor retractions (about which he greatly boasted in the preface), reiterated his earlier position.

Two decades later, in 1553, came the publication of Servetus's magnum opus: *Christianismi restitutio* ("The Restitution of Christianity"). Within months, he was arrested in Geneva, brought to trial, and burned at the stake. Before the flames consumed his body he was heard to cry, "O God, save my soul; O Jesus, Son of the eternal God, have mercy on me." As one bystander remarked, if he had placed the adjective "eternal" before "Son," his life would have never been in danger. The flames of Geneva burned his name indelibly into the annals of European history. His death raised the question of religious freedom and his theology sowed the seed of the dissolution of the Trinitarian dogma.

The execution turned into a *cause célèbre*, evoking the resolute sentiment of a few voices of dissent, notably Sebastian Castellio's *De haereticis, an sint persequendi* and Guillaume Postel's *Apologia pro Serveto Villanovano*. Michael Servetus, instead of being an epilogue, proved to be the beginning of a lengthy line of critics of the Trinitarian dogma. His ideas were picked up, echoed, and spread by disciples who succeeded, in the end, in translating his theological theory into ecclesiastical practice. The critics were strikingly similar. They were men of the second generation of the Reformation and of strong humanist orientation. None was a trained theologian; all were Italian. They found a tolerant atmosphere, and thus a home, in Poland, where in the course of the last third of the century they experienced a modest flourishing of their ideas in a new church, the Minor Reformed church. Also known as Socinianism (after Faustus Socinus, the eminent leader) this group survived into the seventeenth century, when it played a part in the breakdown of orthodoxy.

John Calvin

IN MARCH 1536, A SLENDER BOOK WAS PUBlished under the somewhat nondescript title *Institutes of the Christian Religion*. The author, a Frenchman named John Calvin, had worked hard and fast on the manuscript, and had produced a competent, if inconspicuous, work. The book was a success, but hardly more so than dozens of Protestant theological tracts published in that age of religious ferment; yet the author was to dominate the theological Reformation for the next three decades.

John Calvin became one of the most eminent reformers. Many others were ignored by historical scholarship or even deprived of their theological originality; Calvin's stature has always been recognized. In the Anglo-Saxon world his impact has been widespread and his thought has often been synonymous with the Protestant tradition. He was the great theological system-builder of the Reformation, quite in contrast to Luther, who rambled through the theological thicket with the vigor of an exuberant genius, who was neither fearful of paradox nor hesitant of overstatement.

This historical significance must be rightly understood. The site of Calvin's reform activity was modest and insignificant: Geneva, no matter how influential in the Swiss Confederation, was a small city-state, picayune when compared with the real centers of power in Europe, England, Spain, and France. What took place in that small commonwealth, even with regard to the matter of ecclesiastical change, was quite unimportant. Although most histories of the Reformation recount the course of events in Geneva in striking detail, there is no more justification for doing so than for narrating the events in Strassburg, Basel, Augsburg, Nuremberg, or any other of the numerous towns in central Europe in similar fashion. The history of the Reformation in Geneva can well be slighted. Of primary significance is the thinking of the Genevan reformer, transferred in a remarkable way from the town of Lake Leman to the four corners of Europe, to France no less than to Scotland, Poland, Hungary, and Holland. Calvin's thought had a centrifugal quality that made it, within a few short years, the normative vocabulary of those who adhered to the new faith. Throughout Europe Calvin's beliefs took on flesh and blood. Men formed new churches, suffered pain and martyrdom, and went into exile because they were persuaded that John Calvin, who had never taken a formal course in theology, propounded the authentic Christian message. In several countries, notably in Scotland, France, and the Low Countries, the fabric of Calvinist thought interwove intricately with the political aspirations of the people so that the cause of the Reformation (which was Calvin's Reformation) became, once again, inextricably linked to the broader history of society.

Recalling on his deathbed the struggles during his years at Geneva, Calvin observed that "the Lord our God so confirmed me, who am by no means naturally bold (I say what is true), that I succumbed to none of their attempts." "Who am by no means naturally bold"—no description of Calvin sounds more unbelievable:

we envision him as a cold, stern, even tyrannical person. Perhaps Calvin himself sensed the astounding character of his words for he added, "I say what is true." What he meant by those words was that his natural disposition was alien to the demands of the official responsibilities he exercised in Geneva. But he was persuaded that God had called him to do the work, and he was going to do it. The notion of a strong divine vocation hovers over Calvin's life.

Like his great reforming counterparts, John Calvin had a penchant for work. His literary output does not quite equal that of Luther (who often wrote while he was still clarifying his thinking), but still it was enormous. In addition, Calvin was involved in the routine of ecclesiastical affairs in Geneva, corresponded prolifically, and preached countless sermons from the pulpit of St. Peter's Church. About 2,000 of these sermons are extant, preached over a ten-year period, which accounts for the highly impressive average (especially when one is aware of the content) of 200 a year. Such activity, coupled with a persuasive theology, carried Calvin's message far beyond the city walls of Geneva.

Obvious factors help to explain its success. During the time of Calvin's ascendancy Lutheranism was not only engaged in a bitter life-and-death struggle, but also was forced to cope with serious theological dissensions within its own ranks. By the force of external circumstances Lutheranism, for all practical purposes a German phenomenon, became inner directed. In the German situation the alignment of religion and politics, so typical of the Reformation, meant the pursuit of certain ecclesiastical concerns on the part of the territorial rulers in the German Diet.

Calvinism found itself in a different situation for two reasons: the French background of John Calvin himself and the geographical proximity of Geneva and France. Calvin had no greater aspiration than to lead his native land to the true understanding of the Christian gospel. In addition to this emotional involvement was the practical fact that the language of his theological tracts and his letters of counsel, inspiration, and exhortation was, as a rule, in French. He could speak directly to the French people, in the way Luther had been able to speak to the Germans, and the geographic location of Geneva added its own particular significance.

Another element was that the sites of vigorous Calvinist expansion were also places of political and constitutional turbulence, and this had profound consequences for the inner history of Calvinism. Virtually all reformers had agreed on the right of the lower magistracy to resist the upper magistracy. In Germany this line of thought had provided the theological rationale for the founding of the League of Schmalkald. Elsewhere in Europe, however, notably in France, the issue was considerably more complicated, for there the situation was characterized by not only a prolonged and frustrating struggle for the legal recognition of the Protestant faith, pursued under intermittent persecution, but also by the presence (at several places) of a real constitutional crisis. This precipitated reflections on the relationship of the Christian to the secular authorities. Calvinist theologians offered some striking answers to make their position congenial to political upheaval and change. Calvinism, in other words, was at the right time and place when certain issues arose and demanded an answer. This was its destiny and, in a sense, its historical significance.

Calvin was a strange man—both timid and stern, modest and aggressive, an unusual combination of opposites. Above all, however, he was a brilliant theologian. The second generation of the Reformation may have called for men of this type and Calvin brought impressive credentials, foremost, of course, being a profound mind. Much has been written about his theology and there can be little doubt that it was one of the eminent achievements of the century; one can say this without engaging in the kind of parochial hagiography that so often inflates denominational founding fathers to bigger-than-life positions of historical prominence. Compared with the other outstanding reformer, Luther, Calvin was more systematic and less paradoxical.

Several themes occupy more than a cursory place in Calvin's theological exposition. The assertion of divine sovereignty is one; predestination is another; the righteousness of faith, yet another. The difficulty is not so much the acknowledgment that these are important, but the assessment of their relative significance. Possibly the common thread is the systematic delineation of the theological ramifications of a rigid notion of justification by grace alone. The spectrum of Protestant opinion in the sixteenth century shows that this principle lent itself to a variety of expressions, and Calvin's exposition is therefore neither the only nor the authentic one.

There is an interesting phrase in Calvin's dedicatory epistle to Francis I: "How does the kingdom of Christ come to us and remain among us?" The majesty of divine sovereignty seems to be the leitmotiv of Calvin's theology. God's sovereignty over little things as well as big ones, over good as well as evil, over man's damnation as well as his salvation, forms the constant theme of Calvin's *Institutes of the Christian Religion.* Creation and man point to the glory of God.

Predestination was the radical application of justification by grace alone. To the assertion that God's grace, and not man's works, effects man's redemption, Calvin added the insistence that God is utterly free to bestow this grace upon whom he pleases.

We say rightly that [God] foresees all things, even as he disposes of them; but it is confusing everything to say that God elects and rejects according to his foresight of this or that. When we attribute foreknowledge to God, we mean that all things have always been and eternally remain under his observation, so that nothing is either future or past to his knowledge: he sees and regards them in the truth, as though they were before his face. We say that this foreknowledge extends throughout the circuit of the world and over all his creatures. We call predestination the eternal decree of God by which he decided what he would do with each man. For he does not create them all in like condition, but ordains some to eternal life, the others to eternal damnation.

This was Calvin's notion of predestination. God did not merely allow the fall of Adam; he willed it. Calvin saw this as the teaching of Scripture, but he conceded the difficulties: "We ought not to seek any reason for it because in its greatness it far surpasses our understanding." Calvin was persuaded that this doctrine was taught in Scripture. He asserted that it guaranteed man's redemption as nothing else could. The certainty of redemption was related to the certainty of election, which, in turn, was the consequence of Christ's redemptive work. And this redemptive work of Christ—the death on the cross of God's Son—was as impenetrable a mystery as the mystery of predestination. Although Calvin was reluctant to speak about the possible verification of election, he cautiously acknowledged that there were signs of it, fallible to be sure, but indications nonetheless. Among these were the external acceptance of the gospel and the reception of the Lord's Supper. There was also the new life of the believer.

Wherever Calvin's religion gained entrance, there prevailed a serious determination to follow the rule of Christ. Perhaps the other reformers gave in a bit too easily, or were too greatly overcome by theological scruples about the use of the magistracy to achieve moral reform. Calvin, however, saw his goal and pursued it relentlessly. No wonder that John Knox found Geneva "the most perfect school of Christ since the days of the Apostles." Geneva was different, and those who went there were quite aware of it. Whether all the people were different is impossible to say from this distance, though the reports (such as the one by Knox) were uniformly exuberant. Clearly, however, the authorities both endorsed the Calvinist ethos and determined to put it into practice.

Calvin's Life and Labors

JOHN CALVIN WAS BORN IN 1509, THE SON OF Gerard Calvin, secretary to the bishop of Noyon, and procurator of the cathedral chapter of the town. Both year and parental background are important: Calvin was a man of the second generation of the Reformation who reached theological maturity when the period of storm and stress had passed. Moreover, he spent his youth in the urbane and cultured setting of a cathedral town, the *haut monde* of ecclesiastical life. In 1531 Calvin moved to Paris, where he undertook humanistic studies. His main preoccupation was a commentary on Seneca's treatise *De Clementia*, which was published in April 1532. "At length the die is cast," he wrote a friend. "My commentaries on the books of Seneca, *De Clementia*, have been printed, but at my own expense, and have drawn from me more money than you can well suppose. At present, I am using every endeavor to collect some of it back." Since this work was not theological and antedated Calvin's Protestant orientation, it has generally been overlooked by scholarship. It is important, in that Calvin's notion of natural law undoubtedly was derived from Stoic thought, and the exegetical approach of the commentary—using grammar and parallel passages—laid the foundation for his subsequent mastery of biblical hermeneutics.

In May 1534 Calvin traveled to Noyon to surrender his ecclesiastical benefices. An event of importance must have compelled him to cut his ties with the church, and there is reason to believe that a conversion had been the precipitating factor. The sources are scarce, and the most pertinent document is Calvin's own *Commentary on the Psalms* (1557), in which he wrote that "God by a sudden conversion subdued and brought my mind to a teachable frame." Much depends on the meaning of "conversion." If we take the term to mean a religious reorientation and simultaneous break with Catholicism (as seems most obvious), the event must have occurred sometime between August 1533, when Calvin attended a Catholic meeting at Noyon, and May 1534, when he resigned his benefices. In any case, Calvin's Protestant conviction made his continued stay in France dangerous; in the fall of 1534 he moved to Basel. He read further in theological works and corresponded with some of the reformers, but mainly he worked on the *Institutes of the Christian Religion*, the book that led him to his destiny. He was truly *vir unius libri*, a man of one book. After 1539 a second edition appeared, substantially enlarged—the original six chapters were expanded into seventeen—and this new edition revealed the theological brilliance of the author. Further editions appeared in 1543, 1550, and 1559, each followed by a French translation.

In the summer of 1539 Calvin happened to travel through Geneva, then a small town on the westernmost tip of Lake Leman, relatively unimportant and undistinguished. The woodcut in Sebastian Münster's *Cosmographey* of 1564 shows a few dozen houses, together with the steeples of three or four churches. Geneva had its share of political problems in the opening decades of the sixteenth century (mainly caused by the oppressive policies of the dukes of Savoy), but in addition the city experienced religious ferment. At issue was the propagation of Protestant ideas, personified by Guillaume Farel, who arrived in the fall of 1532. He was a Protestant firebrand with a bit of explosive and ebullient Gallic temper in him; he knew neither weakness nor patience, only a zealous pursuit of the things of God. "At no time did any man preach the Sacred Word of God purely without being persecuted and denounced by the world as a rogue and an impostor," he said on one occasion; his life provided abundant illustration for his own contention. The monument erected in his memory in front of the cathedral of Neuchâtel shows him with arms raised high, holding a Bible: the figure could be Moses hurling the Ten Commandments against the golden calf, and the similarity is more than coincidence. Some would have called him a rabble-rouser, for he always left traces of tension, strife, and turmoil. He was the prototype of the militant Protestant. In Geneva his agitation was successful; in May 1536, the Protestant faith was officially introduced. With upraised arms, the citizens voted for the new faith. An edict of the city council extolled the "Gospel and the Word of God" as the norm of life and faith.

John Calvin passed through this city two months later. Before the day was over his life had been altered and Geneva had become the site of his destiny. He later recalled with characteristic reticence that Farel sought to keep him at Geneva, proceeding "to utter an imprecation that God would curse my retirement, and the tranquility of the studies which I sought, if I should withdraw and refuse to give assistance, when the necessity was so urgent. By this imprecation I was so stricken with terror that I desisted from the journey which I had undertaken."

Calvin's activities began with the interpretation of the Pauline Epistles "with great praise and profit." He spoke of himself as *"professor sararum literarum in ecclesia Genevensi,"* a somewhat high-sounding title that obscured his modest role in the ecclesiastical affairs of the city which was more aptly expressed in the minutes of the city council for 5 September 1536: "Master Guillaume Farel points out the necessity of the lectures begun by that Frenchman at St. Peter's and requests that he be retained and supported. He was told that such support would be taken under advisement." Calvin drafted a church order that dealt with worship, as well as with such matters as marriage and the celebration of the Lord's Supper. A short time later he completed a catechism based upon the *Institutes* and a confession of faith based upon the catechism.

A provision in the church order stipulated that all citizens should publicly subscribe to this confession "so that it can be seen who agrees with the Gospel and who would rather belong to the Kingdom of the Pope than of Jesus Christ." In March 1537 the Large and Small Councils approved the church order. The subscription to the confession, however, proved to be a different matter and despite repeated efforts most burghers were recalcitrant and refused to subscribe. At that point, Farel's rashness and Calvin's inexperience precipitated a fateful development.

In February 1538 elections to several municipal offices were held and the opponents of the recent ecclesiastical changes made a clean sweep. Calvin called it a "most miserable situation," forgetting that in part it had been caused by his own obduracy. The showdown came over the use of ordinary or unleavened bread at Communion and the use of the baptismal font. Calvin and Farel conceded that these were insignificant matters, but they saw a basic principle at stake. For political reasons, namely to effect closer ties with Berne, the city council favored the use of unleavened bread and the baptismal font. The ministers were furious over this governmental usurpation of ecclesiastical authority.

Communion was to be celebrated on Easter. Farel and Calvin refused to use the Bernese form and were promptly forbidden to preach; Calvin preached anyhow. Two days later the two men were ordered to leave the city. Calvin continued the journey begun two years earlier. His public ministry, reluctantly begun but vigorously pursued, had ended in failure. Farel found a home at Neuchâtel and Calvin accepted an invitation to serve a congregation of French refugees at Strassburg. For three important years that city was his home; indeed, it was more than that. It was his school of theology and ecclesiastical statesmanship. At Strassburg Calvin saw a Protestant community in action, without the kind of problems that had perturbed Geneva.

In July 1539 he received Strassburg citizenship; without doubt he had every intention of making the city his permanent home. Meanwhile Geneva was experiencing tensions. The summer of 1539 had brought a bitter dispute over a treaty with Berne. The city was divided between two factions, the Artichauds, who approved of the articles of the treaty, and the Guillermins, the followers of Guillaume Farel, who opposed them. Early in 1540 the Guillermins succeeded in obtaining the majority on the Small Council. In June riots occurred over this issue and shortly thereafter one of the leaders of the Artichauds was executed in an enigmatic exercise of justice. The relationship between Berne and Geneva deteriorated.

If the political situation of Geneva was in a precarious state, religious affairs were hardly better. No strong leadership existed and the clergy were a sorry lot, characterized by shocking behavior and professional incompetence. Some Genevan citizens thought wistfully of Calvin. His return began to be advocated by the Guillermins, and in September 1540 the city council issued its first invitation. Calvin could not have been less interested: "I would prefer a hundred other deaths to that cross." But eventually he yielded. On 2 September 1541, he journeyed into an unknown future. He carried a letter from the Strassburg authorities, who gave him a leave of six months. Whether or not he meant to stay only until calm and order had returned, the six months stretched into twenty-three years; more than once Calvin must have wondered about the wisdom of his return.

Calvin and the Genevan Church, 1541–1564

AT THIRTY-TWO, CALVIN WAS STILL A YOUNG man in 1541. But he came as the leader of the Genevan church, a far cry from the subordinate position he had occupied five years earlier. Geneva gave him an opportunity to translate his theological theory into ecclesiastical practice. To be sure, even in Geneva the real always fell short of the ideal, and Calvin's relationship with the city was never more than a *mariage de convenance* where neither of the partners was particularly happy, though both found it acceptable and valuable. Calvin was too one-sidedly concerned about religion to be fully appreciated by the Genevan citizenry, and Geneva was far too worldly to gain Calvin's full respect.

On the day of his return Calvin asked the city fathers to consider a church order. He left little doubt about what was foremost on his mind, namely, the formulation of a comprehensive order for the Genevan church. On 20 November 1541 the people of Geneva approved the new order without opposition.

The *Ordonnances ecclésiastiques* were Calvin's contribution to the issues of practical churchmanship. Influenced by the practice in Strassburg, their assumption was that the New Testament contained a clear-cut and explicit paradigm of how a congregation should be structured. Four congregational offices were noted: ministers (*pasteurs*), teachers (*docteurs*), elders (*anciens*), and deacons (*diacres*). The ministers, collectively known as *venerable compagnie des pasteurs*, were responsible for preaching and the administration of the sacraments. The teachers saw to the religious instruction of the congregation, taught the young, and trained future ministers. The elders supervised the lives of the faithful to assure that the principles of Christian demeanor were properly exhibited. The deacons, twelve in number, cared for the sick and the poor.

Of all the provisions of the *Ordonnances ecclésiastiques* none has been as famous—or infamous—as the institution of the consistory, composed of the ministers and the elders. It was the heart of the *Ordonnances*, the instrument, as Calvin observed, of "the supervision of the congregation of the Lord so that God might be honored purely." It met weekly and considered a large variety of offenses: Catholic practices, blasphemy, immorality, dancing, nonattendance at church —some trivial, others important. There is pathos, sadness, and even humor in the records of the consistory meetings; for example, a *femme fatale* who, cited because of improper dress, retorted that those who did not want to see her that way should close their eyes.

A careful ecclesiastical supervision of the citizens was thus established. This fact must not lead to the conclusion that there existed a clerical tyranny, for the consistory was not a clerical body. The majority of its members were laymen. Moreover, such supervision was hardly new, for public regimentation of morality was a characteristic of general late medieval society. The uniqueness of the Genevan situation was that such regimentation was administered by a body that spoke for both the ecclesiastical and the political community. The prerogative of the church to supervise the lives of the citizens was forcefully asserted. There were long, difficult, but successful battles to establish that prerogative. The opposition came from the secular authorities, who objected to what seemed to be an ecclesiastical usurpation of civic jurisdiction.

Calvin died on 27 May 1564, and Theodore Beza, his successor, recorded that "as the sun went down, the greatest light in this world was taken up into heaven." The funeral was simple, for so Calvin had wanted it—no hymns, no eulogies, no tombstone. This expressed his conviction that his person possessed no significance. As one contemporary said, "No man knoweth his resting-place until this day." Those who would seek out John Calvin in Geneva today may walk from the university, the successor of the academy, across the Promenade des Bastions to the famous Reformation Monument, where the statues of Calvin, Farel, Beza, and Knox symbolize the events of the sixteenth century and the tradition that Calvin founded. The figure of Calvin is only slightly taller than the others, a striking expression of the way he himself wanted his place understood.

6 The Political Consolidation

Years of Transition

WITH THE DIET OF WORMS BEGAN A NEW AND different chapter in the ecclesiastical controversy. This was not only for the reason already noted, that the proclamation of a single man was increasingly echoed and reechoed throughout Germany. More important was the fact that the Edict of Worms turned the affair of Luther into an affair of state. Any resolution of the matter from then on had to be in the realm of politics as much as of religion.

The man who was to undertake the administration of the edict was absent. The splendid oratory of Worms, when Charles had confronted the territorial rulers with his uncompromising assertion that he was ready to pledge his life and property to the eradication of the Lutheran heresy, had disappeared like smoke. Charles departed for Spain in what seemed a wise and necessary move after having attended, at his first German Diet, to the pressing political problems in the empire. He had settled the problem of the *Reichsregiment*; he had turned over the Austrian lands and the claims to Bohemia and Hungary to his brother Ferdinand; he also had disposed (on paper, that is) of the heretical menace. Accordingly, he directed his attention to Spain. There his election to the imperial throne had been received with ill-concealed dismay. The prospect of an absentee ruler and of higher taxes, necessary for Charles's exercise of the imperial office, was hardly calculated to arouse warm feelings. In May 1520, the *comuñeros* revolt (a rebellion of the towns against the nobility) had broken out and, even though it was quickly suppressed, there is little doubt that Charles's return seemed highly necessary.

Germany was like a pilotless ship, a fact that was to have profound consequences for the subsequent course of events. At the time Charles could see no reason why the Lutheran menace would not be swiftly crushed. Heresy, after all, had always been crushed. One suspects that Charles left Germany in the spring of 1521 with a feeling of satisfaction and accomplishment. But he overlooked two important facts: the intensity of popular support for Martin Luther and the inability of the *Reichsregiment* to function effectively—which meant failure at Nuremberg to enforce the Edict of Worms. Its representation rotated all too frequently for any long-range policy to be practicable. There was also a disposition to stay aloof from such a heated controversy and to let events run their course. Only the dogged determination of Duke George of Saxony led in January 1522 to a mandate that prohibited all changes in existing ecclesiastical practice. Since the Edict of Worms had, in effect, declared the same, the mandate was probably gratuitous; it was certainly as ineffective.

In 1523 the estates demanded a council as the means of settling the religious issues: a general assembly of the German people should convene at Speyer in November to arrive at a temporary settlement. The emperor voiced a veto; he was shocked, he wrote to Germany, by this incredible venture proposed by the "pious German people." He demanded that the Edict of Worms be administered and that "all discussion, explanation, or interpretation of the Christian faith" be stopped. In cooperation with the pope he would seek to bring about a general council.

The emperor's prohibition settled the matter; November 1524 came and went, and no council gathered at Speyer. But some Germans did gather, casually at first, but then with increasing intensity and determination: the German peasants, restless and discontented, rallied to express their grievances. Germany, already in the throes of religious controversy, became the site of the political and social turmoil of the "Peasants' War." The conflict had not come overnight: from the late fourteenth century onward Germany had been beset by periodic peasant unrest. Though the peasants' demands and grievances were many, a single theme ran through them: the demand for the restoration of traditional custom and law. The peasants resented the new way of life, the new taxes and obligations, the new laws, the new judicial procedures, and, above all, the increasingly autocratic tendencies of the rulers. What evoked their indignation was not economic need or social oppression, but a changing and alien legal order. A few propounded a vision of a society governed by the principles of the divine law, in which the peasants' place would be determined not by arbitrary laws but by the very law of God. Vassalage would be abolished, for God had created all men free; and the fruits of creation would be used by all, for God had created them for all. When the storm broke in southwest Germany in the fall of 1524 there were a few skirmishes and numerous acts of brutality on both sides, but that was all. The final outcome half a year later, however, was disastrous. Though exact figures are beyond reconstruction, the number of casualties among the peasants may well have reached 100,000. The peasants were militarily naïve and lacked competent leaders; they never had a chance.

The multitude of peasants killed, houses burned, and land devastated left little doubt that the toll had been heavy, indeed catastrophic. Initially, the peasants' demands had been moderate and the possibility of a pacific resolution of their grievances existed. Here and there agreements were actually reached between peasants and lords. But by and large violence, not compromise, determined the course of events.

Some of the pamphlets that appeared in the early 1520s had called for a reform of society no less than of the church. Although not actively pursuing this sentiment, Luther paid lip service to it in his *Open Letter to the Christian Nobility* and never openly dissociated himself from it. It was inevitable, then, that the peasants should take up his words. There was a connection between the proclamation of Martin Luther and the aspirations of the peasants, who with halberds and sickles went forth to translate their dreams into reality. Exciting new thoughts and slogans such as the common man had not heard before had come out of Wittenberg. Luther had spoken about the freedom of the Christian man, who was a "perfectly free lord of all, subject to none." He had asserted that even the simple could understand the Gospels and that the high and mighty of the world had perverted this precious treasure. Luther had proclaimed the priesthood of all believers, and had insisted that all Christians were spiritual equals. The tracts expounding the Lutheran gospel no longer derided the peasant, but presented him as a paradigm for an authentic insight into things spiritual.

After the initial peasant uprising Luther sought to clarify his relationship to the peasants with his *Friendly Admonition to Peace Concerning the Twelve Articles of the Peasants* of April 1525. He was bitter toward the stubborn rulers and favorably disposed toward the peasants' demands, which seemed right and proper to him, though as a minister he felt not competent to judge. Experts in the fields of law and economics should do this. What evoked his indignation, however, was that the peasants supported the demand for the alleviation of economic grievances with references to the Gospels. This was an abomination and Luther spared no words of vehement denunciation. "And even if they [the demands] were proper and right according to the natural law, you have forgotten the Christian law, since you do not seek to attain them with patience and prayer to God, as becomes Christian men, but with impatience and blasphemy to force the authorities."

Three weeks later Luther took to the pen again. His tract *Against the Murderous and Plundering Hordes of the Peasants* was of a different tone. The peasants had proceeded to violence, insurrection, and bloodshed; law and order were disrupted. This was bad enough, but what made it demonic was the peasants' utilization of religion for their political purposes, an abominable misunderstanding of the Gospels, which admonish man to turn the other cheek, and a repudiation of political authority as well, which had been ordained by God to provide for law and order. Luther used some harsh and almost hysterical words in the tract, but this he always did when he thought fundamental issues at stake. It was as if Luther had written his pamphlet with indelible ink. Theologically his case may have been consistent as well as sound; linguistically, it was a failure. No wonder the peasants found little love lost between themselves and the man who wished for their stabbing, slaying, and killing. One cannot measure the religious allegiance of the sixteenth century peasant who had no leader, no platform, and no literary expression. To talk about what he did after the Peasants' War is therefore as gratuitous as to suggest what he had done before. The assertions are many, the facts lamentably few. Whether the Peasants' War signified the end of the popular dimension of the early Reformation cannot be said. That general enthusiasm waned is incontestable, but natural; the exuberance of the initial period was bound to end sometime.

Speyer, 1526

THE YEAR 1525 HAD BROUGHT GREAT TURBU-lence to Germany, and many saw the violence and bloodshed of that spring and summer as a sign of the last days. Luther thought so, as did Elector Frederick of Saxony, who died during the height of the Peasants' War. The many victims of the uprising, the destruction and devastation, created a feeling of despondency.

This turbulence symbolized the significance of the year in the German Reformation, for in several important ways 1525 was a watershed. It was a year of clarification, for Luther's involvement in the Peasants' War and the emergence of radical dissent tended to define more sharply the movement for ecclesiastical reform. The period of ecstatic exuberance, during which Luther's camp was overcrowded with well-meaning, if uninformed, partisans, came to an end.

The Peasants' War had significance not only for Luther's loss of popular support, but also for the larger course of the Reformation. The rulers were naturally concerned about a future uprising and, with a kind of self-evident logic, rallying together suggested itself as the best means of preventing one. Since Luther was widely viewed as the spiritual mentor of the rebellion in spite of his criticism of it, any protective effort was bound to have an anti-Lutheran character. What was directed on the surface against the peasants could easily be interpreted as aimed at the suppression of the Lutheran movement. This fact proved to be of utmost importance for subsequent developments, for it also suggested to those rulers with Lutheran propensity the need for collective action. The uniting of Catholic rulers made this inevitable.

Therefore, the two parties of the religious controversy began to face one another, not merely as proponents of differing theological points of view, but also as warriors preparing for battle. The Reformation became a political phenomenon and the character of the course of events changed. If the first phase had been the spontaneous popular response to Luther's proclamation, and if the second phase had been characterized by the haphazard administration of the Edict of Worms in individual territories, the third phase brought the emergence of two political blocs, the one loyal to the Catholic church, the other committed to the new faith.

A diet was convened to meet at Speyer in 1526. It opened in June. On the first day mass was celebrated in the cathedral, as this had always been the custom; yet there were differences. Some of the Lutheran sympathizers had the initials VDMIE on their coat sleeves, the abbreviation for *Verbum Dei Manet in Eternum* ("The Word of God Remains Forever"). Philip, Landgrave of Hesse, had an ox butchered and roasted on a Friday, the day the Catholic church exhorted the faithful to abstain from meat.

The most important item on the agenda was the enforcement of the Edict of Worms. The cities stated bluntly that this simply could not be done and afterward proposed that the emperor should be so informed. Their point was obvious: in the emperor's absence no decision could be made, neither for nor against the Edict of Worms.

The subsequent decree of the diet proposed a delegation to the emperor to acquaint him with conditions in the empire, requested a "free general council or at least a national council," and advised the territorial rulers how the religious issues should be handled in the meantime: "In matters concerning the Edict so to live, rule, and act as each estate could hope and trust to answer before God and the Emperor." The proposed delegation to the emperor never materialized, and the most important matter to come from the diet was the sentence just cited. Here, needless to say, everything depended on interpretation. The diet had meant the provision to be a temporary solution, as a truce until the religious problem could be solved, it was not a recognition of Lutheranism, nor an acknowledgment of the right of the territorial rulers to do as they pleased. At issue was only the enforcement of the Edict of Worms.

Yet the essence of any truce is brevity. If it lasts too long it becomes unalterable. So it was with the decree of Speyer. The continuing absence of the emperor, together with the absence of a general council, postponed the final resolution from month to month and year to year. This, in turn, made the organizational consolidation of Lutheranism inevitable, and the recess of Speyer formed the rationalization for this development. The decree of Speyer, and thereby the history of the Reformation, might have been altered by a new turn of events: the emperor's intervention or return to Germany, the convening of a council. But nothing happened, and the truce became a peace. The religious schism developed to a state beyond repair.

Here lies the tragedy of Charles V. His absence from Germany, prompted by his complex involvement in Spanish and, indeed, all of European politics, created a vacuum in Germany and decisively influenced the fate of the Reformation. Charles, if anyone, should have been the one to stem the tide of the Lutheran heresy. But he was far away in Spain, waging war against his archfoe Francis I. He won a splendid battle at Pavia, but afterward he lost the peace at Madrid. In short, his concerns were those of the *rey catholico* of Spain rather than of the *Kaiser* of Germany. Whether or not his presence in Germany would have altered the course of events, his absence certainly did not make matters better.

Speyer, 1529

AFTER AN INTERVAL OF THREE YEARS THE German Estates gathered again. The emperor's summons had singled

86

out action against the Turks as the principal item for consideration, though it also noted that the religious situation had deteriorated and therefore required action.

The deliberations among the estates revealed extensive disagreement. The first draft of a decree called for the convening of a general council within eighteen months; until that time the territories that had accepted the new teaching should undertake no further changes. The Lutheran estates voiced opposition, but the majority clearly favored a tough line. The situation was different from that of 1526, when affairs had been in a state of flux. In 1529 the issues were clearly defined: the long duration of the controversy and the temporizing that increasingly turned into permanent arrangements called for a definitive resolution. The majority of the estates proposed to rescind the decree of 1526, renew the Edict of Worms until a general council, and prohibit any ecclesiastical change.

The adherents of the new faith promptly voiced a protest: since the recess of 1526 had been passed unanimously, it was "honorable, proper and legal" to rescind it only by a unanimous vote. They would not accept the proposed decree, "since in matters pertaining to the honor of God and the salvation of our souls each man must himself stand before God and give an account so that no one can excuse himself with the decision and doings of others, be they many or few."

The occasion was hardly spectacular. Whether majority opinion could be imposed upon the minority was legally an open question; but more was at stake than legality. The minority raised the voice of conviction against political odds. The medieval world, with its ideal of the *corpus christianum,* the one Christian body, fell apart. In 1521 a single monk had faced the dignitaries of the empire and had demanded freedom for the exercise of his conscience. Almost to the day eight years later a group of territorial rulers echoed this sentiment and cause. Politically, the situation had become explosive.

While the diet was still in session, negotiations were conducted between several Protestant rulers. In April a plan for a defensive alliance was proposed. If any partner was attacked "for the sake of the Word of God," the others would come to his assistance. Many questions went begging since not all the parties had the same understanding of the significance of the proposal. The emperor was not mentioned, which meant that the critical problem of what should be done if he were to suppress them was ignored.

Augsburg, 1530

THE EMPEROR SOON SUMMONED ANOTHER DIET
to meet in 1530. His invitation was astoundingly conciliatory.
Concerned about the restoration of religious concord for the sake of
both religion and political stability, Charles agreed to "hear, understand, and consider everybody's opinion in love and grace." He
offered his assistance "to consolidate all opinions to one Christian
truth and to remove everything which is not properly interpreted on
either side." During the discussion of the agenda the Protestants
successfully demanded that the religious problem be considered before
the discussion of Turkish aid. A Protestant refusal to supply aid
against the Turks, if the religious problem was not satisfactorily
settled, hung like a cloud over the diet and reminded the emperor to
be realistic in his religious policies and plans.

The emperor's willingness to "hear everyone's opinion" suggested
the formulation of a Protestant "opinion." Since no systematic
delineation of the new faith existed, Philipp Melanchthon drafted a
statement of faith on his way to Augsburg. By the middle of June he
had completed his work.

This Augsburg Confession has come to be considered the classic
theological statement of Lutheranism—ironically so, for the intent was
quite different. The confession did not stress the theological divergence
between the old and the new faith; its argument was that the major
differences consisted in "externals"—the Communion cup for the laity
or clerical celibacy. The confession showed that attitudes had not yet
become hardened beyond repair.

The draft of the recess of the diet gave the Protestants until 15
April of the next year to return to the Catholic church. Until that time
the recess of the recent diet at Speyer was to be observed. A general
council, to be convened within a year, would consider ecclesiastical
reform. The tenor of the draft was conciliatory. The reasons were
obvious: lacking strong support from Rome for a council the emperor
realized that he could hardly be successful in his efforts. Moreover, he
was politician enough to recognize (as did the Protestants themselves)
that he depended on Protestant support for any military action
against the Turks.

The Protestant estates rejected the draft, which on 19 November
1530, became the formal decree of the diet. By that time, however, the
diet was a rump gathering comprised of the emperor and the Catholic
estates. Twice, in a little over a year, the efforts to bring the adherents
of the new faith back to the Catholic church had proved unsuccessful.
The Protestants had a breathing spell of only six months.

The first full-fledged effort to achieve a theological conciliation of the two sides took place at Augsburg. The uniqueness of the effort lay in the fact that to some extent its driving force was neither the Catholic church nor the Protestant bodies, both of which appeared resigned to the split, but the political authorities. This fact was to become typical for the next two decades. Naturally, the absence of official religious endorsement circumscribed the maneuverability and raised the specter of official ecclesiastical disavowal.

Some of the emperor's Erasmian advisers had made him aware of the need for reform, but in part his pursuit of a policy of religious conciliation was political. He wanted religious peace to have the political stability indispensable for safety against the Turks and for freedom toward France. In short, it was not Charles, the son of the Catholic church, but Charles the emperor who doggedly, if sporadically, pursued conciliation.

The issue at Augsburg was whether the disagreement between the two sides pertained to substantive theological issues or merely to the correction of abuses. Opinions differed. At one point, only the issues of the Communion cup and of clerical celibacy were unresolved, and today we know that Rome was conciliatory even in these matters. The negotiations failed rather over questions of "ecclesiastical abuse."

Augsburg revealed an ambiguous situation, more hopeful than some had dreamed, more discouraging than others had feared. More had taken place than merely a discussion concerning the execution of the Edict of Worms, such as had characterized the two previous diets. There had actually been a semblance of theological discussion, an indication that the situation was flexible after all, but it failed. The Protestants had presented division: not only were there Lutherans, Zwinglians, and those traveling the narrow road between these two, but there were also those of irenic and not so irenic temperament. The latter distinction could also be found among the Catholics. There could be little reason for optimism when the diet adjourned.

The League of Schmalkald

FOR THE PROTESTANTS THE DIET CREATED A perturbing situation. The emperor seemed determined to use force after the expiration of the period of grace, and this danger prompted a determined reaction on their part. Philip of Hesse had hardly returned home from Augsburg when he invited the Saxon elector to discuss the possibility of an alliance. Few questioned the political advisability of such a move, but the theologians agonized over the legitimacy of opposing the emperor. After an initial reluctance Luther affirmed the right of resistance. He had been influenced by Philip, who pointed out the difference in the constitutional status of the emperor and the territorial rulers: the former was elected and had specific responsibilities; the latter had inherited their offices. The argument was that any resistance of territorial rulers against the emperor emanated from the exercise of their own authority.

The deliberations resulted in the League of Schmalkald, a defensive alliance to protect the signatories if attacked for religious reasons. The constitution of the league provided for a common treasury for military defense, military aid, a force of 12,000 men, and a council of war. But the bickering of the signatories in subsequent years revealed the extent of the political disintegration of the empire, since even the common religious profession (allegedly the *raison d'être* for the league) did not result in common political action. Despite this shortcoming, however, the league constituted a major factor in German politics no less than religion for over a decade. After the formation of the league the alternative to religious conciliation was force.

When 15 April 1531 arrived—the deadline for capitulation—the political situation had changed so drastically that Charles had no choice but to pretend that the date had never been mentioned. Wherever he looked, he faced problems: the reluctance of the pope to convene a council; the obstinacy of the Protestants; the Turkish threat; the uncertainty of relations with France. Pope Clement's promise to convene a council formed a major element in the emperor's plans to solve the religious problem. Yet it increasingly became obvious that this promise was hardly worth the paper on which it was written. A council was as far off as ever. Rumors about an imminent Turkish attack upon Vienna were circulating, and as long as the need for territorial support against the Turks persisted, Charles could ill afford to alienate the Protestants.

Moreover, the formation of the League of Schmalkald had altered the political picture. It showed that the Protestants were committed and determined. Charles's most prudent policy might have been to grant the Protestants coexistence; this was indeed suggested to him by Cardinal Loaysa, who told him that his difficulties were insurmountable and that he should "accept the heretics and have them be subject to your brother as the Bohemians are." The acceptance of religious diversity for the sake of political unity was a fateful suggestion; Charles would have none of it. He expressed his willingness to recognize the status quo, if the Protestants would aid him against the Turks. He still held two cards, and either might yet prove to be a trump: a peace with the Turks would free his hands for a firm policy toward the Protestants, while a peace with the Protestants would enable him to pursue an aggressive policy against the Turks.

Then Charles was reminded that one of his best friends was his greatest enemy. In the fall of 1531 his brother Ferdinand attacked Hungary. Ferdinand's move was intended to give him the advantage of controlling a strategic area and the prestige of military victory. It was unsuccessful and only increased the tensions between Suleiman II and the West. Suleiman was aware of Charles's determination to fight the Turks as soon as the opportunity presented itself, but he also knew that the religious turmoil in Germany tied Charles's hands. For Suleiman, the opportune hour had struck. On 26 April 1532, his trumpets sounded and a mighty military force marched westward, crossing the Hungarian border in June.

A diet had convened at Regensburg a few days before Suleiman began his campaign, and for the first time in a decade the religious problem was not paramount in the deliberations, but rather the Turkish threat. The emperor hoped to obtain aid from the estates. The Protestants in turn were willing to contribute, but demanded substantial ecclesiastical concessions: the revision of the Augsburg decree and toleration. Had the emperor received strong support from the Catholic estates, Protestant aid would have been unnecessary. But the Catholics insisted on a strict enforcement of the Augsburg decree, and at the same time refused to contribute aid. As far as they were concerned the Turkish threat was not very real. They demanded that the emperor set a good example by supplying troops of his own and argued that Ferdinand's attack gave them little confidence in the ability of the Hapsburgs to handle the admittedly precarious situation.

Negotiations at Regensburg quickly reached a stalemate. The real sites of action were Schweinfurt and Nuremberg, where talks were held between the representatives of the emperor and the League of Schmalkald. The Protestant demand for a religious peace and the emperor's request for aid against the Turks were the issues. Several months of negotiations brought no agreement, but then the Protestants became more flexible, mainly demanding the assurance of toleration and the suspension of religious litigation before the *Reichskammergericht,* the imperial supreme court, until the time of a general council. The possibility of a Turkish attack still called forth common solidarity. Luther admonished the estates to harmony in such troubled times and, according to an interesting (if erroneous) tradition, intended the first stanza of "A Mighty Fortress Is Our God" to be a battle song against the Turks.

In the end the Protestants granted their support and the emperor promised what they had asked. The agreement is known as the Peace of Nuremberg. It was a major achievement for the Protestants, the first step away from the policy of a rigid enforcement of the Edict of Worms. The peace had been prompted by the precarious political situation; it was conceded by the emperor to be a legal move (which had no bearing, of course, on the theological assessment of the differences), and it was meant to be temporary.

After the adjournment of the diet the forces of the empire proceeded to Vienna to meet the Turks. The emperor, barely recovered from serious illness, yearned to follow the troops and lead them into battle. He dreamed of a victory by which his name would be forever remembered. "Should I be defeated," he said, "I will leave a noble name behind me in the world and enter into paradise; should I be victorious, I will not only have a merit before God, but would also possibly restore the ancient boundaries of the Empire and obtain immortal glory." But Charles was thwarted in his aspirations. A small fortress in western Hungary, Güns, resisted the Turkish attacks for twenty-one days, sapping the strength of the onslaught. When Charles arrived, no battles could be fought nor victories attained.

Had he then returned to Germany, events might have taken a different course. Charles made his way to Italy, for good reason. In Germany a truce prevailed, an uneasy one, to be sure, but one that had temporarily calmed the situation. The Turks had been repelled and relations with France were tolerable. The religious issue remained unresolved, and Charles gave it priority. He knew that short of the use of force against the Protestants the only hope for a resolution of the conflict lay in a council. Since the pope was the key to the convening of a council, Charles hoped to persuade him to action. "I met with His Holiness," he wrote in his memoirs, "but without the full success I had anticipated." His verdict is true, even though the meeting at Bologna in February 1533 was amicable and papal cooperation disarming. Pope and emperor agreed on the need for a council and pledged themselves to secure the cooperation of France and the German Protestants.

Charles had seemingly been successful; but no council was to meet during Pope Clement's pontificate. The emperor's seeming hour of triumph was really one of tragedy.

Political Crisis in Switzerland

MEANWHILE, EVENTS IN SWITZERLAND PRECIPI-tated an ominous confrontation. The ecclesiastical changes effected in Zurich in 1525 brought a Catholic reaction: the Catholic cantons demanded that the Edict of Worms be administered throughout Switzerland and sought, moreover, the involvement of Austria in Swiss affairs. They threatened that deeds would promptly follow their words.

Zurich countered by seeking allies of its own to establish a balance of power in Switzerland. It was successful in December 1527, when it concluded an alliance with Constance. Berne became Protestant and other places showed Protestant leanings, among them Glarus, Appenzell, Graubünden, and Basel.

The Catholic cantons concluded a "Christian Alliance," *Christliche Vereinigung,* with Austria. The political situation in the Swiss Confederation deteriorated steadily. Both sides shrank from armed conflict, but their language was evasive. Zwingli asserted with strikingly timeless words that "the peace so eagerly sought by some is war, and not peace; and the war, for which we so eagerly prepare ourselves, is peace, and not war." He sought to broaden the political strength of the Swiss Protestants. He envisioned a European-wide anti-Hapsburg alliance. His persistent effort to reach a theological understanding with Wittenberg concerning Communion was influenced by his political plans. He was convinced that only a politics of strength safeguarded the new faith.

The showdown came quickly. The tensions between the Catholic cantons and Zurich took a turn for the worse and in April 1531 Zwingli asked for a declaration of war against the Catholic cantons. His proposal received no support. Within a month, however, an economic blockade was inaugurated against the Catholic cantons to deprive them of essential goods and thereby force them to submission.

In August a fiery comet was seen in the sky over Zurich and people pondered its significance, as sixteenth century man always did when confronted with unusual natural phenomena. Queried as to its meaning, Zwingli was said to have ominously replied that "many a man of honor, including myself, will be paying dearly." As though in fulfillment of his prophecy, war came in October, declared by the five Catholic cantons, which were determined to throw off the choking economic blockade. Zurich was ill prepared. The city had more than 12,000 men of conscription age, yet on the day of battle a mere 700 constituted its fighting force, together with 1,200 advance troops. There were no horses to pull the artillery, and both the morale and the pay of the soldiers were low. Twenty-one mobilizations between 1524 and 1531 had taken their toll.

On the morning of 11 October 1531, the Zurich forces went into battle. Among them was Huldreich Zwingli, who accompanied the troops with sword and Bible. In the afternoon the soldiers reached Kappel, ten miles south of Zurich, and the skirmish began. Twice the

Zurich forces were able to repulse the enemy; then they were overrun. Zwingli, who probably fought in the brunt of the battle, was mortally wounded. "What is it? The body they may kill, but not the soul," reportedly were his last words. Catholic soldiers discovered him on the battlefield, quartered his body, and burned it to ashes—the punishment of the day for a man who was thought both a traitor and a heretic.

By the middle of November peace negotiations were in progress, and toward the end of the month peace returned to the Swiss Confederation. This Peace of Kappel provided that the individual cantons could determine the religious faith within their boundaries. Any further expansion of Protestantism, however, was prohibited. The new faith was recognized in Zurich and the other Protestant cantons, but it was destined to remain a minority religion within the Swiss Confederation. The new faith had found legal acceptance almost a quarter of a century before such an accommodation was reached in Germany, but the dream of a Swiss Confederation, united in the new evangelical faith, had died, like Zwingli, on the battlefield of Kappel.

Yet something had happened. After the theologians had failed to persuade one another, the parties had marched to the battlefield, there to resolve their theological conflict. A Roman adage spoke of war as *ultima ratio regum,* the final reasoning of kings. The battle of Kappel offered eloquent proof that in the sixteenth century war could also be the final reasoning of theologians, or, to vary Clausewitz's famous definition, the "continuation of theological controversy by other means." Europe had watched with eagerness.

A New Church Emerges

BY THE EARLY 1530s THE ECCLESIASTICAL CONtroversy had reached the point where an element of permanence increasingly characterized the scene. No matter what the professed commitments of the Protestant reformers concerning the unity of the church, the harsh realities of life spoke a language of their own: sermons had to be preached, the sacraments administered, ministers educated, and congregations organized. In short, a new church had to be nurtured and exposed to the biting winds of life. This was the eminent task of Protestant churchmen in the 1530s and 1540s.

The formation of Protestant churches was a slow and haphazard process that suggests that the break with the Catholic church was not understood as an inevitable parting of the ways. It soon became evident that the break was permanent, or at least that one could proceed as though it were. This meant more comprehensive changes and entailed the establishment of new organizational structures, in short, the formation of new churches. As matters turned out, whereas certain external changes were undertaken with relative speed, alterations in temperament were long in coming. The process of Protestantization took the better part of the century.

In short, the process of initial change had been relatively untheological, moderate, and lacking in revolutionary fervor. Those characteristics underscore that the change lacked the quality of deliberate confrontation and break. They suggest haphazardness, an unwillingness to confront categorical alienation. What had been avoided, however, turned out to be the reality, and the pious hopes of the mid-1520s had faded, ten years later, like flowers on a sultry summer day.

The course of events proved to be different from what the reformers had anticipated. The Catholic church had not been open to the kind of change and reform they had desired. The reaction, indeed, had been one of hostility and even persecution. Nor had conciliation been possible. The parting of the ways, at first unconscious and unreflected, became petrified and no amount of effort seemed capable of bridging the gap. This meant that the heavy burden of permanence settled upon the new Protestant churches. The more time passed, the more reconciliation was out of the question even as the frantic eschatological sentiment of the early sixteenth century likewise waned and no longer afforded any grounds for nonchalance. The new churches were forced to settle down to everyday routine.

Three specific tasks were involved in the organizational consolidation. One pertained to the local congregation, its organizational structure and form of worship. A second aspect was the restructuring of the many social functions, such as the care for the poor, which the church had carried out in the past. Finally there was the matter of the broader organizational pattern of the church. In Germany the question of the form of the local congregation was greatly influenced by Luther's nonchalance in this respect. He wrote several orders of worship, but his *German Mass and Order of Service* of 1526 asserted that "in sum and substance this order and all others are to be used in such a way that, if there is abuse, they are promptly abolished and a new one put in its place." Luther sought to emphasize the centrality of the local congregation in ordering its life, from the selection of the minister to the form of the service. He had expressed this notion in his 1523 treatise *That a Christian Congregation or Gathering Has the Right and Authority to Judge All Teaching*. When a fellow reformer proposed a council to bring about ecclesiastical uniformity among those adhering to the new faith, Luther retorted that such uniformity was neither necessary nor advisable. Structures and forms would issue spontaneously and creatively from the local congregation. In a few instances this actually was the case: Thomas Müntzer wrote an order of worship for Alstedt, and Johann Lang one for Erfurt. But most congregations simply did not have the creative talent necessary for this purpose.

Some of the problems could not be solved on the local level. This fact inevitably placed the governmental authorities in the key position, for they alone could assume broad responsibilities. Governmental authority supervised the external ecclesiastical affairs, the training of the clergy, their remuneration, the supervision of the faithful. Luther conceded the ruler's role in ecclesiastical affairs only with great reluctance. His preface to the *Instruction of the Visitors for the Clergy* of 1527 indicated that he had given up the idea of effecting the building of a new church by way of a spontaneous evolution of forms, structures, and patterns on the local level. The territorial church was to be built with the help of the ruler. Luther's rationale was the emergency situation that existed. His exhortation was gratuitous and, if anything, showed the clash between theological reflection and political realities. The political authorities were already exercising a considerable role in ecclesiastical affairs, from the inspection of the clergy to the disposition of church property.

The laity generally had no voice in church affairs. Among the territories, a measure of congregational participation existed only in Hesse, where the organizational structure was less bureaucratic than elsewhere. The same held true for the imperial cities, influenced no doubt by the limited geographic confines and the representative character of the city councils. Of course, the priesthood of all believers continued to be espoused as a splendid ideal, but in actual practice churchmanship differed little in Protestant or Catholic lands.

Not all of the Protestant clergy were men of achievement, and Protestantism no less than Catholicism had its share of men for whom spiritual commitment was as much a mystery as theological competence. Philipp Melanchthon told about a minister who, when asked if he taught the Decalogue, answered that he had not as yet been able to purchase the book. Nor was moral demeanor always the norm. In 1541 the Hessian superintendents requested Landgrave Philip for a radical cure of clerical immoderation: "Whereas there is much complaint about clergy who cause considerable offense by their immoderate drinking and other vices and yet remain unpunished as well as unchanged, we recommend that a jail be established in the monastery of Spisskoppel and the unrepentant clergy be given the option of either leaving their parishes or being confined in that jail with water and bread to bring about their correction."

Needless to say, there also were many dedicated and competent ministers who carried out their responsibilities with proficiency and conscientiousness. They translated Protestant theory into practice; they were the field officers of the Reformation. They proclaimed the new gospel, nurtured their congregations, dealt with the political authorities. In sum, they added religious vitality to theological pronouncements. Though Protestantism had espoused the notion of the priesthood of all believers, in practice it became a *Pastorenkirche,* a church guided by the clergy.

The task of the ministers was to preach and administer the sacraments. Little difference with Catholicism existed with respect to the reception of the latter, except it tended to be less frequent. The emphasis upon preaching altered traditional precedent and placed a heavy responsibility upon the minister. There had been a good deal of preaching before the Reformation (that there was none is one of the stereotyped Protestant misconceptions), but the sermon had not occupied as important a place as subsequently among the Protestants. This Protestant stress on preaching was easier postulated than put into practice, and it speaks for Luther's practical sense of churchmanship that as early as 1522 he published a church postil to provide examples of scriptural preaching. Within his lifetime this "Wartburg Postil" saw almost thirty editions, a proof of its usefulness. The sermons of the postil were to be used by the ministers as an aid in the preparation of their homiletical exercises or as their "own." The zeal for the gospel was more important than questions of authorship. Thus, the words of Luther or Melanchthon were heard from many a Protestant pulpit in the sixteenth century, even though Luther never darkened the door of that church and the name of Melanchthon was never heard. The people were probably edified by such plagiarism.

Continued Protestant Expansion

FOR NINE LONG YEARS, FROM 1532 TO 1541, Charles V was absent from Germany, during which time Protestantism formalized its achievements. To be sure, the time of Protestant *Sturm und Drang* was over, but the list of territories and cities that embraced the Protestant faith during the 1530s is long and impressive: Württemberg, Pommern, Mecklenburg, Dinkelsbühl, Hannover, Nassau, Bremen, Osnabrück, and many others, especially in north Germany. These ecclesiastical transformations did not happen overnight; they were long in coming, and were, as often as not, merely the formalization of a state of affairs which had prevailed for some time. Many territories and cities had bided their time in view of the uncertainty of the decrees of 1529 and 1530, which had made a public acceptance of the new faith unwise.

At stake was not so much the dynamic acceptance of Protestant tenets on the part of the people, but a change in the formal ecclesiastical structure: the repudiation of episcopal jurisdiction, the dissolution of the monasteries, the secularization of ecclesiastical property, the discontinuation of the mass, and the introduction of what was called "evangelical preaching." These formal changes could now be undertaken, for the existence of the League of Schmalkald meant that any use of force on the part of the emperor would be met by force. At the same time, the Peace of Nuremberg seemed to offer toleration to Protestants. At long last, the formal acceptance of Protestantism in a territory no longer entailed ominous political consequences; quite the contrary, there were distinct advantages to ecclesiastical change. A new kind of Protestantism emerged from these achievements: self-conscious, political, institutional. Its spokesmen were the councillors of the League of Schmalkald; its expression was the formalized church order that gave permanent form to the changes undertaken. Still, no firm legal basis for the changes existed; to obtain it was the foremost objective of the Protestants.

The expansion of Protestantism created problems. The new Protestant territories demanded that the provisions of the Peace of Nuremberg should also be applied to them. The Catholics disagreed, holding that the peace applied only to those territories that had been Protestant in 1532. The *Kammergericht* followed a staunchly Catholic line and kept the Protestants in legal trouble. Then, in the late 1530s, the atmosphere in Germany appeared to undergo a change, and conciliation seemed, once again, the primary concern of the two parties. Charles V had really never given up hope that rapprochement might be possible, and on the Protestant side Martin Bucer's conciliatory efforts persisted.

Thus, after more than twenty years of bitter controversy, the hope for an amicable resolution of the religious conflict had not subsided. In both camps were men who thought it possible to achieve conciliation. The problem was that the ensuing colloquies did not take place under the aegis of the church and thus lacked authority and ecclesiastical stature. Agreement, even had it been reached, would have amounted to very little. If Zurich, Geneva, England, or Sweden had concurred with an agreement, not to speak of the German Protestants, the only consequence would have been a different psychological atmosphere. Such, however, would have been a noteworthy accomplishment, indeed.

Of course, not all was pristine purity at Hagenau, Worms, or Regensburg, the sites of the colloquies. Over the colloquies hovered a peculiar mixture of political and religious considerations, and the former may even have been more important than the latter. The emperor considered religious concord in Germany to be of utmost importance for his political plans (France, Denmark, and even England were flirting with the League of Schmalkald), though at the same time his understanding of his imperial responsibility as the arbiter of Christendom was an important factor in his thinking. The Curia was an uneasy bystander. The possibility of a religious agreement without Curial participation was real.

The first colloquy convened at Hagenau in 1540, but the participants could not even agree on the formulation of an agenda, a discouraging beginning. The second colloquy got under way at Worms in the same year and this time, after lengthy debates on procedural questions, theological questions were indeed discussed. Surprisingly the discussion of original sin brought agreement. Behind closed doors secret conversations were held between Martin Bucer and Johann Gropper, both men of irenic temperament, congenial choices to pursue conciliation. After the modest success at Worms, the talks were to continue at the diet to be held at Regensburg, this time in the emperor's presence.

By that time a military resolution of the religious conflict must have been already on Charles's mind, though at Regensburg, in the spring of 1541, conciliation dominated. Charles was the heart of the conciliatory effort, even though the theologians dominated the scene. The basis of the colloquy was a secret agreement reached at Worms, introduced under mysterious circumstances as the *Regensburg Book*. Its affirmations were broad and contained the proper sprinkling of biblical and patristic references, and thus seemed to promise a resolution of the disagreements.

Agreement was reached on several points, including justification. Though broadly formulated, the theological substance of that agreement was that justification is by faith and works, by grace and deeds of love. The accomplishment was enormously significant. For two decades justification had been the cause of heated disagreement: at Regensburg both sides found it possible to agree to a common formulation. The initial reaction was one of rejoicing. The emperor remarked that "God has been pleased to enlighten" the participants, a statement that implied that generally God chose not to inspire the theologian. Calvin found the agreement evasive, but accepted it, as did a number of other Protestant theologians.

Then the wind shifted. From Wittenberg, Luther responded negatively to the "vast and patched thing," and Cardinal Contarini, who had stressed the Catholic character of the agreement, discovered that the Curia did not agree with him. These negative voices turned out to be decisive, especially since the ongoing negotiations soon reached an impasse. When the emperor asked the participants to provide him with a summary statement, he received two, since no agreement had been reached on most points. The situation was hopelessly chaotic, for, in actual fact, there were four factions: the die-hard Catholics and Protestants as well as the conciliatory theologians from the two sides. The specter of a threefold division among Catholics, Protestants, and those accepting mediation hung over the diet and indicated that anything less than an enthusiastic and full agreement was bound to be unsatisfactory.

In June the emperor submitted this meager "result" to the estates. The Catholics rejected whatever agreement had been reached and the Protestants followed suit. The hope, sometimes faint, sometimes optimistic, that the schism between the two sides might be healed had gone, vanished, as one observer sadly remarked, "even as smoke." General hopelessness and confusion followed.

The decree of the diet expressed once again the hope for a council and provided that a national council should convene if no general council was possible. The Protestants were told to accept the articles on which agreement had been reached. The Peace of Nuremberg was to continue until the next diet.

The failure had been, above all, the emperor's. But he had little time to ponder his failure, for conflict had broken out in other parts of his realm. Francis I declared war, the fourth such exercise between the two monarchs. Francis thought he had chosen a perfect time and splendid circumstances. The theater of operations was the Low Countries, which were attacked from three sides: by the French from the south, by the Duke of Cleves from the east, and by the Danish navy from the north. Charles's sister Maria, the regent of Holland, put up a gallant fight, courageously marshaled the defenses of the land, negotiated a treaty with England, and increasingly tipped the scales in the emperor's favor. When Charles threw his forces against the Duke of Cleves, victory came quickly. In the Treaty of Venlo of September 1543, the duke agreed to the end of ecclesiastical reform in his territory. Actually, this latter point was a minor provision, but the victory strengthened Catholicism in northwest Germany.

The Road to War

"THIS EXPERIENCE OPENED THE EMPEROR'S eyes and convinced him that it was not only not impossible, but indeed very easy, to subdue such insolence by force—if done at the proper time and with the necessary means." These words were Charles's own, after the military campaign had ended in amazing success. Charles began to wait for "the proper time" and the "necessary means" to wage war against the Protestants. The failure of the negotiations at Regensburg convinced him that, as matters stood, no theological compromise was possible. Since the Protestants were recalcitrant, only force remained, and Charles was prepared to solve the religious problem in Germany by force.

Slowly, the figures in the emperor's game were falling into place. By making peace with France in September 1544, the emperor had eliminated one important obstacle. In May 1544, he successfully negotiated a truce with the Turks. Only the pope stood in the emperor's way of settling the German religious problem. The two viewed each other with distrust, but since the conciliation between France and the emperor had created a new situation for the papacy, Paul III accepted Charles's offer of peace.

A diet, meeting at Worms early in 1545, pursued possible avenues of religious conciliation. Behind the scenes, however, the emperor held negotiations with papal representatives to secure support for the military showdown. The decree of the diet voiced regret over the impossibility of conciliation and announced that another theological colloquy would attempt agreement.

After some delays, that colloquy got under way at Regensburg in January 1546. An air of futility hung over the venture, for the emperor was not serious and the Protestants were hardly optimistic. The two sides went through the routine of trying to settle their differences. There had been some difficulty finding Catholic participants, but finally Johannes Cochlaeus, together with three lesser-known theologians, agreed to represent the Catholic side. All of them were staunch Catholics and differed in temperament from the irenic men who had been at Regensburg in 1541. Disagreement over the agenda occupied the most attention.

The diet itself opened in June, and for a while the situation was what it had been for as long as anyone could remember. The imperial proposition spoke of the need for religious peace, but Catholics and Protestants disagreed about almost everything. The prospect seemed to be another stalemate, as had happened so many times in the past. There were also perturbing rumors about the emperor's armaments, and by the middle of the month the Protestants boldly asked Charles for an explanation. The emperor replied only that he meant to deal with disobedient estates as became the authority of his imperial office. This begged the question and the Protestants persistently asked for his definition of "disobedient." This time the emperor's answer was clear:

those who under the pretense of religion disregarded law and order were the "disobedient." The handwriting was on the wall.

On 20 July Charles pronounced the ban over Philip of Hesse and John Frederick of Saxony, the two bulwarks of the League of Schmalkald; this could only mean war. The ban said nothing about religion, but cited three violations of law and order, one of which, the Pack affair, dated back to the late 1520s. The major charge pertained to the feud of Philip and John Frederick with Duke Heinrich of Braunschweig over the city of Goslar, a complex situation in which Philip and John Frederick used a semblance of legal justification for a blunt exhibition of power politics.

This was only a pretense for the emperor, who thought of the war as being fought for the cause of religion. Yet the matter was not quite that simple, for some of his allies were Protestants to whom he had guaranteed the retention of the ecclesiastical status quo until the time of a council. Thus, full suppression of Protestantism could not have been his immediate goal. That it was his final goal, however, is clear. Charles was engaging in the kind of temporizing in which he had become an expert. He hoped to defeat the major Protestant territories first, and later deal with those Protestants who were his allies.

While Catholics and Protestants sought to settle their differences at Regensburg, Martin Luther died. There is a bit of irony in that his death came while Bucer expounded the doctrine of justification at the diet. The day was 18 February 1546, and the place, by a strange coincidence, Eisleben, where he had been born sixty-two years earlier. An errand of love had taken him there to mediate—successfully, as it turned out—a feud between the Counts of Mansfeld.

Luther had become a bit more insolent and argumentative with age, but his warmth had never left him, as can be seen in his last piece of writing, found after his death: "No one can understand Virgil's *Bucolics* and *Georgics* unless he was, for five years, a shepherd or a farmer. No one understands Cicero's letters, I suppose, unless he occupied an eminent public office for 20 years. No one can understand the Scriptures sufficiently unless he guided the church with the prophets for a hundred years. There is something exceedingly wonderful about John the Baptist, Christ, and the Apostles. Do not manipulate his divine Aeneas, but venerate its footsteps. We are beggars, this is true."

Luther lived to witness the full consequences of his work, and it surely must have been to him both blessing and curse: the former because his conviction about his faith became ever more definite as the years passed, the latter, because he witnessed that the Protestant churches were not exempt from that historical pattern woven with threads of strength and weakness, of vitality and abuse, into one fabric.

The War

ONCE WAR HAD BEEN DECLARED THE LEAGUE OF Schmalkald moved with astonishing dispatch, mobilized its troops, and agreed on the general conduct of the war. Only the theologians, who believed that a defensive war alone was legitimate, dragged their feet and advised against precipitate moves.

Action commenced slowly. For several months no outright fighting occurred, only insignificant skirmishes here and there. In the late summer of 1546 both sides seemed unsure of what course to take. In the case of the emperor, this was an expression of his vacillating temperament; in the case of the members of the League of Schmalkald it was a matter of incompetent leadership. Either side could have scored a decisive victory, especially the Protestants. Their earlier blunders, their naïveté concerning the emperor's intention, even their internal squabbles could have been things of the past. The prize was to be had for the asking. In the fall both sides committed blunders that kept them from attaining victory. But since both engaged in this gratuitous exercise, the outcome changed nothing. An acute financial crisis beset the league in November, and before the month was over its forces were compelled to retreat from south Germany. By that time a new element had entered the picture. Swayed by the emperor's promise of the Saxon electorship, Duke Maurice of (Albertine) Saxony had allied with the emperor and, together with King Ferdinand, prepared to attack Saxony.

The winter months passed without decisive military developments. The emperor was in control of south Germany and one Protestant territory and city after the other surrendered. In January 1547 the pope announced the withdrawal of his troops from Germany, and two months later he approved (or instigated) the move of the general council to Bologna. Charles was furious, especially since the pope had been less than discreet about the details of their treaty and had announced the stipulation that "Protestants and Schmalkaldians" were to be subjected, if necessary by force, to the true religion and to obedience to the pope. Since Protestants were in the emperor's phalanx, they were hardly pleased to hear about the true purpose of the exercise they had aided.

At this juncture the two friends became enemies. Both pope and

103

emperor had viewed each other with ill-concealed distrust, annoyance, and even anger. The pope, for one, considered the emperor's various ecclesiastical involvements (aside from that of using force for the unconditional suppression of the heretics) as intrusion, while the emperor was dismayed over papal indifference regarding the resolution of the conflict in Germany.

One major area of disagreement (or misunderstanding) was the recently convened general council. After years of striving and futile efforts, Pope Paul III at last succeeded in convening a council at Trent in December 1545. The emperor, who for almost decades had pleaded for such a gathering, found himself in the paradoxical situation of having to acknowledge that at this particular juncture he had no use for it—especially if its pronouncements and decrees were to convey an uncompromising Catholic position.

As Charles V saw it, the Council of Trent was prepared to do just that. While the disagreement concerning the agenda was resolved by a compromise which stipulated that doctrine and reform were to be considered simultaneously, the fact was that the council defined several important doctrinal issues—tradition, original sin, and justification—within a short time. This meant that the council had, virtually overnight, accentuated and formalized the existing doctrinal differences between Protestants and the Catholic church, and this at the time when Charles put his sophisticated scheme into action: first to subject the Protestants militarily by force, and then to bring them to a voluntary return to the Catholic fold by a mediating formula and the assurance of ecclesiastical reform. The last thing Charles wanted in 1546 was the formalization of ecclesiastical and theological differences.

When hostilities were resumed in the early spring of 1547, an indecisive state of affairs continued. Late in March, Charles moved northward to join the forces of Maurice and Ferdinand. On 23 April he reached Mühlberg and had come within a stone's throw of the Saxon soldiers. Since the waters of the Elbe flowed majestically between the two armies, the Saxon elector thought himself safe. It was a Sunday, and afterward people recalled that it had been *Misericordia Domini,* an apt commentary by the ancient liturgical tradition of Christendom on the events of the day. Fog hung over the landscape when the emperor's soldiers reached the river. The Saxon elector was attending church and the news that enemy soldiers had been seen on the other side of the Elbe disturbed him little. Since he thought the Elbe to be an insurmountable obstacle, he saw no reason to leave church or forego a leisurely breakfast.

John Frederick was woefully mistaken. A few days before, his soldiers had confiscated two horses from a peasant who took revenge by showing the Spaniards a passage across the river. Suddenly the enemy was upon the Saxons and wild fighting began; the Saxons sought their salvation in flight and John Frederick was taken prisoner.

The rest is quickly told. In June Landgrave Philip of Hesse surrendered to the emperor; for all practical purposes the military power of the League of Schmalkald had been broken. A few north German cities continued their resistance, notably Magdeburg. The emperor realized that trying to subdue these cities was like biting into granite, and in the larger course of events their resistance made little difference. He ignored them and in June he made his way to Augsburg to hold a diet that would deal with the situation created by his military victory.

Uneasy Peace and Final Decision

TWO CONCERNS WERE ON THE EMPEROR'S MIND at Augsburg: the solution of the religious problem and a change in the political structure of the empire. Charles was persuaded that his victory over the Schmalkaldians had put him into a position to do both. Politically, he sought to strengthen imperial power in Germany by means of an association of the territories that would redistribute power in favor of the emperor. In light of the balance of power in the empire, it may have been a hopeless venture from the beginning; but Charles clearly was too impatient. Although powerful, he was by no means the undisputed master of Germany. Had he made haste more slowly, content to achieve his goal of a league through evolution, the outcome might have been different.

It is notable, from a religious point of view, that Charles did not decree the immediate and full restitution of Catholicism in Germany. Such would have been the natural solution, though also the most difficult one. The emperor's Protestant allies would hardly have liked such a procedure, and Charles stood in need of their support. At the same time he sensed the intensity of Protestant conviction.

The tenor of the proposed solution was Catholic; the section on justification merely used Protestant terminology to express Catholic sentiment, but the section on the mass sought to accommodate Protestant feelings. The Communion cup was temporarily allowed, as was clerical marriage. The other provisions of the twenty-six-article document followed by and large a Catholic line. When the document was made public opposition came from both sides. The Catholics objected that concessions had been made to the Protestants and denounced the emperor for having usurped ecclesiastical prerogatives.

They refused to be included in the provisions of the document, since as Catholics they had no need to modify their faith; only the pope had that authority. The Protestants, on the other hand, were displeased with the Catholic orientation of the document. On 30 June 1548 the so-called Interim became law, applicable only to Protestants. The death warrant for German Protestantism seemed to have been delivered.

The Interim, however, was a failure. Since it was the emperor's last attempt to settle the religious problem in Germany, its failure meant his decisive defeat. Opposition came from everywhere. There was no support from the pope, little from his allies, and only militant repudiation from the Protestants. Some of the opposition was politically motivated, and in some instances, there may have been economic considerations. Protestant resistance was the crucial factor.

In addition to the political authorities, the Protestant theologians, those "minor" reformers who had labored in their communities to introduce and consolidate the Reformation—Johann Brenz, Martin Frecht, Ambrosius Blaurer, Martin Bucer, Andreas Osiander, and the rest—did their share in opposing the Interim. To their names should be added a host of simple ministers, whose identities have long been forgotten, but whose resolute opposition spelled failure to the Interim. Their stand was impressive. The intensity of the popular opposition against the Interim, when the rulers were quiet and some of the eminent Protestant theologians accommodating, shows the strength of the Protestant faith in Germany.

It was a spattered picture: resolute opposition, unwilling acceptance, seeming success, blatant failure. Before the lasting vigor of the religious resistance could be measured, the course of political events all too speedily provided the final answer to the question of the success of the Emperor's solution of the religious problem.

In March 1550 Charles convened a diet to meet at Augsburg. A changed man came to the south German city that ranks so prominently in the history of the German Reformation. Three years before, Titian had painted the victorious emperor, depicting him as the victor of Mühlberg: high on a horse, clad in shining armor, a lancet in his right hand, confident and determined. In 1550 Titian painted the emperor again, but this time in a painting of the Last Judgment, in which the emperor appeared as one of the many who stood before the throne of God. Astutely, the artist captured the change: then the pride of the victor, resolutely determined to impose his will upon the conquered; now the dejection of failure, turning increasingly to spiritual concerns.

The imperial proposition made much of the papal willingness to reconvene the Council of Trent and decried the widespread disregard

106

of the Interim and its provisions for ecclesiastical reform. The decree of the diet of February 1551 ordered the continued administration of the Interim, but agreed that the objections against it would be considered at a future date. The emperor's intent to suppress Protestantism had alienated his Protestant allies and angered his Protestant foes. His intent to restructure the relationship between emperor and territorial rulers had precipitated even greater difficulties.

It was Maurice of Saxony who crystallized the latent opposition against the emperor. Formally a Protestant, Maurice had fought in the War of Schmalkald on the side of the emperor. This would indicate that religion was hardly a serious matter for Maurice. He was not unreligious, but his policies were prompted by considerations of *realpolitik* rather than any commitment to his interpretation of the Gospels. Maurice had rallied several Protestant territories into an alliance directed against the emperor. This venture saved Protestantism in Germany.

The saviors of German Protestantism were Elector Maurice and his princely confreres, few of whom were concerned about religion. The bonds of alliances and the tensions of opposition were oriented by other factors. Strong religious sentiment continued to prevail on both sides, but the great issues of the day were of a different character: the territorial rulers were concerned about their own political interests.

After almost thirty years of extemporization, the situation in Germany demanded a definitive solution. The emperor's military tour de force against the Schmalkaldians had ended in failure. The Protestants demanded a formal recognition of their faith. The emperor, however, was as yet unwilling to concede defeat, though he did convene a diet to be held at Augsburg to seek a solution and asked Ferdinand to represent him there. Ferdinand would only approve such decisions as he could accept in good conscience. (Later Charles himself protested "against everything that would offend, hurt, weaken or endanger our true old Christian and Catholic religion," and subsequently refused to offer an opinion about the ongoing negotiations.)

The contested issues at Augsburg were many, but one stood out: the permanence of the settlement. The two other important questions were ecclesiastical jurisdiction and church property. The Catholics could neither acknowledge the abrogation of the former nor the secularization of the latter without surrendering important affirmations of their faith. The Protestants, on the other hand, saw the acknowledgment of ecclesiastical jurisdiction as the retention of ecclesiastical authority contrary to that of the ruler. Ecclesiastical property, in turn, had been used in Protestant territories for the support of education and religion, and its restitution was practically impossible. The Protestants accordingly demanded the acceptance of the secularizations.

On 25 September the estates agreed to "a permanent peace"—permanent, that is, unless a future council would bring conciliation. The basic provision was the right of the territorial rulers to determine the official religion within their territories. Before the end of the century the famous phrase *cuius regio, eius et religio* ("he who rules determines the religion") was coined to describe the significance of the provision. Subjects disagreeing with the accepted religion of their territory had the right to emigrate. The so-called *reservatum ecclesiasticum* provided that the religious change of any ecclesiastical ruler after 1552 (in other words, the acceptance of Protestantism by a ruler who exercised political authority by virtue of his ecclesiastical office) was a "personal" conversion only, which would not affect the ecclesiastical and political status of that territory. The Protestants yielded at this point, but they were paid well for their concession. All ecclesiastical changes up to 1552, including the secularization of church lands, were formalized, and the "ecclesiastical jurisdiction" in Protestant territories was "suspended" until a future conciliation.

Few happenings of Reformation history were more significant than the document promulgated on 25 September 1555. All the flowery oratory of the occasion could not obscure the fact that the tedious negotiations, the inevitable compromise, and stubborn determination had produced a haphazard document. In theory, there were many alternatives but all but this one had been tried and found wanting: only the permanent recognition of Lutheranism remained, since neither of the two religious factions was politically strong enough to force its will upon the other.

The peace established the legal recognition of Lutheranism and thereby the religious division of Germany. For sixty-three years—until the Thirty Years' War in 1618—peace would prevail in Germany, and even when war came, it had other more pertinent causes than religion. Germany was spared, therefore, the kind of religious-political turmoil that would characterize the situation in France or Holland.

Full religious freedom had not been achieved even for Lutherans and Catholics. Only the territorial ruler had this privilege; his subjects had to accept his ecclesiastical decision or pack their belongings and emigrate. Accordingly, German ecclesiastical life developed along territorial lines, even as did the political life of the empire. There was deep significance that both pope and emperor were absent from the deliberations at Augsburg. Karl Brandi, the biographer of Charles V, was prompted to call this "the most perfect expression for the dawn of a new era." Both had lost their ability to influence the course of action in Germany. On paper the traditional concepts of universal church, emperor, and pope were still invoked, but obviously they had lost much of their meaning. The territorial ruler assumed a new responsibility, politically autocratic and ecclesiastically important, powerful over church no less than state.

The climax of these events came a few weeks after the adjournment of the diet. On 25 October Emperor Charles announced his abdication. On that occasion he reviewed his life—from the day, forty years earlier, on which he had been declared of age—his successes and his failures, lamenting his failing health and the absence of peace. Stark symbolism lay in Charles's selection of his birthplace, Brussels, as the site of his abdication. He had returned to the beginning.

The following August, Charles left Brussels for Spain. Toward the end of November, he saw for the first time the palatial house built for him adjacent to the monastery of San Jeronimo de Yuste, not far from Madrid, which from February 1557 to 21 September 1558 would be his home. He had reached the end of the road and found solace in his religion and in the things of the world to come. To be sure, his life at San Yuste was by no means ascetically simple. He had attendants, counselors, cooks, physicians, and all the rest, but these made little difference to a man who had left behind the turbulence of the world.

There are many legends about Charles's sojourn at Yuste—that he occupied himself with synchronizing his many clocks or that he ordered his own requiem mass to be celebrated in his presence. No legend is ever without some substance, and though not fully accurate these stories may convey something of his temper at the time. In his final weeks he often sat in front of Titian's monumental canvas *Gloria*, which depicted mankind appearing before the judgment seat of God. Titian had included Charles and his late wife in the huge throng, with Charles's head bare of the imperial crown.

The life of Charles V was inextricably linked with the course of the Reformation. With uncanny irony the years of his public activities paralleled those of the German Reformation: in 1519, when he was elected emperor, the case of Martin Luther became an *affaire d'état*, and in 1555 his abdication came in the wake of the formal recognition of Lutheranism in Germany. But more was involved than chronological proximity. Charles exemplified the interaction of religion and politics that characterized so much of the Reformation era. He was both a Catholic and the emperor and he thought, following the ideas of his chancellor Gattinara, that these two functions could be in perfect harmony. That they could not was Charles's tragedy. Had he been less a dreamer of noble dreams and aspirations, less a devout

Catholic, less a disciple of Charlemagne, he might have been more a man of action. As matters went, Charles was a failure at what mattered most to him—perhaps all the more blatant a failure because he lived in an age so rich in achievements.

7 The Reformation in England

The "King's Great Matter" and Other Affairs

KING HENRY VIII TOWERS OVER THE HISTORY of the English Reformation exactly as Hans Holbein's famous painting shows him: bold and confident, determined and resolute. The Reformation is unthinkable without the king. Thomas More had once counseled Thomas Cromwell to tell Henry always "what he ought to doo, but never what he is able to doo; so shall you shewe your selfe a true, faithfull servaunt and a right worthy Counsailour; for if a Lyon knew his owne strength, harde were it for anye man to rule him." The advice was gratuitous; Henry did know his own strength and events in England derived their momentum from this fact.

The Reformation in England followed the continental European pattern: theological revolution, reformative zeal, and organizational consolidation by the strong hand of the ruler. The uniqueness of the English situation lay in Henry's conservative theological temper, which under ordinary circumstances would hardly have disposed him to any kind of ecclesiastical change. Quite the contrary, by temperament and previous record he seemed predestined to excel all other sovereigns in his jealous zeal for the Catholic faith. Yet it was to end quite differently.

Henry provides the cue for England's ecclesiastical changes, but his ecclesiastical maneuvering would not have been possible without a congenial religious atmosphere (if a historian may conjecture so positively). Moreover, the English atmosphere was influenced by the religious upheaval on the Continent, and thus two factors, in addition to the heavy hand of the king, must be cited as important elements: the religious ferment in the land and the continental precedent. It is dubious that these factors would have prevailed against the king, however, for nowhere did a religious settlement take place against the will of the ruler.

The first official recognition of Lutheran ideas came from none other than the king himself. Henry had read Luther's treatise *The Babylonian Captivity of the Church* with indignation, and, amateur theologian that he was, he published a reply, *Assertion of the Seven Sacraments*, which, while hardly one of the eminent publications of the sixteenth century, was a competent treatment of the traditional Catholic doctrine. In September 1521 a special copy was presented to the pope, who expressed his admiration for the king's erudition and one month later conferred the title *"Defensor Fidei"* ("Defender of the Faith") upon Henry.

The king's noble efforts notwithstanding, the incidence of Lutheran ideas in England became more numerous in subsequent years. In 1526 William Tyndale's English translation of the New Testament, printed at Cologne and Worms, found its way across the Channel. In England, even as on the Continent, the awareness of the potential damages caused by the vernacular Scriptures in the hands of the Protestants led to their denunciation. Tyndale, indeed, offered more than a translation: preface, notes, and marginal annotations were extensive, and they were pure Luther. The work was vastly influential.

There was also the so-called Society of Christian Brethren, a somewhat enigmatic enterprise, which sought to distribute religious books, even heretical ones. Whether this meant the conscious colportage of Lutheran ideas is another question. At Cambridge a group of young dons met at the White Horse Inn, at what was on the surface a harmless discussion circle on matters of current theological interest. Little is known about this group; the only source is a brief passage in Foxe's *Actes and Monuments*, and those historians who have discussed it have used imagination rather than evidence by listing those then in Cambridge whom they would have expected to attend, such as Barnes, Gardiner, Fox, Heath, Lambert, Latimer, Ridley, Shaxton, and Tyndale. The group included future heretics and ecclesiastics, future bishops and martyrs. Not all of them became reformers, and at the time they probably were more excited by Erasmus than by Luther,

112

though soon the group was tellingly dubbed "Germany." Then, as always, it was chic to discuss the latest in theological fashion.

The dissemination of the vernacular Scriptures reduced the willingness to listen to official ecclesiastical pronouncements and confirmed the religious autonomy of the individual. People could read the Bible themselves and decide which side was right or wrong in the theological controversy. They may have been mistaken in their conclusions, and since they lacked theological training they probably often were; but such lack of training did not keep them from adding their marginalia to the Sacred Writ. The Protestants argued that it was erroneous to hold that Scripture could not be understood by simple men and women.

Alongside the vernacular Bible stood a host of other publications. Tyndale translated not only the New Testament but also wrote several theological tracts. He had many comrades in arms. John Frith published *A Pistle to the Christian Reader: The Revelation of Antichrist* (1529) and *A Letter unto the Faithful Followers of Christ's Gospel* (1532). George Joye wrote an *Answer to Ashwell* in 1531, a discussion of justification by faith. From the pen of William Barlow came *A Dyaloge Descrybyng the Orygynall Ground of These Lutheran Faceyons* (1531), and William Roy published *A Proper Dyaloge betwene a Gentillman and an Husband Man* in 1530.

In all, some forty Protestant books were published between 1525 and 1533. While this figure is too modest to warrant the assertion of a widespread impact, it is sufficient to suggest an intrusion of the new theological currents into the country. The English religious scene was more turbulent than it had been ten or fifteen years earlier.

There is also considerable evidence that Lollardy, the heretical movement tracing back to John Wycliffe, had not only survived in various groups and conventicles into the early sixteenth century, but also appears to have increased in its numbers. Whether Lollards constituted a noticeable element in the English ecclesiastical scene in the early sixteenth century is difficult to say; their existence clearly denoted the presence of restlessness.

There was also the influence of Erasmus. Humanism stood in more than chronological proximity to the Reformation, and the line between the humanist critique of ecclesiastical abuse (real or imagined) and the Protestant repudiation of Catholic religion was so thin that many contemporaries never perceived the difference. In England (as elsewhere) humanism supplied both defenders and opponents of the Catholic church, an indication that its theological propensity was ambiguous. Some, like Stephen Gardiner or Thomas More, criticized the church until they realized that they were only adding fuel to the

113

fire of the heretics. Then they stiffened in their attitude, became unwilling to acknowledge any ecclesiastical shortcoming, and were indisposed to explore new ways of theological reflection. Others, like Robert Barnes or John Hooper, turned into ardent Protestants.

The religious scene in England in the 1520s was in lively and exciting ferment. Its three ingredients—Lollardy, Erasmian humanism, and the new theology coming from Germany—indicate that religious life might undergo turbulence, if not change. A conjecture about whether these forebodings would have become reality is rendered unnecessary by the sudden introduction of a new element.

In 1527 Henry VIII informed his wife that they were not truly husband and wife and could not continue to live together. Since the two had been married for seventeen years, this was astounding news for Catherine of Aragon. Henry's quest for a "divorce" was to overshadow, for the next half-decade, the foreign and domestic affairs of England and eventually lead to the severing of the English church from its Roman matrix.

Catherine had come to England in 1501 to be betrothed to Henry's elder brother Arthur. Political considerations had prompted the match and since these persisted after Arthur's unexpected demise, Henry was asked to take his brother's place. But Canon Law forbade marriage with the widow of one's brother, though it was possible (under certain conditions) to receive a papal dispensation. Such a dispensation was indeed received, the impediment of affinity existing between Henry and Catherine removed, and the two were married.

At some point, Henry began to have doubts about the legitimacy of the dispensation (and thereby his marriage). What prompted this insight is difficult to say. The absence of a male heir may have set him pondering and undoubtedly became a factor of major importance. Catherine had become pregnant eight times during the first ten years of her marriage, but only one child, Mary, had survived infancy. In the end neither Henry's vow to lead a crusade against the Turks nor the counsel of Spanish physicians was able to alter the inevitable. There was no male heir. Since Henry had sired a bastard boy, the evidence seemed to put the blame on his wife. As matters stood, the succession would fall on Mary, and Henry shuddered at that thought.

The king claimed that the study of Scripture had convinced him that he was under a divine curse for having violated the law of God. "My conscience was incontinentlie accombred, vexed, and disquieted," he said, "whereby I thought myselfe to be greatlie in danger of Gods indignation. Which appeared to be (as me seemed) the rather, for that he sent us no issues male: and all such issues make as my said wife had by me, died incontinent after they came into the world, so that I doubted the great displeasure of God in that behalfe." A literal

114

reading of Lev. 20:21 ("And if a man shall take his brother's wife, it is an unclean thing: he hath uncovered his brother's nakedness; they shall be childless") suggested that he was under a divine curse.

Another version was offered by Reginald Pole, who charged that Henry's "passions for a girl" had been the reason. The girl was young and vivacious Anne Boleyn. The Venetian ambassador reported that "madam is not one of the handsomest women in the world," and, judging from her portrait, Anne indeed was no beauty. Love makes one blind; Henry fell madly in love with her but she kept him at arm's length. Surely in the beginning Henry had no idea of the interminable complications facing his amorous fancies. He confidently thought that the Catholic church would grant his request for an annulment of his marriage. After all, his services to the church had earned him the title of "Defender of the Faith."

But there were complications. Henry's argumentation ran counter to the consensus of a formidable array of canonists who claimed that, given certain conditions, a dispensation to marry one's brother's widow was proper and did not conflict with either natural or divine law. Henry's case was by no means unique (how could it be, with generations of canonists exploring every minute aspect of marriage law?) and a forceful consensus stood against him. Whatever peripheral ambiguities there may have been—as, for example, whether the marriage between Arthur and Catherine had been actually consummated—were summarily removed by a second dispensation, discovered in the course of the "divorce" proceedings. Practically, Henry wanted to be "divorced" from Catherine; technically, he wanted the pope to withdraw the original dispensation and thereby declare that an impediment existed between him and Catherine.

Henry's case, already weak because of the tradition of Canon Law, was made even weaker by the political situation. Almost simultaneously with Henry's dramatic announcement to his wife, the troops of Charles V conquered Rome, making Pope Clement VII virtually a prisoner. Charles, as nephew of Catherine of Aragon, was interested in the "divorce" case and used every conceivable pressure to have the decision go in Catherine's favor. This put Clement VII in a difficult position, worsened by his characteristic slowness in making decisions. "I have never seen him so slow," wrote Stephen Gardiner and Henry's "great matter" provided Clement with a splendid opportunity to demonstrate his tendency to procrastinate. The pope must have thought that by postponing action he could resolve the difficulty, though he entertained little doubt about its seriousness. There is no evidence that he was ever willing to make an uncanonical decision, even though Charles and Henry, each in his own way, exerted pressure. Clement thought that if the decision were postponed long enough the matter would, somehow or other, resolve itself. Little did he know the king's dynastic concern and his amorous passion.

Cardinal Wolsey, the king's chancellor, thought, too self-confidently, that Henry's request would encounter no complications in Rome; but it did, and after a year or so, Henry realized that he could expect no help from that quarter. This meant failure for the man who had pursued his policy. In October 1529, Wolsey was indicted for violation of the statutes of *praemunire*. Known by this Latin term which simply means "strengthen," these thirteenth century statutes vaguely prohibited Englishmen from acknowledging any foreign power. Wolsey, of course, was hung for having acknowledged the pope. Eight days later he lost the chancellorship, to be succeeded by Thomas More.

Since More opposed the king's "divorce," Henry conceded that he would not have to be involved. Thereby the king's highest official remained aloof from the major political issue of the day.

Parliament, which had not met for years, convened in November 1529. The business at hand seemed routine, though several bills dealt with ecclesiastical matters and were bluntly anticlerical in tone. Probate fees of mortuaries were restricted and pluralities of benefices were prohibited, as were all efforts to secure papal dispensations for such pluralities. This last provision placed an English statute over papal prerogatives. The language of the act was cautious, all the same, for only the effort to obtain a dispensation was prohibited and nothing was said about papal authority as such.

By that time another development was in the making. Thomas Cranmer, a Cambridge don, suggested that the real issue of the "divorce" was theological: it was not the canonists of bygone centuries that mattered, but the teaching of Scripture. The theological consensus of the universities could set aside the edict of the papacy. The suggestion fell on fertile ground with the king, who remarked that Cranmer "hath the sow by the ear."

A grandiose canvass of the citadels of higher learning began. Oxford and Cambridge were sounded out first and the situation there proved paradigmatic of things elsewhere. There was no clear-cut position, however; accordingly, the confusion of the academicians had to be resolved by royal intimidation. As a rule the opinion of a university depended on its geographical location: Spanish universities decided in favor of the papal dispensation and French seats of higher learning against it. In the end the results were impressive, but inconclusive. Henry could comfort himself that formidable opinion favored his "divorce," but the sentiment was by no means unanimous.

And so more time passed since the king had first voiced his pangs of conscience. He had engaged in legal maneuvering, had pleaded and pressured, but without avail. The means utilized thus far had proved unsuccessful. There was a deadlock, and he probably had no clear notion of how to break it.

In December 1530 the attorney general filed charges against the English clergy. The nature of the charges is not exactly clear—whether the clergy were indicted for mere complicity with Wolsey for having accepted his legatine authority or for recognition of foreign authority (the pope). The clergy were stunned, but in convocation they quickly regained their equilibrium: "subsidies" were offered as grants to the king in gratitude for his defense of the faith. In plain language, these grants were meant as bribes. Henry needed the money, but he wanted more: the clergy had to acknowledge their guilt and the king's position as "protector and only supreme head of the English Church and Clergy." John Fisher, bishop of Rochester, suggested the insertion of the phrase "so far as the law of Christ allows," and this was the way it was accepted by a convocation.

This acknowledgment of royal headship was in a way nothing more than the extension of existing trends involving the ever greater political control over the church. There is evidence of Henry's preoccupation with ecclesiastical affairs during that time, of a growing awareness on his part of the nature of royal authority. The Henrician "Caesaropapism" developed parallel to but quite distinct from the quest for the "divorce." There was talk, startlingly new, about the ancient privileges of the English church or about the true nature of Henry's "imperial" office as it related to the church.

The years between 1529 and 1532 were a time of transition, when the novel tools for a revolutionary change in policy were very much present, but Henry, a staunch if conventional Catholic, grappled for traditional means of resolving the deadlock over the "divorce." In 1531 even an indefatigable optimist had to admit that the king was not any closer to his goal than he had been in 1527. Time was running short and Henry grew impatient. The final effort to cajole the papacy—on its weakest point, namely, money—came early in 1532, when Parliament passed the Conditional Restraint of Annates which prohibited the payment of annates to Rome. Henry meant to tighten the financial screw and deprive the pope of his English revenue. The lesson was unmistakable: no "divorce," no money.

In March the Commons presented a supplication to the king that had all the appearances of a grievous sigh of a people oppressed by the church. The twelve complaints included both the sublime and the ridiculous—that minors were given benefices and that there were too many holy days, especially at the harvest time, "upon which many great, abominable, and execrable vices, idle and wanton sports be used and exercised." The heart of the matter was stated at the beginning: the clergy make laws, the king was told, "without your knowledge or most royal assent," none of which were "declared unto them in the English tongue."

The clergy, when confronted with this matter, submitted to the king. "Having our special trust and confidence in your most excellent wisdom, your princely goodness and fervent zeal to the promotion of God's honor and Christian religion, and also in your learning, far exceeding, in our judgment, the learning of all other kings and princes," the clergy agreed to obtain royal assent for all new constitutions, canons, and ordinances. The following day Thomas More, pleading ill health, resigned from his office as chancellor. Something dramatic had happened. Chapuys, the Spanish ambassador, reported that there was "a new papacy made here." The clergy were now inferior to shoemakers, he said, for these latter could at least make their own statutes.

Henry's man to carry out the policy was Thomas Cromwell. He had been Wolsey's secretary and, somewhat unexpectedly, had weathered the fall of his master. After attracting the king's attention, he was for ten years or so his right-hand man. Recent research has demonstrated that Cromwell possessed the genius of mind and the singularity of purpose that enabled him to be the eminent figure of the 1530s. He stepped into a vacuum and he filled it splendidly. His counsel to Henry was that as sovereign of an "empire" he possessed supreme authority in both church and state. Early sixteenth century England experienced the clash between two concepts of government, the one medieval, characterized by ultimate ecclesiastical supremacy over kings, and the other modern, characterized by the supremacy of the positive law of the state over any claims of the law of nature, God, or the church. Cromwell proved to be the capable proponent of the latter view, seeing in Parliament the manifestation of the nation and realizing the possibilities which this offered.

Henry's patience, strained by the inconclusiveness of the "divorce" proceedings, was all the more put to task by the presence of a scheme that offered a solution. Those who had ominously prophesied that it would be all over with the pope's authority in England if the king's request were denied could comfort one another with the accuracy of their prediction.

Parliament erected the hurdle to keep Catherine from appealing to Rome. The Restraint of Appeals prohibited, with allusions to historical precedent, any appeal abroad by declaring England to be an "empire" whose king could adjudge all spiritual and temporal matters in his realm. Practically, the Restraint kept the "King's great matter" in England; theoretically, it culminated the delineation of a new concept of government. A perfunctory trial, presided over by Cranmer, declared the marriage between Henry and Catherine

118

invalid. A week later Anne Boleyn was crowned queen of England.

The preoccupation with the "King's great matter," as the affair was euphemistically called, and the introduction of ecclesiastical change by parliamentary statute must not lead to the assumption that England was bereft of theologians and theological reflection. Neither the pursuit of the "great matter" nor the parliamentary fiat would have been so smooth had there not been a concomitant religious restlessness and anti-Roman agitation. England had its reformers, men who had accepted the new interpretation of the Christian gospel and propagated it. One must not bestow undue creativity and brilliance on these men, or suggest that they played an important role in the course of events; but they brought about religious ferment, and thus theirs was an indispensable role in the English Reformation.

Initially their message consisted of a vague echo of Lutheran commonplaces, of those sweeping assertions that reformers everywhere propounded with disarming self-confidence and naïveté: the stress on Scripture and salvation by faith, the rejection of works-righteousness and human traditions. Afterward came a more sophisticated delineation of the new theology, though the king's own conservative temper, dramatically illustrated by the conservative Six Articles of 1539, always tended to keep matters in check.

From 1534 on, anti-Catholic propaganda was not only tolerated but actively encouraged. Theretofore the Protestant tracts had been printed on the Continent and were smuggled to England; now they could actually be printed in England. A tract entitled *Of the Olde God and the New*, probably by Miles Coverdale, was prohibited at its first publication in 1529—and officially endorsed five years later. Protestant propaganda moved freely, though an element of precariousness continued to be present. Henry wanted antipapal propaganda and support for the notion of royal supremacy. At the same time, he was firmly Catholic in his theological orientation and the outright propagation of salvation by faith or of a non-Catholic understanding of the sacraments was to him an abomination; he would have none of it.

To propound theological notions in Henry's England after the break with Rome was rather like walking a tightrope. The argument had to be both antipapal and pro-Catholic, a combination of ingredients that required an exquisite measure of theological balance or versatility. Still, a multitude of writings—several hundred theological books, devotional tracts, primers, plays, and poems—issued from the printing presses during the last dozen years of Henry's rule. The tenets of the Protestant Reformation were widely expounded.

Since the king himself seemed unsure of the direction of his ecclesiastical policy, official encouragement (or repudiation) of specific theological positions remained haphazard. Indeed, for a while the key word was ambiguity, as the subsequent sequence of official theological documents, from the *Bishops' Book* to the Six Articles and the *King's Book,* made abundantly clear. England steered a middle course between the Scylla of Henry's staunch Catholicism and the Charybdis of the repudiation of Rome.

One religious option of the time seemed to supply this strange mixture up to a point: the thought of Erasmus, which made an even greater impact on the English scene after the break with Rome. While the official endorsement of Erasmianism did not come until 1547 with the stipulation that the clergy should study the *Gospel Paraphrases* of Erasmus, his informal influence was felt long before then. Several of his treatises had been published in England in the early 1530s, notably his *Exhortation to the Diligent Study of the Holy Scripture*, which subsequently was included in Tyndale's 1536 edition of the New Testament.

On the surface ecclesiastical life continued as it always had. The familiar prayers were offered, the traditional services performed, the Catholic faith expounded and confessed. The difference was that the bond uniting the English church with Rome had been cut. The major change was tied to the repudiation of papal jurisdiction, for this meant that ecclesiastical authority had to be newly defined. Several parliamentary statutes passed in 1534 sought to do so. The Ecclesiastical Appointment Act dealt with filling ecclesiastical appointments; the Dispensation Act placed all authority for dispensations with the archbishop of Canterbury; the Act of Submission of the Clergy transformed into statute the earlier acknowledgment of convocation not to legislate without the king's consent; the First Act of Succession vested the English crown in the issue of Henry and Anne and thereby bestowed parliamentary sanction on the king's divorce; the Supremacy Act transformed the acknowledgment of convocation that the king was the supreme head of the church into a parliamentary statute; the Treasons Act made it a criminal offense to question the king's titles or to suggest that he was a heretic.

If the elements in the English religious scene in the early 1530s are obvious enough, their relative importance in the precipitation of ecclesiastical change is enigmatic. Often the king's "divorce" has been singled out as the factor of primary importance, which suggests that Henry's determination to free himself from Catherine of Aragon at all costs brought about the breach with Rome. One can also cite the religious ferment in England (either of indigenous origin or imported from abroad) and argue that the Henrician Reformation by statute constituted only the legal foil for profound religious changes. One can also assert the priority of constitutional considerations, in the sense

120

that the king developed a growing awareness of the proper scope of the royal office, an awareness that increasingly entailed the notion that kingship included authority over church as well as state.

The best way to characterize the scene is to stress the interplay of these factors. All of them were present, and their collective presence, their mutual forcing as well as thwarting of the course of events, made for the developments in England. Had not all of them been present, there would undoubtedly have been other expressions: a confrontation between king and pope, but resolved amicably; religious agitation, but no outright introduction of the Protestant faith; a quest for a "divorce," but a shying away from final consequences.

Still if any factor was decisive, it was the "divorce" that alone provided the element of urgency and inescapable pertinence. That Henry did not enjoy the full prerogatives of kingship could be pondered and then forgotten; that some reform was called for in England likewise could be ignored. Only the absence of a male heir was a cruel reality which assumed, with each passing day, greater urgency and relevance.

In all this, the common people in England could discern little evidence of ecclesiastical change. They had a new queen (whom they despised as a harlot), their king had the new title of "Supreme Head of the Church," and the pope's authority had been called into question. The people in the pews, faithfully (or not so faithfully) attending divine services, were neither asked to believe something different concerning the faith nor confronted with a different form of worship. Aside from subtle changes, the same prayers were offered and the same affirmations made as before.

Understandably, there was little opposition to the legal changes undertaken, even as there was no need for government to be stern in its enforcement. There was one spectacular incident of opposition and persecution: the trial and execution of Thomas More, the learned humanist and former Lord Chancellor of the realm. More was a hesitant opponent and he was brought to the executioner's block because of the king's vindictiveness—as the ancient adage said, "The wrath of the king is death." The same must be said about another trial, that of Cardinal Fisher.

The irony of More's trial was that he appealed to the same ultimate authority as did Luther at the Diet of Worms, the existence of an objective moral and metaphysical order which man, if he were to be true to his destiny, was compelled to accept. The issue, in other words, was not subjective dissent but the acknowledgment of the truth of that order which could be no less denied than the fact that the sky was blue and the grass green.

121

The Reformation Enforced

WITH THE TRIALS OF MORE AND FISHER, THE curtain fell on the first act of the Reformation in England. It could have been the last. Though theological ambiguities existed, further religious changes did not, and the general pattern of ecclesiastical life might have continued. But there was a second act, even more spectacular than the first, prompting Nicholas Harpsfield, a contemporary chronicler, to reflect that the king could no more keep from further changes "than it is possible for a man to roll a millstone from the top of a high hill and afterward to stay it in the midst of its course." By parliamentary fiat the English monasteries were dissolved.

Henry's financial problem was the major cause. The cost of government had risen substantially during his rule because of several factors, not the least of which was his extravagant involvement in European power politics. The Restraint of Annates had diverted into the royal exchequer moneys that had theretofore gone to Rome, but this was only the proverbial drop in the bucket. More was to be had from the church for the asking. A simple statistic indicates the relationship of monastic wealth to the king's pecuniary troubles: at the end of Henry's reign the annual rental value of the monastic lands was more than double the annual expenditures of government. The confiscation of monastic wealth promised to end the crown's financial embarrassment. Cromwell's scheme was to use the property as a permanent endowment.

In the summer and fall of 1535 a visitation of the monasteries was undertaken. Afterward, the visitors produced a report that depicted the monasteries as iniquitous dens of vice, corruption, and superstition. The king himself appeared before Parliament to relate the sorry tale, and his performance must have been impressive. Hugh Latimer recalled many years later that "when their enormities were first in Parliament house, they were so great and abominable that there was nothing but down with them." The king told Parliament that the monasteries were wealthier than necessary and that many no longer served a proper spiritual purpose.

To disentangle fact and fiction in the report of the visitors is impossible, though there seems little doubt that English monastic life was hardly a paragon of spiritual vitality in the fourth decade of the sixteenth century. This did not make the monasteries dens of iniquity, however; in all likelihood, most monasteries were fulfilling their functions in about the way they had for some time.

Early in 1536 Parliament passed the Act for the Dissolution of the Lesser Monasteries, which were those with an annual income of less than £200. Intriguingly, not the number of the religious in a house nor even in specific monasteries, but the "clear yearly value of two hundred pounds" marked the dividing line between those houses "wherein (thanks be to God) religion is right well kept and observed" and those abounding in "manifest sin, vicious carnal and abominable living." The act provided that the property of the monasteries was to go to the crown. The religious had the choice of transferring to larger monasteries, serving as secular clergy, or giving up their clerical vocation. In 1539 the larger monasteries were also dissolved.

The impact of the dissolution was far-reaching. By 1540 an institution that had been at the heart of the English religion for centuries ceased to exist. Thousands of monks and nuns became homeless and without vocation. Enormous wealth changed hands. The composition of the House of Lords was altered by the disappearance of the monastic abbots. There were also social and economic consequences, since the monasteries had provided, especially in less populous places, lodging for the traveler and alms for the poor. On the other hand, there was a profit to learning, since monastic funds, some at least that is, were used for educational purposes, such as the endowment of professorships and the establishment of cathedral schools. Cromwell's scheme to keep the monastic lands in the hands of the crown did not materialize, for pressing fiscal needs (caused by the wars against France and Scotland) forced their sale, which, in turn, created a group with a vested interest in the retention of the break with Rome.

The summer of 1536 brought much rain in England and an age disposed to regard anything unusual as an ominous foreboding of the future promptly offered its interpretation: rains were God's vengeance on behalf of the victims of Henry's religious policy. The first month would, so the prophecy went, "be rainy and full wet, next month death, and the third month war." There was war; an uprising occurred in the north. It was quickly subdued, but others occurred in places many miles apart.

There were differences between the various uprisings. In Lincoln the townspeople were the banner bearers; in York, the gentry. The grievances were a motley assortment of economic, social, and religious concerns. The common motif, with the exception of the uprisings in Cumberland and Westmorland, was indignation over the recent religious changes in the land: the royal supremacy, the new bishops, and the dissolution of the monasteries.

The uprisings came to naught. By matching shrewdness with dishonesty, Henry survived the most serious crisis of his rule. The northern uprisings revealed the extent of discontent in the land. It was not only that the king had broken with Rome. Catherine of Aragon had been a popular queen and her shoddy dismissal in favor of a "fair

123

wench" hardly endeared Henry to the people. The trials of Fisher and More, the other executions, and the attack on the property of the church helped arouse discontent and prompt restlessness among the people.

The task of guiding the new church in England was Thomas Cromwell's. As the royal vicegerent he looked after ecclesiastical affairs and demonstrated his administrative competence. At the same time he showed himself to be a skillful proponent of the king's ecclesiastical cause by launching an extensive propaganda effort. He was joined by Thomas Cranmer, the new archbishop of Canterbury; but the king was never far away. He was erratic and unpredictable; his interest in theological matters oscillated between active interest and nonchalance. Cromwell was so efficient because his policies agreed with those of the king.

The initial official statements concerning ecclesiastical policy (aside from the cluster of parliamentary acts promulgated in 1533 and 1534), the First and Second Royal Injunctions, were doctrinally vague and addressed themselves to matters pertaining to the broader social involvements of the church. Of far-reaching import was the stipulation of the Second Injunction that "the very lively word of God" which everyone must "embrace, believe, and follow, if he look to be saved," should be read and, moreover, "one book of the whole Bible of the largest volume, in England," put into all parish churches. This was a new development. A few years earlier Henry had issued a proclamation which had denounced "the divulging of this Scripture at this time in English tongue," insisting that it would be more to "further confusion and destruction than the edification of their souls." By 1538 the situation was different, and the influence of the Protestant gospelers was evident.

This stipulation called for an official version of the English Bible. Cromwell decided to produce one and entrusted Miles Coverdale with the task. Coverdale, who had published an English Bible in 1535, knew no Hebrew and only little Greek and simply translated from German and Latin. What he could not get from Luther's translation or the Zurich Froschauer version, he lifted out of Tyndale. He was neither a biblical scholar nor even a translator, but a gifted stylist who knew how to turn a smooth phrase. The result of his efforts was the so-called Great Bible, first published in April 1539 and republished six more times before the end of 1541. The title page pompously stated that it was "the Byble in Englyshe of the largest and greatest volume," and the ornamentative woodcut placed the king in that gloriously prominent center place theretofore reserved in similar title pages for God, who now found a place—a small place—near the top of the page. The practical problems thwarting the general use of the English

124

Bible were many. The price was high and, of course, literacy was necessary to make use of it. The provision that a copy of the Bible was to be put into all parish churches overcame certain practical difficulties. The impact must have been substantial.

The End of an Era

    IN 1539 PARLIAMENT PASSED THE SIX ARTICLES Act, the "whip with six strings," as Protestants called it. The theological ambiguities of the earlier measures were drastically removed. As matters stood, neither the "gospelers" nor the conservatives had been content and the pendulum had to swing one way or the other. It swung in the conservative direction, influenced by the king's own religious temperament and, perhaps, by his awareness that the country still preferred the old way. The six points of doctrine (transubstantiation, Communion under both species, celibacy, vows of chastity, private masses, and auricular confession) affirmed by the act expressed traditional Catholic sentiment.

    There is no reason, however, to speak of a general conservative reaction during the last years of Henry's reign. Naturally, the Six Articles proved a profound shock to the gospelers in England and their comrades-in-arms on the Continent; their aspirations seemed to have come abruptly to naught. Even Cranmer felt sufficiently frightened to return to a state of practical celibacy by sending his wife back to her native Germany. The close chronological connection between the Six Articles and Cromwell's fall suggested that this was part of a comprehensive scheme, perhaps even plot, to eradicate Protestantism in England.

    One doubts if Henry intended such a reversal of his ecclesiastical policy. He had become concerned about the all-too-formidable barrage of Protestant propaganda, and, good Catholic that he was, he could view this development only with dismay. The Six Articles were meant to stabilize the religious situation in England on the basis of the status quo. They were to be a "yellow light" for all would-be reformers, but no additional measures of anti-Protestant suppression followed. Above all, the ferocious penalties (the death penalty was prescribed for the denial of transubstantiation or marriage by one who had vowed chastity) of the act were not enforced.

    Almost to the day a full year passed between the promulgation of the Six Articles Act and Cromwell's fall. His conservative foes of long standing, notably the Duke of Norfolk and Stephen Gardiner, had

125

been able to persuade the king of his responsibility for the ill-fated royal marriage with Anne of Cleves, that nonentity on the pages of Tudor history. A court camarilla that despised him, as did Norfolk, because he was an upstart without noble birth, and that detested him, as did Gardiner, because he favored Protestant ideas, abruptly gained the king's ear and brought about his fall. "I crye for mercye, mercye, mercye," Cromwell had written to the king, but without having been heard—one of the witnesses at his trial was Richard Riche, who had already distinguished himself by perjurious service for the king in More's trial—he was condemned. John Foxe, the martyrologist, called him a "valiant soldier and captain of Christ" and provided a moving, though apocryphal, account of Cromwell's last moment: "He patiently suffered the stroke of the axe, by a ragged butcherly miser, which very ungodly performed the office." In his last words Cromwell protested his orthodoxy and offered a prayer for the king. Soon thereafter the reformer Robert Barnes was executed and the irony of the occasion was that on the day of his execution two other Protestant sympathizers were burned, and three priests were hanged, drawn, and quartered for having denied the king's supremacy. "What a country England was to live in," a foreign observer remarked, "when they hanged papists and burned antipapists." To have executed an equal number of Protestants and of Catholics on a single day is an undue manifestation of the *via media* Henry was disposed to travel.

During the next years the king carefully mediated between the conservatives and the Protestants, temporarily moving in one direction, but always reverting to the other. The last doctrinal pronouncement of the reign, the *Necessary Doctrine and Erudition for Any Christian Man*, came in 1543. It is known as the *King's Book*, because Henry had not only called for its drafting but also contributed the preface, for him a splendid opportunity to demonstrate his pedestrian theological competence. Theologically it was a conservative book.

That same year the authorization to read the Bible was taken from the "lower sort" and restricted to the upper classes of society. The act that provided for such restriction had the interesting title, Act for the Advancement of True Religion, and the parallel note in the *King's Book* observed that the reading of the Bible had led some "to sinister understanding of Scripture, presumption, arrogancy, carnal liberty, and contention." A revision of service books was ordered in 1543, and a book of homilies was submitted to convocation but not published. In 1545 a book of vernacular prayers was authorized, while an act empowered the king to seize the last bit of ecclesiastical property, the so-called chantries, and to use it to pay for the war with France. That year Henry also made his last appearance in Parliament. He had words of commendation for his loyal subjects (after all, Parliament had "nationalized" the chantry endowments), but also biting criticism: "Charity and concord is not amongst you, but discord and dissensions beareth rule in every place." The king spoke harshly: "One calleth the other Heretic and Anabaptist, and he calleth him again, Papist, Hypocrite and Pharisee. . . . Thus all men almost be in variety and discord and few or none preach truly and sincerely the word of God, according as they ought to do. You of the temporality be not clean and unspotted of malice and envy, for you rail on bishops, speak slanderously of priests, and rebuke and taunt preachers."

What occupied Henry's mind during those last months of his life when sickness increasingly burdened his worn-out body is impossible to know. Perhaps he was concerned to ward off a possible attack of Charles V upon England after the successful conclusion of the military conflict with the League of Schmalkald. Perhaps he intended a full introduction of Protestantism in the land, such as John Foxe suggested when he wrote that "most certain it is and to be signified to all posterity, that his full purpose was to have repurged the state of the Church." On the other hand, it is possible that Henry thought that his hybrid of ecclesiastical complexities, which produced shaking of heads on the part of everyone except Henry himself, could survive as a stable creature. Perhaps he saw the answer precisely in the continuation of his own formula; after all, he was always a bit self-confident and vain, besides being an astute statesman. The strange composition of the council of regency that was to rule during the minority of his son complicates conjecture, though the most obvious explanation·is that Henry was concerned to thwart a submission to Rome—in which event his son, Edward, would have been considered a bastard and the Tudor dynasty conceivably removed from the English throne. On the other hand, to allow the Protestants to triumph would have been squarely against Henry's own theological temper.

Henry took the secret with him when he died, and what is more, he could well ponder that one cannot rule from the grave. The two tutors of his sons (who had been inconspicuous humanists) turned into ardent Protestants and, most importantly, the Council of Regency did not at all conform to his anticipation.

In the early morning hours of 28 January 1547, Henry died. His last request had been to see Thomas Cranmer. When the archbishop arrived, he found the king in the throes of death. The king stretched out his hand and for the last time the two men, so unlike in character, locked their hands. Cranmer asked the king for a sign of his trust in Christ, and with one last thrust of his ebbing strength the king pressed his hand.

So died a strange man. Few men in the sixteenth century pursued policies more erratic and bizarre, more brilliant and disgusting. And

127

yet, when the Lord Chancellor announced his death to Parliament, there were tears in his eyes.

The Edwardian Revolution

"THE TRUMPETS SOUNDED WITH GREAT MEL-ody and courage to the comfort of all them that were present." So the chronicler reported the scene at the king's passing. Henry's nine-year-old son, Edward, ascended the throne, the sixth English king to bear the name. He was a handsome youth, with an angular face that resembled his mother's. His own *Literary Remains* show that he was intelligent and devout, though a bit perplexed about what was going on about him.

The change in England's rule could not have been more dramatic. The crown passed from a strong ruler to a child, and power in the land to a group of councillors, sixteen in number, designated as Council of Regency. Henry had provided for equality on this council, but the Duke of Somerset promptly saw to his own appointment as Lord Protector and within two months the council had been transformed into his advisory group. The people called Somerset the "good duke" and he was indeed conscientious, intelligent, and able. But the country was beset by more problems than he could handle: a precarious financial situation, restlessness among the peasants, and uncertainty about religion. To solve them required more ability and luck than Somerset could muster.

With respect to the religious problem the continuation of Henry's policy suggested itself as the best solution. Somerset professed to this approach when he announced that "he would suffer no innovations in religion during the king's mastery's young age." But Protestant sentiment was widespread and Henry's powerful personality no longer kept matters in check. A host of would-be reformers who had lived with an uneasy truce between outer conformity and inner persuasion during the Henrician rule advocated substantial religious change. On the council the sentiment was divided between Protestants and Henrician Catholics; Somerset's own religious convictions tended in the Protestant direction.

Parliament met in November 1547 and repealed the Six Articles Act, the statutes against heretics and Lollards, and removed all restrictions on the printing and reading of Scripture. Catholics, previously under the threat of the Treason Act, and Protestants, previously under the threat of the acts against heretics, could breathe

128

more easily. Aside from testifying to Somerset's own religious perspective this parliamentary move may be interpreted as an effort to still the waves of religious excitement; but the easing of legal restrictions unleashed a flood of Protestant propaganda.

In January 1549 Parliament approved the introduction of *The Booke of the Common Prayer and Administration of the Sacraments*. The *Book of Common Prayer* surely is one of the most famous documents of the English tongue. One reason is its beautiful form: while its theology is often ambiguous, the polish of its prose has rarely been matched. It spans centuries and oceans, and the cadences of its prayers have expressed beautifully the piety of the Anglican tradition and indeed of English-speaking Protestantism.

The sources of the *Book of Common Prayer* were many and heterogeneous; but the whole was greater than its parts. The several sources were fused into a creative unity. While the medieval tradition provided the basic outline, everything remotely resembling Catholicism was omitted.

The Act of Uniformity which introduced the *Book of Common Prayer* prohibited the use of other forms of worship; this was the extent of religious conformity imposed. At issue was public worship and only the clergy were held responsible for compliance. No effort was made to establish conformity of belief, to require attendance at worship, to supervise the lives of the faithful. Catholic worship was abolished, but within the framework of the *Book of Common Prayer* various theological interpretations were possible. Somerset, whose imprint on the course of ecclesiastical events was obvious, was a latitudinarian at heart and he found a kindred soul in Cranmer. There were others, such as William Turner, who argued in their pamphlets that diversity of theological views need not entail persecution.

Still, the act may have precipitated an uprising, the deeper causes of which reached back into the early part of the century. Prices had risen drastically; according to some observers they trebled in the first half of the century. Population had increased much faster than did productivity, and this, too, constituted a problem. One problem was the so-called enclosures, a result of the effort on the part of landlords to deprive tenants of their land and convert it into sheep pasture—English wool was a highly sought commodity in Europe.

Social reformers, the so-called "Commonwealth Men," were propounding their remedies concerning the alleviation of social ills. Though in actual fact the sheep enclosures were quite insignificant, except in the Midlands, the noise made by the pamphleteers drowned out the economic realities. People thought this to be a problem, and their sentiment made all the difference. Hugh Latimer, John Hales, and Thomas Smith were the outstanding representatives, and the eminent document was the *Discourse of the Common Weal of This Realm of England.* The call was for a greater concern for the welfare of the common man.

In the summer of 1549 several uprisings occurred, in Devon and Cornwall in the west and in Norfolk in the east. The demands of the rebels, formulated in fifteen articles, revealed a curious mixture of economic and religious concerns. The mass was to be reinstituted; the Six Articles were to be restored, as was the use of Latin in Scripture and the divine service. Cornishmen, so it was argued, could not understand English any better than Latin.

Within weeks of the suppression of the rebellion Somerset was arrested and sent to the Tower by order of the council. Thereby the first phase of Edwardian rule came to an end, and John Dudley, Earl of Warwick, the main instigator of Somerset's fall, began to dominate. Dudley was an egotistical opportunist, willing to engage in whatever intrigue seemed most advantageous to him. Henry VIII had beheaded his father for conspiracy: the son may have been congenitally predisposed to walk the path of intrigue and scheming. In all probability Dudley was without religious conviction, though before his death on the scaffold he confessed that he had always been a Catholic, a surprising statement from the lips of a man who led England on a distinct Protestant course. He had profited from the religious change and its revocation would have had disadvantageous consequences for him. Moreover, he was a man greedy for power, and he may have sensed that only the consolidation of Protestantism would thwart Mary's accession to the throne which event would be the most serious threat to his power. Under the influence of Dudley, religious policy in England became pronouncedly Protestant. Even Cranmer, up to that time a moderate Protestant, began to move to a more aggressive position, responsible, perhaps, for a major revision of the *Book of Common Prayer.* In March 1552 Parliament passed the second Act of Uniformity, which ordered the introduction of a new prayer book. The new edition had commendable words for the old, calling it "agreeable to the Word of God and the primitive Church," but here obviously the left hand (the preface) did not know what the right (the book itself) was doing, for the changes, particularly in the section on Communion, were drastic. The terms "mass" and "altar" were discarded. Where in the first prayer book the minister, in distributing the elements, said: "The body of our Lord Jesus Christ which was given for thee preserve thy body and soul into everlasting life," the second prayer book had the following: "Take and eat this in remembrance that Christ died for thee and feed on him in thy heart by faith with thanksgiving." The emphasis was on "remembrance." The English church was as distinctly Protestant as it ever was to be.

After the new prayer book had been approved and was already in print, John Knox, the Scottish reformer, began to complicate matters. Knox was temperamentally unable to accept the book as biblical: to kneel when receiving the Sacrament, as the book enjoined, was for him idolatry. He aroused the conscience of the young king in this matter. Since the book was in press, the Solomonic solution was to add an appendix, the so-called "Black Rubric," which explained that kneeling did not mean adoration but gratitude. The "Black Rubric" safeguarded tender consciences as well as theological integrity.

The new prayer book did not lend itself to the same breadth of interpretation as the first one, but the atmosphere of tolerance in England remained. The second Act of Uniformity was stricter than the first, but still sufficiently vague to let matters stand where they had been three years earlier. Church attendance was enjoined upon the people, since many people "following their own sensuality, and living either without knowledge or due fear of God, do willfully and damnably" refuse to attend divine worship. This, however, was the extent of religious regimentation.

After six years of Edwardian rule, Protestantism was firmly embedded in England. Some of this had been accomplished by the foreign divines, notably Martin Bucer, but there were many native reformers to spread the Protestant tidings where they counted most—among the people. From 1548 on, a flood of Protestant writings rolled over the English countryside. Some writers, such as Peter Moone or John Ramsey, were obscure and hardly brilliant. Others, like Hugh Latimer or Richard Cox, were respectable as well as profound. They wrote both distinctly theological tracts and devotional works such as Hugh Latimer's famous *Sermons on the Plough*. These writings increased the dissemination of the Protestant faith in the land.

On 6 July 1553 King Edward, the "godly and virtuous imp," died. For four days his demise was kept secret while Dudley desperately plotted to influence the course of events. Next in line of succession stood Edward's stepsister, Mary, whose accession would spell disaster for the ambitious Dudley. His solution was to eliminate both Mary and her stepsister, Elizabeth, from succession (they could be labeled bastard children) and name the children of Frances Brandon, a niece of the late king, as rightful successors. This in turn placed Jane Grey next in line. Edward had agreed to this scheme, and four days after his death Jane was proclaimed queen. But the very next day Mary asserted her own rights to the crown, and within another two days Dudley's house of cards had tumbled. He had failed to arrest Mary, who was welcomed by the people with spontaneous and enthusiastic support. The Protestant divines at Cambridge had offered fervent prayers for Dudley's success, but no divine intervention came forth—unless, that is, Mary's success be so considered.

The Marian Reaction

WHAT HENRY VIII HAD STRIVEN SO DESPER-ately to avoid occurred in July 1553, when a woman ascended the English throne. It was as if that unfailingly self-confident king had only been teased with his son Edward. Mary Tudor was thirty-seven years of age when she received the royal crown, and those years had left their imprint upon her. Her father had once boasted "this girl never cries," a telling characterization of his daughter. Though by nature gentle and simple, Mary possessed harsh features that were the result of experience. Rejected by her father and mistreated by her brother and his council, hers had been an unhappy life, which found comfort only in religion. Naturally, this was the religion of her mother, Catholicism. Mary had stood aloof from the English scene for more than two decades and did not comprehend that the religious changes undertaken by her father and brother had become accepted by the people. She was mistaken when she took the wave of popular enthusiasm as an approval of her Catholic faith.

Mary ascended the English throne at a time when tranquility had to be restored. Had she understood this, she would have been a good ruler; but history has given her the ugly name of "Bloody Mary." This is ironic, since Mary possessed deep piety, personal integrity, and noble ideals, an uncommon accumulation of qualities for a Tudor. Epitaphs are written, however, for better or for worse, by posterity, and in this instance posterity appeared all too quickly. Had Mary lived as long as her sister Elizabeth, English religious, indeed, political, history might have taken a different turn. After all, rulers usually succeeded, if given time, in determining the religious sentiment of the people. Mary undoubtedly could have done the same. This is not to underestimate the impact of Protestantism in the land, but rather indicates a basic characteristic of the Reformation in Europe: only by attaining political control could Protestantism score formal success. The trouble with Mary's rule was not her religion or anything else but its brevity. Five short years could not assure the advent of a lasting Catholic era in England.

Still, Mary committed more than her share of blunders. She was unable to translate her noble personal qualities into action congenial to the English people. Her attitude was that of a surgeon performing

132

an operation, determined to bring about improvement. The English people had forsaken the Catholic faith, and she was going to rectify this evil. She viewed this as her foremost task, even though her initial statements on religion showed a magnanimity uncommon in the sixteenth century. She was going to leave each one free to follow whatever religion he chose, she said. One suspects that she thought the English people would quickly return to the Catholic faith; the few who did not could be ignored. She mistook the English temper, however, and as soon as she recognized this, the situation changed. Several of the "Protestant" bishops were deprived of their sees and some were arrested. The adamant Protestants emigrated to the Continent, about 800 in all, many of them able and important figures later known as the "Marian Exiles."

Parliament met in October 1553 and passed several bills of repeal pertaining to ecclesiastical legislation. The act that had annulled Henry's marriage with Catherine was rescinded, as were the new definitions of heresy promulgated under Edward. According to the latest version of the law of the land, Mary was the legitimate offspring of a proper marriage. Mary's intention was to take the country back to 1529. There was considerable resistance in Parliament to the changes; one-quarter to one-third of the members dissented, a telling evidence for the extent of Protestant sentiment among its members. At the touchy matter of the restoration of papal supremacy Parliament balked outright, and there was also strong indication that the restitution of monastic property would encounter opposition. Perhaps the two were causally related.

Mary bore the title of "Supreme Head of the Church," even though her documents bear the nondescript "etc." in its stead. The lands of the church continued to be in illegal hands and the pope's sentence against England stood. Upon Mary's succession, Pope Julius III had appointed Reginald Pole as legate to England to bring about reconciliation. When he arrived in England, he proved to be a tough customer, for he insisted on the restitution of the church lands. This would have meant far-reaching repercussions, since the lands had often changed hands and the question of who should make restitution defied an easy answer.

The touchy problem constituted the main stumbling block in the return to the religion of the Fathers. Once it was clear that the formal restitution of Catholicism did not mean the reassignment of these lands to the Catholic church, no formidable resistance remained. As soon as the present owners of church lands realized that their property would remain untouched, they seemed willing to accept the latest change. After having experienced no less than three changes in the official religion (including the two undertaken under Edward, namely from the first to the second prayer book), the English people had tired of the religious controversy and theological squabble, and were willing to accommodate themselves to any policy. The most adamant Protestant partisans were on the Continent; this fact had some bearing on the ease with which Mary's ecclesiastical changes were accepted in England; the men of ardent Protestant conviction were absent.

There was a difference between the formal restoration of the Catholic religion and a genuine interest in Catholicism on the part of the people. The former came easily enough; the latter was nearly impossible. Parliament considered reconciliation with Rome toward the end of November 1554. On the last day of that month came the moment for which Mary had been waiting for over twenty years. Speaking through the voice of Parliament, the English people declared themselves "very sorry and repentant of the schism and disobedience committed in this realm." England was Catholic again. Parliament passed several bills to provide the legal basis for the religious restoration. It revived the ancient law against heresy, and in January 1555 it repealed all of Henry VIII's ecclesiastical legislation, from the Statute of Appeals to the Supremacy Act, explicitly providing for the protection of the holders of church lands.

At that time the persecution of the religious dissenters began, and it did not terminate until four years later when Mary's reign itself came to an end. The instigator was the queen herself, who must have thought she did penance for the heresy of her father and brother. She showed herself thereby a true child of the age, for religious diversity was, in the sixteenth century, a pill too bitter to swallow. Diversity seemed to entail the disruption of order which was feared as much as the possibility that the dissenter might infect others with his heretical venom. Since criminal law was severe, and capital punishment an all-too-common matter, the Marian persecutions were neither particularly unique nor ruthless. The number of victims was actually less than 300.

The pen of John Foxe added a spectacular glow to the persecution; he would not have been so successful, if his work had not touched a sensitive spot. He was far away on the Continent when it all happened, but with indefatigable exuberance he went about collecting his material. Published first in Latin at Basel in 1559, his story appeared in an expanded English version four years later. The title of Foxe's work set the tone for its content, for it was meant to be not a cool and neutral report of fact, but a passionate defense of a great cause: *Actes and Monuments of These Latter and Perillous Dayes, Touching Matters of the Church, Wherein Are Comprehended and Described the Great Persecutions and Horrible Troubles That Have Bene Wrought and Practised by the Romishe Prelates.* In the preface came the inevitable apology to the reader who might feel—together with the author—that in light of the "infinite multitude" of books another publication may be "superfluous and needeles." Foxe's implication was, of course, that it was not superfluous, for he meant not to be a historian but to score a point. He was little concerned, for example, about the details of the "King's great matter," but lengthily narrated how it led to the spread of the gospel. As in the case of other sixteenth century martyrologists, Foxe's credibility has been questioned, though recent research has vindicated his generally judicious handling of the facts.

For several hundred years the *Book of Martyrs*, as Foxe's book is commonly known, was a second Bible for the English people, frequently chained beside the Great Bible in English parish churches. Such fame was hardly only theological. The content made it fascinating both for those who sought spiritual edification and for those who thrilled to read about martyrs writing in their own blood on the walls of their jails, or about persecutors with "monstrous making and misshapen fashion of feet and toes."

The Marian persecution hardly endeared the Catholic faith to the English people, who were shocked by the harsh suppression of a religious sentiment on the part of those who themselves had shared it a few years earlier. The country was perturbed by the burnings and there was public sympathy for the victims; the most illustrious of these was Thomas Cranmer, who on Mary's succession had been deposed as archbishop of Canterbury. Brought to trial, he first confessed to his Protestant convictions boldly; but he soon wavered. A brief recantation which acknowledged the pope to be the head of the Church of England "so far as the laws of God and the laws and customs of this realm will permit" marked the beginning, and five additional and far-reaching recantations followed. In the last one he confessed that he had misused his office and authority, that he had exceeded Saul in malice and wickedness, that he was a blasphemer, a persecutor, and contumelious.

Whether Cranmer was sincere or only grasped at recantation in hopes of saving his life will never be known. He had been catapulted to prominence against his desire. At his trial he recalled that upon receiving word of his nomination to the archbishopric he delayed his return to England for weeks, hoping that the king would forget about him. Henry did not; Cranmer became archbishop, and rose to be the king's trusted ecclesiastical advisor. Cranmer was a scrupulous scholar, ever willing to follow new insights and suggestions. He was persuaded that by divine ordination a sovereign exercised authority in the external affairs of the church and that the people were called upon to render obedience. When Mary ascended the throne and demanded his obedience, he found himself on the horns of a dilemma, created by his temperament and theological perspective—his willingness to change and to be submissive.

On the day of his execution he spoke differently. Every man hoped to give an exhortation at the time of his death, he remarked, and this he wanted to do: "I come to the great thing that troubleth my conscience more than any other thing that I ever said or did in my life, the setting abroad of writings contrary to the truth." He renounced everything that he had written since his degradation: "And forasmuch as my hand offended in writing contrary to my heart, therefore my hand shall first be punished. For if I may come to the fire, it shall be first burned."

It matters little that Cranmer was Protestant and his judges Catholic. If the ecclesiastical labels had been reversed—as they were at other places and at other times during that eventful century—the story would have the same meaning. The lesson of the religious persecutions of the sixteenth century is not only that men then killed for religion as men today kill for political or social ideals but that, in the end, man's integrity is a price beyond treasure. Matthew Parker, archbishop of Canterbury under Queen Elizabeth, offered another perceptive commentary. In the margin of *Bishop Cranmer's Recantacyons* he wrote two words: *homines sumus*—"we are all human beings." Thomas Cranmer, man of high achievements and distressing shortcomings, serves as a reminder that history is not only made by heroes but by human beings, simple and complicated, courageous and weak.

England held its breath. The north was conservative and thus more congenial to the Catholic religion, but even there minor annoyances—about married clergy or monastic lands—cropped up with almost predictable regularity. The English people went about their daily chores showing little enthusiasm for the old religion. There were few zealous Catholics in the land, no eloquent Catholic pamphleteers, no gifted Catholic preachers. The Catholic faith was imposed from the top, a policy that was bound to fail.

In November 1558 after long delays and great reluctance, Mary consented to name Elizabeth as her successor. An air of resignation overcame her and her mind seemed somewhere else. A few days before her death she remarked "what good dreams she had, seeing many little children like angels play before her, singing pleasing notes." In the early morning hours of 17 November 1558, Mary died and forty-three years of an unhappy life came to an end. Later that same day her chief advisor, Cardinal Pole, also passed away, as if one star had governed both their destinies or as if the one was not to face the future without the other.

A little over five years had passed since Mary had come to London. The cheers which then had greeted her had faded and the joyful brightness of that August morning had given way to the dreary cold of November. At Mary's death the English people shed few tears to grace her departure. This was a telling verdict. She had ventured to accomplish great things *ad majorem Dei gloriam* and, outwardly, she had accomplished them. But her zeal had proved a poor guide in the affairs of state; she had pushed too hard too fast. Perhaps this was due to her dogmatic zeal, perhaps to her awareness that she was living on borrowed time. Failure in her religious policy was the end, for even though the Catholic faith had been formally restored in England, the heart of the people had not been won.

In history the seal of success is the permanence of accomplishment, even as the seal of failure is repudiation. Mary Tudor's failure was that her stepsister Elizabeth was to repudiate what she herself stood for. Were it not for the sad fact that she committed the blunder of making martyrs, her name would be written, as has been remarked, as on water.

The Elizabethan Settlement

THE RULER WHO SUCCEEDED TO THE ENGLISH throne in November 1558 was again a woman: Mary's stepsister Elizabeth, twenty-five years of age, tall, full of poise, with reddish hair, not particularly attractive, though with striking eyes. Rather like her stepsister, Elizabeth had had a trying youth. At her birth her father was disappointed over her sex. Soon thereafter her mother had lost the king's favor, and Elizabeth experienced the consequences of being considered a bastard. Her stepsister Mary had despaired over a similar experience; but Elizabeth learned the art of diplomacy—a bitter process—that enabled her to rule England superbly for some forty-five years. When she died England was more powerful for her reign. "I pray God save her Grace, long to reign over us, to the glory of God," a contemporary had written when she came to the throne. So she did.

The foremost problem facing the new queen was what to do about religion. When Edwin Sandys wrote to Heinrich Bullinger in Zurich upon Pole's death, "We have nothing to fear . . . for dead men do not bite," he expressed the sentiment of the gospelers, who felt the time ripe for a change. Whatever her religious conviction in 1558, Elizabeth acted as a good Protestant, though perhaps more because of circumstances than personal conviction. As a daughter of Anne Boleyn she was, of course, illegitimate in the eyes of the Catholic church, and at the news of her succession Pope Paul IV plainly expressed himself along such lines. She would hardly embrace the religion that so labeled her. And what began as political expedience may well have settled as personal habit, though the queen never became a Protestant zealot. Scholars disagree about her religiosity, some seeing her as a bulwark of the Protestant faith, while others suggest that she was what the French called a *politique,* an English-woman first and a religious partisan second. The evidence is inconclusive. Elizabeth kissed the Bible in public, but she was a good actress and may well have done this for the gallery.

She spoke highly of the Augsburg Confession, and a charmingly simple verse, perhaps apocryphal, expressed her view of the Lord's Supper:

> 'Twas God the word that spake it,
> He took the Bread and brake it;
> And what the word did make it,
> That I believe and take it.

If Elizabeth's personal circumstances, her background and religious convictions, were one factor in disposing her to venture yet another alteration of the official ecclesiastical state of affairs, the temper of the English people undoubtedly was another. The inner fiber of Catholicism in England had been damaged beyond repair. For almost a generation England had not really known the Catholic faith (excepting, of course, the five years of Marian rule) and dynamic Catholic leadership was absent. No enthusiastic and youthful partisans had come to the fore during the five years of restored Catholicism.

The practical impossibility of a continuation of Catholicism as the official religion left open the question of the specific nature of the change. Elizabeth, in other words, had the option of moving in one of several directions. At the beginning she intended to reverse the religious policy of her stepsister, but this need not have meant more than the return to the religion of her father. To do more was hazardous and she must have known it. Elizabeth told the Spanish ambassador that she wanted to restore religion as her father left it. The leaders of the church were Catholic and the international situation, in light of the war against France, was precarious. The ardent Protestants were abroad, and even though the English people were weary of the religious persecution under Mary, Catholicism formally continued strong.

The settlement Elizabeth chose was neither the only nor indeed the self-evident one: a settlement at once limited and conservative, one that would allow her to make further changes at a later date. The meager evidence indicates that the Commons wanted the comprehensive reestablishment of Protestantism. Accordingly, demand stood against demand. The outcome was a compromise in which neither got all it wanted, but more than the other side originally was willing to concede.

Toward the end of January, Parliament met. A bill was introduced to "restore the supremacy of the Church of England, etc. to the Crown." The evidence concerning this bill and what happened in Parliament is enigmatic. Obviously supremacy was to be reintroduced; but Elizabeth seemingly was content to let the details of a religious settlement rest until a later time. Such a circumspect policy would allow her to settle the political problems before the religious ones.

When the Protestant Commons received this bill they added enough Protestant riders to make it a comprehensive instrument for religious change. Then the conservative Lords changed the bill back into its original form. The Commons diplomatically passed the bill; simultaneously, however, they approved one bill that reestablished Protestant worship. Thus the Commons had made their sentiment plain. They wanted more than the supremacy and the possibility of additional changes in the future: they wanted the introduction of Protestantism right then and there.

On Wednesday of Holy Week, 22 March 1559, both houses of Parliament had passed the original bill, which needed the queen's assent to become law. Elizabeth had every intention of giving this assent, but then changed her mind. Parliament, instead of being dissolved, was only adjourned until after Easter. The explanation for this change is that the queen had been informed of the peace concluded at Cateau-Cambrésis between France, Spain, and England. The international situation had cleared and Elizabeth could face the domestic issues without regard to possible complications abroad.

Elizabeth may have also realized that there was no likelihood that Catholics would agree to any change, no matter how conservative. The Convocation of Canterbury had voiced a strong protest against the proposed bill, a noteworthy departure from thirty years of ecclesiastical silence and all-too-willing concurrence with varying royal decrees. The leaders of the church would not fall in line. The queen was caught in a dilemma: the Catholic hierarchy was intransigent, unwilling to accept the supremacy, but the Protestants in the Commons were adamant. In the end Elizabeth found it the lesser evil to move into the Protestant direction.

Upon reconvening, Parliament began its consideration of two new bills, one dealing with supremacy, the other with uniformity. The bishops put up formidable resistance, the bishop of Chester asserting that the faith must depend on more than the whims of Parliament, but in the end both houses approved both measures. In substance, the Act of Supremacy undid Mary's repeal of Henry VIII's ecclesiastical legislation: the Act of Annates, the Statute of Appeals, the Consecration of Bishops, and the Submission of the Clergy. In addition, Mary's submission to Rome also was rescinded. For the second time within thirty years England had cut its ties with Rome and the church in England was, once again, the Church of England. The clock had been set back to 1547, though there were a few additional changes. The queen was not designated "Supreme Head" of the church, but its "Supreme Governor." More than semantic subtlety was involved here. Elizabeth was not the self-confident theologian her father had yearned to be. She was a partner of Parliament and her "governorship" was indirect at best. The new title lacked the theological significance of the old one, and, as it turned out, both theory and practice of Elizabeth's rule were different. The Act of Supremacy also redefined heresy, or rather it repealed, to speak more exactly, Mary's Act which had revived the old heresy laws. Scripture, the decrees of the first ecumenical councils, and Parliament acting with the consent of the Convocation, were declared to be the basis on which heresy was to be judged.

The Act of Uniformity reintroduced the second Edwardian Act of Uniformity that had accompanied the prayer book of 1552. A few changes were made in the prayer book. In the litany the minister's petition, "From the tyranny of the Bishop of Rome and all his detestable enormities" was omitted and the "Black Rubric," the unauthorized marginalia of 1552, disappeared. The most spectacular change concerned the Lord's Supper and consisted in the juxtaposition of the words of distribution of the 1549 and 1552 editions. Theologically, this constituted a compromise between the Lutheran view of the real presence and the Zwinglian view of a spiritual presence in Communion.

While the settlement was the result of accident and compromise, it early began to be seen as a profound and wise act. Through the centuries the settlement has shown an amazing ability to be many things to many men, admixing Protestant substance with Catholic principle. Indeed, it delivered what some of the early continental reformers had promised: a reformation only of the recent and blatant errors of the church.

With the statutory settlement of religion out of the way, the theological definition of the Elizabethan church remained as the major unresolved issue. Reformation England had a tradition of theological nonchalance: Henry VIII had waited until 1539 before promulgating the Six Articles and Edward until 1553 before issuing the Forty-two Articles. Convocation addressed itself to the problem in 1563 and came forth with a revision of Cranmer's Forty-two Articles.

After extended discussion seven of these were omitted, the wording of some of the remaining ones was changed, and four new articles were added, to bring this theological revision to the Thirty-nine Articles.

Theologically they were evasive. On the surface they seemed to propound a moderate Protestantism, though in the nineteenth century John Henry Newman thought it possible to give them a Catholic interpretation. The concern of the framers of the document was to invoke the teaching of the early church. Parliament approved the articles in 1566, but Elizabeth declined to give her assent. She soothingly asserted that the articles contained the faith "she doth openly profess" but added that she could not approve them because she disliked their form. Obviously, she had more than stylistic scruples. Her official approval would have formalized the theological character of the settlement of religion in England and she was concerned about possible international repercussions.

Approval did not come until 1571. By then the settlement had for all practical purposes become permanent, and the papal bull of excommunication at long last (in February 1570) was hurled against Elizabeth. The ways of Rome and Canterbury had permanently parted.

The task of guiding the religious settlement between determined and moderate Protestantism was difficult. No sooner had the settlement been concluded than it began to be vigorously assailed. It survived because it was what the queen wanted, but also because of its own remarkable inner strength.

The Puritan Dissent

THE MOST PERSISTENT ATTACK UPON THE ELIZabethan settlement came from the Puritans. "The hotter sort of protestants are called puritans," was the simple verdict of one contemporary. We might call the Puritans the "reformers of the Reformation," for they were persuaded that to realize the biblical ideal, the Reformation itself (in this instance the settlement) had to be reformed. The Puritan William Fuller pointedly wrote to the queen "but halflie by your Majesty hath God bene honoured, his Church reformed and established." The desired reforms pertained either to matters of practical churchmanship or to theological issues, though even the practical issues entailed theological presuppositions. On the surface, the controversy seemed to be about embarrassing trifles.

Much has been written on the question of the Puritan temperament, but the matter remains elusive. In a way, "Puritan" sentiment is timeless, defined as the rigorous insistence on a "purified" church, divested of additions and unbiblical impurities. That one of the medieval heretical movements should have used the very name ("Cathari") is surely telling. William Haller's comment that it is difficult to say who was the first and who may prove to be the last Puritan underscores this point. The historian must be careful to distinguish between "Puritanism" as it emerged in the second half of the sixteenth century and "Puritanism" as it characterized the English scene in the seventeenth century. The former, to be described presently, was devoid not only of the sectarian propensity (the sixteenth century Puritan did not think of leaving the official church; he wanted to reform it), but it was also without that kind of sour-faced drabness and dedication to the proposition that anything enjoyable is sinful which the historian of the seventeenth century Puritans so ubiquitously encounters. Nor did it have the political connotation it was to have in the seventeenth century.

Many suggestions have been made about the matter of Puritan origins: the Lollard heritage, the influence of the vernacular Scriptures, the general revival of learning, the continental Reformation, particularly of the Calvinist variety. The best explanation would take all these factors into consideration and conclude that indigenous (and timeless) sentiment was strengthened by continental influence.

The significance of this continental-Calvinist tradition must not be overlooked. Many of the Marian exiles, who had preferred a residence abroad to the hazards of England, had encountered resolute, comprehensive, dynamic religious reform, different from what they had known in their native land. They had also found a theology that demanded their admiration. Both the faith and the life of the church had been reformed, and the result seemed impressive.

The Elizabethan settlement of religion stands at the beginning of Puritanism, since dissatisfaction with it evoked dissent. Those who later became known as "Puritans" argued that too many vestiges of popery remained in the English church, and they would have none of it. Impatiently they sought further change. The range of disssatisfaction during the next few years was wide: the prayer book of 1549 was the basis of the settlement, the higher clergy lived in pomp and circumstance, wafers were used in Communion, the host was elevated, the service was ritualistic and assigned an inferior place to the sermon, saints' days were observed, and so forth. If a common denominator could be established, one's understanding of the sources of Puritanism would be much better. In part, at least, the first Puritan dissent was a reaction to the lukewarmness of those who approved the settlement.

The Puritan debate engrossed England for the better part of a century, attesting, if nothing else, to the measure of prevailing religious freedom. By and large the Puritan dissenters were able to keep their heads on their shoulders and their pamphlets on the printing presses, though neither task was particularly easy. In all this, one needs to keep in mind that in its initial thrust Puritanism was a clerical movement, spearheaded by the exiles who had returned to England upon Elizabeth's succession. Naturally, they had support among the laity, especially the nobility; the persistent agitation in the Commons for further ecclesiastical change and the establishment of numerous lectureships of Puritan tendency suggests this. Still, the preponderance of the clergy and, more importantly, of clerical issues must be noted. The controversy over vestments and polity would exercise (or excite) especially the men of the cloth.

The first clash occurred over ministerial vestments. The Royal Injunctions of 1559 had stipulated the wearing of "seemly habits, garments, and such square caps" for the clergy. Those who saw such vestments as unbiblical abomination protested. Vestments were a natural point of controversy, for the daily officiating of the clergy formed an ostensible thorn in the flesh of those who abhorred everything that smacked of papal religion. The need for additional ecclesiastical change seemed nowhere more urgent than here.

By the end of 1564 the antivestment cause had its spokesmen: Thomas Sampson and Laurence Humphrey, both from Oxford. Their opponent was Archbishop Parker, who wrote several articles aimed at achieving conformity among the clergy. These *Advertisements* indicated, among other things, the proper "apparel for persons ecclesiastical"; they prescribed an oath for the clergy, exacting the surely laudable promise to read one chapter from the Old and the New Testament daily, and demanded conformity to the vestment provision.

The dissenters were unwilling to yield. Disturbances of worship services occurred and a literary controversy began. A host of pamphlets issued from the printing presses, often distinguished more by zealous devotion than by incisive argumentation. The author of *A Briefe Discourse against the Outwarde Apparell and Ministring Garmentes of the Popishe Church*, for example, thought that the issue lent itself to poetic consideration:

> The Popes attyre, whereof I talke,
> I know to be but vaine:
> Wherefore some men that wittie are,
> to reade mee will disdaine.
> But I woulde wishe that such men shoulde,
> with judgment reade me twise:
> And marke how great an evill it is,
> Gods Preachers to disguise.

The parting of the ways came quickly. In April 1566 Archbishop Parker noted that some "do profess openly, that they will neither communicate nor come in the church where either the surplice or the cap is, and so I know it is practiced." In August, Bishop Grindal wrote to Switzerland that there was talk of withdrawal and the establishment of private meetings. Soon there was additional evidence that separatist conventicles were forming at other places in England. This development raises the question of whether permanent separation was intended. Probably not, though it was inevitable that the dissenters would seek out one another's company. The Puritans hoped that the religious settlement of 1559 was not definitive but could—and would—be changed and modified.

In 1572 the smoldering fire burst anew into flames. In June *An Admonition to the Parliament* appeared, a devastating catchall of assorted antisettlement polemic. Not much of the polemic was new, not all was profound, but everything was advanced with a cocksure conviction that acknowledged no contrary argument. Two young London clergymen—youth was as much a common denominator of Puritan sentiment as was the desire to "purify" the church—named John Field and Thomas Wilcox had collaborated on this *Admonition*. They asked that ministers be "called" by the congregation, that all ministers be equal, and the "titles, livings, and offices, by Antichrist devised," such as archbishop, bishop, and dean, be abolished. The church should be governed by a simple ministry of ministers, elders, and deacons.

Puritan discontent thus received a new focus: the episcopal form of church government. A new leader appeared, Thomas Cartwright, Professor of Divinity at Cambridge. In the spring of 1570 he lectured on the Book of Acts and, measured by this biblical standard, he found the ecclesiastical practice in England sorely wanting. His proposals were that the offices of archbishop and bishop be abolished; that deacons and bishops direct a congregation, the former caring for the physical and the latter for the spiritual needs; that a minister be assigned to a certain congregation that would elect him.

When Archbishop Matthew Parker died in 1575, he was succeeded by Edmund Grindal, a competent and efficient churchman, and a committed Protestant. He had been influenced by Martin Bucer, was a figure of international renown, and basically thought that the settlement of 1559 was open to modification. He ran into difficulties with the queen, who sought to get her own way by interfering directly in ecclesiastical affairs. Grindal reacted with vehemence, if without etiquette, in language the queen had never heard before—and was not to hear again: "I am forced, with all humility, and yet plainly, to profess, that I cannot with safe conscience, and without the offence of the majesty of God, give my assent. . . . Bear with me, I beseech you,

Madam, if I choose rather to offend your earthly majesty than to offend against the heavenly majesty of God. And although ye are a mighty prince, yet remember that He which dwelleth in Heaven is mightier." He was suspended from office in 1577.

John Whitgift, his successor, once appointed to the archiepiscopal office, lost no time in stilling the waves of ecclesiastical discontent. A set of articles was drawn up as the instrument with which to achieve uniformity. The Puritan divines refused to subscribe to the articles. Suppression of Puritan sentiment became more emphatic, and suspensions of nonconforming ministers more frequent.

Deep in his heart the Puritan thought that he could somehow or other persuade the Church of England to revise the settlement of 1559 and accept the pattern which he considered biblical. But as the years passed and this thought increasingly became an illusion, men appeared who were ready to separate from the church. Robert Browne, "dissent incarnate" as he had been called, illustrated the kind of soul-searching and meandering vacillation that characterized those who made the radical break. Twice arrested for nonconformity, he finally crossed the Channel to Holland with a group of faithful followers. Here he published in 1582 his famous pamphlet, *A Treatise of Reformation without Tarying for Anie, and of the Wickedness of Those Preachers Which Will Not Reforme till the Magistrate Commande or Compell Them.* His thesis was simple. The Church of England was so corrupt and unbiblical that true believers had no choice but to go their own way, "be they never so few." Browne denounced the ministers. of the English church as "dumbe dogges, destroiers and mutherers of soules," indeed, as "pope's bastards," and he joined in the denunciation of the polity and the discipline of the Anglican church.

The ecclesiastical climate in England became increasingly severe. In 1593 three adamant Puritans were hanged for sedition. The same year the queen issued an act "to retain the queen's subjects in obedience." To attend meetings of "conventicles" was declared incompatible with the affirmation of the queen's supremacy. Offenders were given a period of grace in which to conform; if they refused, they had to abjure the realm.

There is no need to follow the course of the Anglican-Puritan debate beyond this point. Neither the legal provisions just noted nor the gallons of ink spilled in the publication of the various Puritan and anti-Puritan tracts must mislead us into thinking that the controversy touched the marrow of Elizabethan society. Nothing could be further from the truth. Undoubtedly many lay men and women were drawn into the debate; its main protagonists, all the same, were the men of the cloth, even as the bones of contention were esoteric and hardly of much concern for most people. It was a squabble among theologians.

Only in the seventeenth century did this change—but by then the controversy had ceased to be merely theological. Ostensibly still religious, it was a political matter and as such dominated the English scene for several fateful decades.

8 The Reformation on the Continent

The European Dimension

WHILE SURVEYING THE COURSE OF EVENTS IN England, we have already touched on the fact that the Protestant Reformation was a phenomenon of European dimension, which attests to its vitality and underscores its historic significance. This European Reformation had two distinct aspects. One was the religious component. People throughout Europe heard, read, and accepted a new interpretation of the gospel. They broke with the Catholic church. They developed new religious styles of life, with their own hymns, forms of worship, and literature. In the end, these Protestant congregations either were able to consolidate (as, for example, in Holland) or they succumbed to the use of force against them. Successful or not, theirs always was the gripping story of a religious movement seeking to assert itself.

The second aspect was the kind of political involvement of religion which characterized Germany, that ambiguously religious world of diets, councillors, edicts, and ecclesiastical litigation, concerned with the legal recognition or rejection of the new faith. This was the world of power politics, alliances, intrigues, conspiracies, even war. Here the cause of religious change and renewal intersected the *haut monde* of diplomacy, and religion became a part of political history.

Obviously, these two aspects were interrelated, though they must be distinguished. They were not necessarily the two sides of the same coin, for one could well be divorced from the other: the Anabaptists illustrate the exclusive preoccupation with religion and Gustavus Vasa of Sweden, the preoccupation with politics. Most of the time, however, the Reformation was both. It affected virtually all European countries, from Scandinavia to Italy, from Spain to Poland. Only two countries escaped the turbulence of the Protestant message: Ireland and Spain, both of them nestled along the perimeter of Europe, far from the cradle of the new faith. There is evidence of a few Protestant congregations in Spain, but generally the new religion had little impact.

Several general observations may be made about the expansion of the new theology from Germany to other lands. They presuppose that the Reformation in Europe is to be traced to Luther's proclamation, an assumption by no means universally accepted. Scholars have minimized outside influence and stressed the indigenous elements of reform. In France, for example, the reformative efforts of Bishop Briçonnet at Meaux have been cited as the beginnings of ecclesiastical reform in that country. This perspective would make the Reformation in Europe the simultaneous expressions of reformative change, precipitated by the state of ecclesiastical affairs in the early sixteenth century.

One fallacy of this approach is that it all too easily utilizes a particular definition of "Reformation" as "reform" and thereby defies the complex reality. While there may have been instances in which concern for reform was important, the real aim of the Protestant Reformation was surely not so much "reform" as "reinterpretation" of the Gospels, and it was characterized before long by an inimical stance toward the Catholic church. The Reformation may have built on earlier expressions of reform sentiment; in the final analysis, however, the Reformation introduced an element of discontinuity into these efforts. Nothing illustrates this better than the fact that most of these "reformers" never joined the Protestant cause.

Even a negative conclusion concerning the dependence of the Reformation in Europe on Luther will need to acknowledge that Luther's ideas made their way from Germany to the four corners of Europe. His name became a household word, so to speak, even in France, England, and Sweden. This was possible by a number of means. The heavy flow of traffic between Germany and the rest of Europe enabled a man in Oxford to know what was happening at Basel, and informed the cleric at Strassburg about developments at Wittenberg. Of considerable importance was the correspondence between academicians in which the communication of scholarly news was often an important content: in March 1518, for example, Erasmus sent Thomas More a copy of Luther's Ninety-five Theses, and in April 1519 he wrote John Fisher about the Wittenberg professor.

News and ideas were taken abroad by men who traveled professionally across borders. Foremost, of course, were the merchants, of whose role the English scene offers particularly conclusive evidence. There were also students, especially those returning home from Germany, who brought the news in some instances as mere reporters, in others, as partisans of the new faith. The printers must also be mentioned, for economic interest or conviction (or both) made them send abroad the pamphlets propounding the new faith.

There is evidence for the colportage of Luther's books outside Germany. Zwingli propagated their distribution in Switzerland, Erasmus said that they were read in the Low Countries, and in England they were publicly burned. In February 1519 the Basel printer Froben shipped 600 copies of Luther's tracts to Spain and France, a business and religious enterprise of major proportions. About that time a student at Paris wrote that Luther's writings were received "quite openly" and Luther himself declared that his tracts were read by the doctors of the Sorbonne.

Since Luther's tracts were read in France or England, one is inclined to assume that a situation similar to the one in Germany existed in those countries. However, there were differences. Only the basic notions of Luther could be communicated abroad. Most of his early writings, though addressed to specific issues, were general in nature and did not express a "Lutheran" propensity. Thus, during the early years of the Reformation, Luther did not publish any exposition of his understanding of justification, and of his views on the Lord's Supper only the basic outline—the repudiation of Catholic sacramentalism—was clear. The label "Lutheran," so freely placed upon the proponents of the new theology, was misleading. "Lutheran" was only the affirmation of the primacy of Scripture in the formulation of religious truth, the repudiation of the primacy of the pope, and the minimal value placed on external rites and observances.

In actual fact, Luther's tracts had to be in Latin in order to break the linguistic barrier between Germany and the rest of Europe. The German writings were useless and only his Latin ones afforded a possible means of communication. This meant, of course, that Luther's message underwent an important modification. In Germany Luther had been able to speak directly to the common people. He had done so successfully, as the number of reprints of his vernacular tracts shows. Such direct communication was impossible for linguistic reasons elsewhere in Europe; accordingly, the popular response to the

Lutheran proclamation found in Germany could not materialize in other countries. Only in Germany could there be a popular movement. The transmission of Luther's ideas abroad had to focus on essentials and on catchy slogans—Scripture versus man-made traditions, salvation by grace versus salvation by works.

Despite this handicap, the new theology found active propagators on native soil. Its spread was not dependent upon outside literary influence but could utilize the efforts of indigenous colporteurs who shared the characteristic of youth and Erasmian propensity, men such as Bilney, Tyndale, Barnes, Biros, Wishart, or Petri. Some of them, as, for example, Olavus Petri of Sweden, had actually been in Germany and savored the new theology first hand. Others, like William Tyndale of England, traveled there after their "conversion." All of them were little known and certainly no part of what might be called the academic or ecclesiastical "establishment."

Each country had such native reformers, men who ventured to proclaim the new theology and did so initially against great odds and at great personal danger. Several paid for their faith with their lives and thereby showed the intensity of their commitment: the first Protestant martyrs, two men burned at Brussels in 1523, came not from Germany, but from a place to which the new faith had been imported. The native reformers assured the spread of the Protestant faith in their lands; their efforts transformed the ideas from abroad into a message congenial to the new environment.

The propagation of the new theology took the form of an amalgamation of basic notions of Luther's theology with elements from the native reformers. This synthesis explains the immense variety of theological emphases that characterized the scene, making the Reformation in Hungary different from that in Sweden or Poland. One would hardly expect these reformers to have adopted all of Luther's thought, especially since the "Lutheran" notions reaching them were, as already noted, so general as to require further delineation. Moreover, the men who carried the Protestant message forward in the various countries had pondered theological issues before they encountered Luther. While this encounter proved to be of considerable importance in their theological development, it could not do away completely with the theological background already present. Luther was only one of several factors in their development. The transmission of Luther's ideas was thus twofold, direct and indirect. The former occurred through his writings as these were read in the various European countries, while the latter took place through the native reformers. If the one was pure, but vague, Lutheranism, the other was a mixture of several elements.

An additional consideration pertains to the chronological divergence between the Reformation in Germany and that elsewhere in Europe. In Germany the movement reached its climax by the 1520s, at a time when the Reformation in the rest of Europe was only getting under way. One might say that the German Reformation ended before the European Reformation began. This time lag had two ramifications. For one, it meant that the defenders of the ecclesiastical status quo had advance warning. The defenses could be strengthened and the counterattack launched. The kind of *blitz* so successful in Germany was impossible elsewhere in Europe.

The time lag also helps to explain the important modification of the new theology from what might be described as a vague Lutheranism to a distinct Calvinism. While the Reformation in Germany was eminently Lutheran, in the rest of Europe it was Calvinist. Did this mean that Calvin's thought was more persuasive or that Luther's was too Teutonic? An explanation seems needed and the discrepancy in time between the two Reformations affords an initial clue. At the time Protestantism vied for acceptance in Scotland, England, the Low Countries, or France, Calvinism was the ascending star in the firmament of the Reformation, while Lutheranism was beset by vehement internal strife.

The Protestant goal was to spread the new gospel; it was as simple as that. At the same time, the Protestants wanted the right to live their faith, to worship publicly without legal restriction. Indeed, they strove for the official acceptance of their faith. Such was a legal matter, to be decided by the governmental authorities. Naturally, therefore, the Protestant quest was to obtain a favorable governmental decision. In many instances they were successful: in numerous German territories, in Sweden, in England. In other places they made a persistent effort to sway the ruler's sentiment, notably in France. They were unsuccessful but this very failure prompted another approach in the quest for legal recognition: affiliation with political power in the land in order to force the ruler's hand. In France, Scotland, Poland, and the Low Countries, the Protestants sought to achieve the goal of legal acceptance by allying with the nobility against the ruler. The specific situation differed from country to country, not only with respect to the ultimate outcome of the struggle, but also with respect to its basic characteristics. In France, for example, the Catholic cause, and thus the opposition to the Protestant efforts, was advocated not by the king but by a faction of the nobility. Accordingly, the struggle was between rival factions, with the king occupying an uneasy position between them. In Scotland and the Low Countries another variant can be observed. There the rulers were foreign, and the struggle against them

151

took the form of opposing foreign influence. The Protestant cause became embroiled in a complex political picture and ceased to be a purely religious phenomenon.

Four countries will be singled out on the following pages since events there seemed to have been more significant than elsewhere. Each of these countries, of course, had its own particular Reformation history, each its particular story of Protestant success or failure. These histories have been variously written. To relegate them to collective ·existence is not to minimize their importance, but to assure that the multiplicity of events does not obscure the common lines of development.

The compass to be covered is extensive. Accordingly, the task is frustrating, for to recount the events of decades on a few dozen pages means to slide from generalization to generalization. While important in their own right, it seems that the histories of the Reformation in these countries are primarily significant for their paradigmatic confirmation of general trends of the period. Extension of the study to additional countries probably would not alter the conclusions. Denmark, Hungary, or the Netherlands would have added further names, dates, and theological insights, but contributed little new to the understanding of the nature of ecclesiastical change in the sixteenth century. Parallels and differences in the four countries afford illustrations of the success (or failure) of the Protestant quest for recognition.

France

THE STORY OF THE REFORMATION IN FRANCE can be told in several ways: as the account of a religious movement or of the struggle between competing factions for political power, the influx of Lutheran ideas into the country, or the eventual emergence of Calvinism as the eminent Protestant faction. It is always the same historical reality, though differing emphases will open different perspectives.

Our account will seek to show how the Protestant movement became involved in a fierce political power struggle. The better part of the entire century was necessary to demonstrate that Protestantism could not be victorious in France and the stations along the way were marked by persecution, wars, and bloodshed. The historian, who occasionally, at least, is wiser than were contemporaries, can see the options clearly enunciated from the beginning. Given the saturation of the land with Protestant ideas, the task was to convert the monarch to the new faith; it was as simple, or as difficult, as that. Aside from the possibility that the ruler experienced a religious conversion, as variously happened in Germany, the *raison d'être* for a change of ecclesiastical loyalties might have been the existence of tangible advantages, the case of Henry VIII being the spectacular, if unsavory, illustration. In France no political (or personal) advantages existed. A unique relationship prevailed between the church and the crown. The Pragmatic Sanction of Bourges, promulgated in 1438, had established several important ecclesiastical privileges of the crown. It caused a running battle between crown and papacy which was not resolved until the Fifth Lateran Council, when it finally was declared null and void. But this was a Pyrrhic victory since a concordat, concluded at the same time, granted to the crown virtually the same rights enjoyed before, including the right to nominate bishops, abbots, and priors. In short, the French king possessed extensive power in ecclesiastical affairs. Since this meant, among other things, considerable revenue, he could hardly be lured to break with Rome for the mundane reasons not unimportant elsewhere in Europe.

The alternative facing the Protestants was, accordingly, to force the king to undertake ecclesiastical change because of the widespread presence of such sentiment among the people—and the Protestants tried to do precisely that. Zwingli dedicated one of his major works to Francis, and Calvin followed suit with the dedication of his *Institutes* to the king. The Protestants' minimum program was the legal acceptance of worship in the land.

There was yet another option and that was to seek a change through political means. In the end this is what happened, though it took several decades for such determination (and the political issue) to appear. The course of ecclesiastical change became embedded in political developments. The cause of religion was conjoined to the cause of politics, and the proponents of the one saw advantages in taking up the other: the Protestants saw their cause strengthened by political power, while those concerned with political issues took up the cause of religion for the advantages it would bring.

The first phase of the Reformation in France was characterized by the influx of Lutheran ideas into the country. The simplest explanation of its origins is to see it as the extension of Luther's proclamation. An impressive phalanx of French scholars has dissented from this view, arguing that an independent reform movement existed in France before Luther, evidenced by the widespread propagation of the Bible toward the end of the fifteenth century and the reforming attitudes of Marguerite d'Angoulême or Jacques Lefèvre d'Étaples.

The problem is resolved with a definition of the term "Reformation," which can be applied to a variety of reform efforts in the late fifteenth and early sixteenth centuries. The term can be restricted, however, to the reorientation that had the break with Rome as its most dramatic expression. In this latter sense it is impossible to speak of an autonomous French Reformation. However much Jacques Lefèvre deviated from medieval scholasticism or however close his biblical commentaries came to a view of justification subsequently embraced by the reformers, he was not a Protestant. A humanist, Lefèvre was in many ways critical of the church, but always its loyal son, a fact illustrated by his faithful allegiance to Catholicism after the Lutheran controversy had begun to divide the people. Doctrinal affirmation was less important than the ecclesiastical temper.

Thus the Reformation in France had its beginnings when Luther's writings first found their way into the land. In August 1521 a mandate published *à son de trompe et cri publique* confiscated all of Luther's writings, and in November a royal ordinance prohibited the publication of all writings "favoring and defending the books of Luther." Luther was grouped with such heretics as Wycliffe and Hus, and his *Babylonian Captivity* was compared to the Koran. Lutheranism had taken root.

The defeat of King Francis I at Pavia in 1525 and his subsequent imprisonment by Charles V had repercussions for the ecclesiastical situation. No doubt could exist about the orthodoxy of the French church in order to gain the sympathies (and political support) of the pope, and thereby help effect the release of the king. The Parlement of Paris and the Sorbonne—the one the political, the other a theological authority—strove to excel each other in the persecution of Lutheran heretics.

Personally Francis was of a moderate religious orientation, but he could not afford to be sentimental about the protection of the religious innovators. Charles V was his archfoe, and the support of the papacy was therefore indispensable. Francis would probably have supported the side of the Catholic faith even if the international situation had been different. As matters stood, however, this situation gave him little choice. Politics intermingled with religion from the very outset of the religious controversy in France, and in contrast to other places, such as Sweden or England, political prudence suggested the perpetuation of the ecclesiastical status quo.

Francis opposed deviation within the French church, not only because he wanted to remain in the good graces of the papacy, but also because his struggle with Charles V made a tranquil domestic situation mandatory. His objection was not so much to doctrinal aberration but to the disruption of unity and tranquility. Francis was indisposed to surrender control of the church for the sake of questionable doctrinal adventures which offered little except risks and pitfalls.

Two harmless events precipitated the showdown between the new faith and the old church. One was the speech of a distinguished academician, the other a handbill posted on the door of the king's bedroom. The consequences in both instances were far-reaching.

The oratorical feat came on All Saints' Day, 1533, with a speech of Nicolas Cop, rector of the University of Paris. It was a mélange of Erasmus, Lefèvre, and Luther, theologically quite harmless, yet startling, for it was propounded on an official occasion and given the aura of academic approval. Loyal Catholics were in an uproar and demanded action against Cop, who unceremoniously fled to Switzerland. Afterward Francis I enjoined the Parlement of Paris to suppress the Lutheran heresy. The next twelve months passed with numerous arrests, convictions, and deaths; France increasingly proved an inclement climate for the new faith.

In October 1534 came the second event, the posting of handbills at Paris and various other places throughout the country, including the door of the king's own bedroom at the royal castle at Amboise. The author of this ingenious Protestant propaganda effort was Antoine Marcourt, who considered the mass to be the abomination of abominations, "through which the world, unless God has mercy, will be completely devastated, destroyed, ruined."

Marcourt's move was understandable, but hardly prudent. Since the handbills had been posted at several places at the same time, an organized group was thought to stand behind the coup. The king had to ponder the disquieting thought that the religious innovators had been able to reach the door of his own bedroom. Once again, more was at issue than theological deviation, for the fear that Protestants tended to disrupt law and order haunted the authorities, despite Protestant remonstrances.

Within a month seven persons had been sent to the stake. A stern mandate ordered full censorship. Perhaps the king meant to do no more than teach the Protestants a lesson. His political ties with the League of Schmalkald, as well as his own temperament, kept him from drastic measures. In July 1535 he signed the Mandate of Coucy, which freed the imprisoned Protestants and allowed Protestant refugees to return to France—the amnesty, incidentally, which gave John Calvin the opportunity to return to his native land for the last time. During the next two years Francis was preoccupied with foreign affairs but afterward he had the opportunity to deal with domestic matters. In 1539 and 1540 additional mandates against the Protestant heretics made the suppression of heresy an affair of state.

With the death of Francis in 1547 and the succession of Henry II the efforts at suppression continued with even greater determination. Henry resolutely opposed the French Protestants. He possessed little of his father's empathy for a humanist religion, and he was deeply persuaded that Protestantism constituted a mortal danger for the realm. One of his first measures was to establish a new judiciary body, the *chambre ardente* ("fire court"), which was entrusted with the function "to counter the blasphemous and heretical disturbers of the peace and tranquility of this most Christian kingdom." In the two years of its existence, from December 1547 to January 1550, it rendered over 500 verdicts, most of them death sentences.

In 1551 Henry issued the Edict of Chateaubriand, which sought to render the existing provisions for the persecution of heretics more effective. The edict spoke of the "common malady of this contagious pestilence which has infected many noble towns," and its forty-six articles provided for the judicial treatment of heretics. Once more persecution was intensified, yet success failed to grace the efforts. Some of those who had earlier advocated severity against the Protestant heretics began to have second thoughts, wondering what was to be done if the persecution did not accomplish its goal, whether it were possible to continue the policy of persecution indefinitely, and if not, what kind of rapprochement was possible between the Protestants and the king.

Henry was unwilling to forsake his grim determination to free his land from the heretical pestilence, but he realized his problems: his foreign policy was bankrupt and his dream of conquests abroad, especially in Italy, had not materialized. Governmental finances were in a desperate state and the army was not equipped to launch a major attack upon Spain. The outgrowth was the treaty of Cateau-Cambrésis, signed in April 1559, which ended more than half a century of intermittent Spanish-French conflict.

A few months later the king died unexpectedly. The French Protestants uttered words of relief upon hearing this, for a ruthless enemy of their cause was gone. The twelve years of his reign had been a constant and unyielding effort to crush the Protestant sentiment. The heir to the throne was Francis II, fifteen years of age, hardly capable of leading the affairs of state. The question of regency was hardly discussed, for Cardinal Guise summarily took over the reins of government. Guise's maneuver evoked the protest of the noble family of the Bourbons, who argued that, since the king was a minor, a council of regency should be formed.

This constitutional problem was to have profound repercussions for French Protestantism. There were religious overtones to the tensions between the Bourbons and the Guises: the former sympathized with the Protestants, while the latter advocated a policy of suppression. Thus, a religious note indirectly impinged on the constitutional problem. The French Protestants were drawn into the controversy. They supported the Bourbon claims to the regency and argued that the Guises were usurpers from abroad—most of the Guise lands were in Lorraine—and had to be resisted. The theological rationale for this attitude came from Calvin's doctrine of the right of resistance of the *magistrats inférieurs*, which sanctioned the view that the *princes du sang* (higher nobility) had the right to oppose the unconstitutional moves of the Guises in order to reestablish the constitutional government in France.

During this time there also appeared among the French Protestants the question of whether to resort to arms against the tyrant. This notion of revolution was from then until the end of the century to become a major element in the history of the French Reformation. This was neither totally a departure from previous views nor the ultimate extension of Calvin's ideas. Still, the face of French Protestantism changed. Theretofore, the adherents of the new faith had been committed to a religious cause. They had risked their lives to read the Protestant books or to attend the worship of the Protestant congregations. After the governmental crisis French Protestantism increasingly found its adherents among men who had other than religious reasons to follow its banner. Nobles flocked to its ranks. Before 1559 Protestants tended to be martyrs; after 1559 they were revolutionaries.

The setting of this change was important. A constitutional question perturbed the country and the charge of usurpation of legal rights was raised. Opposition to the Guises could be justified on constitutional grounds, and this political rationale could be supported by religious argumentation. French Protestantism did not change its political ethics in a vacuum but rather in a definite societal context.

Religiously, the situation seemed favorable for the Protestants. In May 1560 a new mandate allowed personal freedom of religion but prohibited public assemblies. Two persons were responsible for this change of policy: Catherine de Médicis, wife of Henry II, and Michel de L'Hôpital. Catherine was not deeply interested in the religious questions which perturbed the time. Niece of Pope Clement VII, she was no doubt a great woman, though she was neither very pious nor very learned, nor even very principled; but she was an astute politician. She also possessed a good deal of feminine charm that brought success where a man might have failed.

Michel de L'Hôpital, the new chancellor, was a man of ability and talents. Catholics had stereotyped contempt for him, Protestants reserved awe. He is said to have been part of the growing faction of the "politique," comprised of moderate adherents of both religious groupings, who were persuaded that the country needed, above all, a strong monarchy to end the religious strife. L'Hôpital would have betrayed his insight had he relegated religion to an inferior place. But his religion was neither staunchly Catholic nor aggressively Protestant; it was of that evasive, yet powerful, version propagated by Erasmus. It consisted of simple precepts and essentially was a way of life. L'Hôpital thought that this religion was the answer to the religious problem facing France. He was persuaded that the use of force against the heretics was bound to be unsuccessful, and that the Catholic church should concern herself with the Calvinist charges and answer them. His goal was irenic concord. The king's unexpected death changed the political picture overnight. The successor was Charles IX, the second son of Henry II, eleven years of age. This time there was no question that a regent was needed; it was to be Catherine de Médicis.

Catherine had a notion of how the religious problem could be solved. Convinced of the strength of Protestantism, she sensed the futility of continued persecution and thought it possible to clear the air with a truce. Afterward a council, either national or general, might effect conciliation. In short, hers was the program of L'Hôpital and exemplified the same weakness. The Catholics were hardly receptive to such a course of action and neither were the Calvinists. Catherine might have learned a lesson from the futile efforts of Emperor Charles V, whose mediating policy had satisfied neither side. The weakness of her policy was the inability to rally supporters; its strength was an astute understanding of the realities of the situation: the country could not be pacified with a substantial segment of the populace in opposition.

In January 1562 Catherine issued the Edict of Saint-Germain, which permitted the Protestants to hold worship services outside fortified cities. This was an epochal concession. After almost forty years of struggles and persecution, the French Protestants received the right to worship publicly. The tradition of only one religion in the realm was broken. No longer was it possible to speak of *une foi, une loi, un roi,* since two faiths were officially recognized. How long this arrangement would last was another question. The preface spoke of "reunion and return to one fold, which is all that we desire," suggesting that the edict was to be temporary. That the French crown was willing to consider a temporary suspension of the notion of the *corpus christianum,* the society where church and state were one, was truly revolutionary.

This turn of events did not herald the resolution of the controversy. Indeed, for the remainder of the century the French countryside was filled with the sounds of battle and the sights of destruction. The Wars of Religion began and lasted intermittently until the Edict of Nantes was issued in 1598. After theological arguments no longer persuaded and diplomacy no longer restrained, the battlefield was to render the final verdict. Such had been the case in most places where the Protestant faith sought legal recognition—in Switzerland, Germany, the Low Countries, Scotland. France followed such precedent, though there the ensuing conflict lasted longer and was more catastrophic than anywhere else. Moreover, in France religion constituted only the veneer in those wars: men exploited the sacred in order to pursue the profane. To be sure, the lines were always neatly drawn, with Catholics on one side and Protestants on the other, but often neither Catholics nor Protestants were greatly concerned about religion. Other factors impinged upon the action and made lip service to one brand of religion both easy and prudent.

In a real sense the war was caused by the failure of the crown to assert itself against the two religious factions. Catherine's program was one of conciliation, but she had received no response. The Protestants thought themselves too strong and the Catholics too threatened to enter upon the path of compromise. The outbreak of hostilities was by no means deliberate, determined, or planned. The transition from peace to war was surprisingly smooth, and the country found itself in a fratricidal conflict before this was realized. Voices of warning, particularly from Geneva, had gone unheeded.

The Peace of Amboise, in March 1563, terminated the first round of hostilities but hardly cooled tempers and left the Protestants dissatisfied. Initially, Condé, their leader, had demanded the reinstatement of the Edict of Saint-Germain, but the Protestant nobility, rather unconcerned about those not of noble rank, failed to support him. Accordingly, the peace granted religious freedom only to the nobility. Commoners were allowed to worship at one place in each bailiwick, though outside the town. No Protestant worship was allowed in Paris.

The peace was a step backward compared with the more liberal provisions of the Edict of Saint-Germain. The war had shown most Frenchmen still to be good Catholics, or, to put the matter in a slightly more dramatic way, a great many Frenchmen turned Catholic again upon seeing the ruthless Protestants in action. The problem was that not all of those who fought on the Protestant side were men of deep religious commitment. Before the war, Calvin had warned his French compatriots lest their impatience bring the Protestant cause to naught. He was not mistaken.

A word must be said about the political reflections of the French Protestants. Influenced by a variety of sources, including, of course, John Calvin, but molded by the sequence of political events from the constitutional crisis of 1559 to the Massacre of St. Bartholomew in

159

1572, the thinking of French Protestants underwent a striking development. There had been a few impatient ones all along who groaned under the oppressive persecution and longed to repay in kind, taking to force to obtain the victory of their gospel; but most of the Protestants were moderate, influenced by Calvin, who incessantly counseled that God had called them to patience and suffering rather than the use of force. He rejected those who, as he put it, sought "to convert the universe in an instant." But the continuous persecution, the constitutional crisis, and especially the Massacre of St. Bartholomew reoriented the Protestant attitude. Theretofore, French Protestants had emphasized loyalty toward authority. The new pamphlets argued differently, even as many hardly espoused religious concerns. Sharply antiroyalist in tone, they saw royal power not as absolute, but as dependent upon legitimate use. Francis Hotman's *De furoribus gallicis* (1573) was an account of the massacre and a vehement indictment of the crown. His *Franco-Gallia*, of that same year, showed that in the past the people had exercised sovereignty and that the absolute exercise of royal power was a recent development. The theme of an anonymous work, *A Defense of Liberty against Tyrants* (1557), attributed to Philip du Plessis Mornay, was the proper attitude toward authority: whether the orders of a sovereign would have to be carried out, even if they were contrary to the law of God, or whether resistance against a sovereign were permissible. The tract asserted that the *officiarii regni* ("officials of the realm") had the right and the responsibility to resist a king who violated the law of God. Kings were not above the people: "Seeing that the people choose and establish their kings, it follows that the whole body of the people is above the king, for it is a thing most evident, that he who is established by another, is accounted under him who had established him." A tract entitled *Du droits des Magistrats sur les sujets,* by Theodore Beza, argued that an unfaithful king had to be removed from office.

In 1584 the country, already beset by constitutional woes, was faced with a new issue: the problem of the successor to Henry III, who was childless and (after the death of his younger brother) the last of the Valois. Next in line stood Henry of Navarre who, as leader of the Protestants, was bitterly opposed by all Catholics. This gloomy prospect rallied the Catholics. The Catholic League allied with Philip II, while Pope Sixtus V excommunicated Henry of Navarre and deprived him of all claims to the French crown. Still, the last of the Wars of Religion in France that broke out in 1585 demonstrated the confusion of religion and politics. Henry III increasingly resented the power and influence of the Guises, so much so that he instigated the assassination of Duke Henry of Guise and Cardinal Louis of Guise in

December 1588. The following summer a rabid Catholic sought revenge by assassinating the king.

On his deathbed Henry asked the army to swear the oath of obedience to Henry of Navarre, who took the appellation of Henry IV, as his successor. With Henry of Navarre the French Reformation and the Wars of Religion reached their end. Though a Protestant and a leader of the Protestants, Henry was hardly a religious person. Beyond the routine of religious exercises, especially before and after battles, he gave no evidence of religious conviction, except a coolness —surprisingly, considering his leadership of the French Protestants— toward rigorous Calvinism. Had he lived in Geneva, his problems with the consistory would have been unending; he was hardly a model Calvinist. His goal was to be a Frenchman, and his conversion to Catholicism was less a traitorous default of the Protestant faith than a wise political move.

In July 1593 Henry abjured his Protestant beliefs and professed the Catholic faith, uttering, according to tradition, "Paris is well worth a mass." The point, if authentic, was well taken: Paris was the citadel of Catholicism, Henry could never hope to rule the city as a heretic, and Paris was France. Henry realized that only as a Catholic could he unite the country. Decades of indecisive civil war were ample evidence. Henry's acceptance of Catholicism did not change the political picture overnight. A long struggle was necessary before he finally controlled the country. His conversion brought the more moderate Catholics into his camp, even as it freed the country from the threat of war with Spain. An astute use of force, persuasion, and money brought the nobility to his side. The Protestants, though shocked by his ecclesiastical turnabout, remained his loyal subjects, and the antiroyalist sentiment that had become so widespread among them during the days of Charles IX and Henry III disappeared.

On 13 April 1598 the king took the decisive step of settling the religious problem by promulgating the Edict of Nantes, the last of a long list of edicts and mandates that began with the Edict of Chateaubriand in 1551. Within certain limitations, the edict granted freedom of worship to Protestants. They were allowed to worship in places where they had done so in 1596 and 1597; elsewhere, Protestant worship was restricted to one place in a bailiwick. Paris continued to be forbidden to Protestants, as were episcopal and archiepiscopal seats. The edict decreed the full equality of Protestants in governmental offices, and guaranteed them 100 places of safety for a period of eight years. This last provision seems particularly noteworthy since it revealed the character of the edict: though issued by the king, it was essentially a contract between two political powers.

The edict marked the end of the Reformation in France. For the first time the notion of religious freedom was embodied in a document of state. As had been anticipated by the Edict of Saint-Germain, it repudiated the principle of the *corpus christianum*, of whatever ecclesiastical coloring. It was a departure from more than a thousand years of Western history, during which a citizen had been, by the fact of his citizenship, a Christian of the kind prescribed by his sovereign. The Edict of Nantes ended this, heralding a development that was to encompass all of Europe. In Germany such toleration came after the end of the Thirty Years' War, in England, after the Glorious Revolution. Yet in France, herald and forerunner of this development, the revolutionary beginnings were subsequently reversed. In 1629 the political and military provisions of the Edict of Nantes were rescinded, and in 1685, three years before the Toleration Edict in England, Louis XIV revoked the religious provisions. The notion of national unity, even in religion, was to be victorious once more.

At the time of the Edict of Nantes, the Protestants probably comprised about one-tenth of the population, a figure which shows they could hardly force their will upon the land. The edict gave them the maximum that could be attained under the circumstances. France had come a long way since that day in August 1523, when the Parlement of Paris and the theological faculty of the university there had joined hands to suppress the ideas of Luther. The ensuing seventy-five years had brought the failure of those efforts, and the Edict of Nantes safeguarded the accomplishments of Protestantism. Yet Protestantism had failed in its foremost goal: to convert the country. That the decisive battles, theological as well as military, were fought in the second half of the century, when a revived Catholicism had replaced the weariness of an earlier generation, undoubtedly was an important element. Above all, the explanation must point to political factors, and especially the role played by the monarchs. Without the benefit of a real political issue, Protestantism was not strong enough to win.

Sweden

IN SCANDINAVIA THE REFORMATION EXPANDED and consolidated in a unique fashion. At the outset of the century the Catholic church was lively and little popular criticism was voiced. The Renaissance prelate, the immoral monk, or the absentee bishop was an unknown figure. The monasteries were centers of spirituality and important places of learning. Surprisingly, it was in Sweden that the ecclesiastical transformation was most comprehensive. It succeeded in achieving quickly what elsewhere came only after tense and tedious development. The explanation is to be sought neither in the bankruptcy of the old church nor in the forcefulness of the Protestant proclamation.

At the outbreak of the Reformation the incumbent on the throne of the Union of Kalmar, which comprised all of Scandinavia, was Christian II, one of the most remarkable rulers of the century. Christian was a typical Renaissance ruler, literate, learned, and cultured, but ruthless and egotistical. He opposed the higher clergy and nobility, though it is hard to say if he was guided by a progressive temper or by absolutist tendencies. One of his main goals was to bring Sweden into closer submission to Denmark. In so doing he favored and supported the pro-Danish faction in Sweden, represented by the archbishop of Uppsala, Gustav Trolle, who was bitterly feuding with Sten Sture, the administrator, or *rigsforstander,* in Sweden. In 1517 the Swedish Estates, convened by Sture, deposed the archbishop, whose influence in Rome, however, caused Sweden to be placed under interdict and brought about Sture's excommunication.

Christian collected arms and men, and in January 1520 invaded Sweden under the pretense of defending the church. Sture was defeated. Magnanimously announcing an amnesty for those who had fought against him, Christian invited the nobles of the realm to Stockholm to join him in the coronation festivities. Unsuspecting, they came, but a scheme, arranged between Christian and Trolle, brought their downfall. The archbishop announced that the royal pardon had not affected the ecclesiastical censure and requested Christian to punish the nobles on behalf of the church. Christian complied. Over 600 nobles and clergy were executed.

This "Massacre," or "Blood Bath," of Stockholm was to have serious repercussions. The church, in the person of Archbishop Trolle, had become intimately involved in political strife and had done so on the side of those whose interests seemed to be foreign rather than Swedish. The political picture changed quickly. Christian seemed to have scored a decisive victory, but it proved to be short-lived. Gustavus Eriksson Vasa, scion of the Sture family, began to garner the support of the remaining nobility and the peasants, and set out to throw off the Danish yoke. His first success came in 1521 with the defeat of Trolle; two years later he was in control of most of the country. That same year Christian II himself was deposed in Denmark, whereupon Stockholm surrendered and Gustavus was elected king of Sweden and Finland.

At his election Gustavus gave the customary assurances about maintaining the "privileges, persons and possessions of the holy Church," but there was a hollow ring about this assurance, since this church had sided with his political opponents, and his words conveyed an uncommon element of magnanimity. In the spring of 1523 the king nominated the papal nuncio John Magnus, a conscientious but weak figure, as archbishop of Uppsala. In addition, four other bishops were nominated, all loyal Catholics, but politically on Gustavus's side. In September he requested the papal confirmation of these nominations, asking, at the same time, for the suspension of the payment of the annates. The country was too destitute to pay and would pledge "greater obedience" in other matters. Pope Adrian continued to support Archbishop Trolle and, moreover, appointed a foreigner to one of the vacant sees. Gustavus found that appointment unacceptable and threatened that, if necessary, he would procure the confirmation of his bishops "from the only and high priest, Jesus Christ." The threat was obvious, yet Adrian's successor, Clement VII, showed himself unwilling to engage in this kind of ecclesiastical blackmail. He confirmed only one of the royal candidates and turned down the request for the suspension of the annates. Unknown at the time, this was the last communication between Rome and Sweden.

In Sweden the initial phase of the "Reformation" entailed nothing more than the repudiation of papal authority, which took place against the backdrop of a spread of Lutheran ideas. Laurentius Andreae, archdeacon at Strengnäs, illustrated the new theological orientation of believers and not of prelates. If this sounded like Lutheran heresy, Andreae added, those who so argued should first check whether their own teaching was scriptural.

Andreae became an advisor to the king—he had been appointed the king's secretary and chancellor in 1523—and he established himself as a staunch partisan of the new faith. An astute politician in addition to being a competent theologian, he persuaded the king that the acceptance of the Lutheran faith offered benefits without liabilities. A sure indication of a new direction came in January 1525 with the promulgation of a mandate which stipulated that the income of the church was to go to the king. One month later, Olavus Petri, a minister in Stockholm and perhaps the foremost theological exponent of Protestantism in the land, married.

The country meanwhile continued in a state of crisis. Gustavus was hard pressed by his foreign creditors, yet he had no money and new taxes were out of the question. Convening a diet at Vesterås in 1527, he confronted the assembled estates with the news that the country was at the verge of bankruptcy. This was hardly novel; what was new, however, was the insistence that the solution lay in the confiscation of the property of the church. One of the bishops retorted that to touch the property of the church was to touch the authority of the pope. Gustavus seemed impressed by the argument and told the estates that under the circumstances it would be best for him to abdicate. He "would move on his way," he said, "never to return to this unreasonable, perverted, and ungrateful fatherland."

After some hesitation the estates agreed that they had nothing to lose from the king's proposed action—nothing, that is, except their faith. Gustavus waited until he had been implored three times not to abdicate before he agreed to change his mind. The recess of the diet handed the episcopal castles and lay-fiefs over to the king, who, in effect, was given the authority to decide what the needs of the church were. All ecclesiastics were placed under the authority of civil courts for civil offenses. The "pure Word of God should be preached" and the Scriptures read in churches and schools. Together with the recess an *ordinantia* was issued which spelled out the relationship between the spiritual and the temporal realm. The existing structure of the church was retained, though episcopal jurisdiction and the authority of the bishops were restricted and replaced by that of the king. The bishops, who had put up a valiant resistance, eventually acknowledged his authority.

The Diet of Vesterås was the real beginning of the Swedish Reformation. Royal authority in ecclesiastical affairs was strengthened and the ties with Rome were broken. Otherwise, however, ecclesiastical life in Sweden was hardly altered. The bishops continued their episcopal functions even as the clergy continued their accustomed round of activities; only the stipulation of the *ordinantia* that the Word of God be preached introduced a new, if vague, element into the situation. The Roman orientation of the Swedish church was repudiated, as were the legal prerogatives which the church had theretofore enjoyed; but the new church could not have been labeled Protestant, and many years were to pass before it became so. The obvious parallel of the Swedish events with the maneuvering of Henry VIII in England comes to mind, for in both instances the sovereign acted in response to a specific need against the backdrop of the existing Protestant sentiment.

The royal usurpation of ecclesiastical power (and property) hardly evoked any repercussions, Gustavus's position was stable, and his decision to be crowned was the outward expression of this consolidation of power. A few days before his coronation, in 1528, Petrus Magni, the bishop of Vesterås, the only one confirmed by Pope Clement VII in 1524, ordained three bishops and this provided for formal apostolic succession. Since he was not a Protestant, he had the three episcopal candidates assure him, perhaps somewhat gratuitously, that they would seek papal confirmation at the earliest opportunity.

The ecclesiastical transformation in Sweden was smooth and undramatic. There was no drastic change, no sudden upheaval; Catholicism had simply faded away. Thus, the monasteries were not forcibly closed down, as had been the case in England. Deprived of their economic base, they decreased in significance until they disappeared. Church services were in the vernacular, but they closely followed the Catholic practice. The Swedish church did not adopt a theological statement until 1593. Then it was the Augsburg Confession of 1530, a document known for its irenic stance.

Scotland

IN SCOTLAND THE LOLLARD TRADITION PROvided the same semi-indigenous backdrop for the Reformation as it did in England. Although its impact upon Scotland has not been thoroughly explored, Lollardy had surely survived into the sixteenth century. The principal cause of the ensuing religious ferment, nonetheless, was Luther, whose writings were disseminated in Scotland as they were elsewhere in Europe.

In the mid-twenties Patrick Hamilton began to proclaim the Lutheran gospel. He had been abroad on the Continent to study and had encountered there the wave of enthusiasm for Luther's proclamation. When he returned to Scotland, he forcefully preached the gospel according to Wittenberg. With "Master Patrick Hamilton," so John Knox wrote in his *History of the Reformation in Scotland*, "our history doth begin." Hamilton penned a little treatise, written in Latin and translated into English under the title *Dyvers Frutful Gatheringes of Scrypture Concernying Fayth and Workes*. It is known as *Patrick's Places* and was an impressive exposition of the Protestant faith.

Convicted of heresy, Hamilton was executed in February 1528. For a while afterward, the evidence for Reformation activity in Scotland is scant. Then, in 1546, a dramatic event gave evidence for the existing restlessness, once again in the typical juxtaposition of religion and politics. A group of Scottish noblemen assassinated David Cardinal Beaton, who combined the highest office in the church with a brief claim to political power by serving as regent during the minority of Mary Stuart. Their chaplain was John Knox, whom Samuel Johnson called one of the "ruffians" of the Reformation, and, true enough, there was a kind of uncouthness about him which prompted a recent biographer to speak of him as the "thundering Scot." That God had chosen him to proclaim his message

166

constituted the very marrow of Knox's life. Had there been no Calvin in the sixteenth century to stress the profundity of God's election, John Knox would have taken his place, for the conviction of God's omnipotent rule was real and deep for him. His association with Beaton's assassins caused him to be sentenced for almost two years to a French galley, to row across the North Sea, between Scotland and France, France and Scotland. In later years Knox rarely spoke about his experience, but when he did his words abounded in pangs of sorrow. "I knaw how hard the battell is betuix the Spreit and the Flesche, under the heavie cross of affliction," he remarked at one time, "whair no warldly defence, but present death dois appeir. I knaw the grudgeing and murmuring complaynts of the flesche; I knaw the angir, wraith and indignation, which it conceiveth aganis God, calling all his promisis in doubt, and being ready everie hour utterlie to fall frome God."

Released in 1549, Knox became the minister at Berwick, an English town near the Scottish border. It was a rough place, unruly and chaotic, full of homeless men, refugees, mercenaries, and others attracted to such places. It was an arduous assignment, but Knox was persuaded that he handled it well. Afterward followed a lengthy sojourn on the Continent, part of which was at Geneva. He was impressed with what he saw there, which prompted the famous and exuberant eulogy that Geneva was "the maist perfyt school of Chryst that ever was in the erth since the dayis of the Apostillis; in other places, I confess Chryst to be trewlie preachit; but maneris and religioun so sinceirlie reformat, I have not yit sene in any uther place."

In the meantime the situation in Scotland itself deteriorated steadily. Politically, the country was divided between the regent Mary of Lorraine, who pursued a pro-French policy, and the Scottish nobility, who favored close ties with England. The marriage treaty between Edward and Mary Stuart, concluded in 1543, had been voided, to be replaced by a new treaty involving the French dauphin Francis. Their marriage in 1558 seemingly made the ties with France insoluble. Again, the Catholic orientation of the ruler made the converging of political and religious considerations possible: those who desired political change saw the cause of the new faith as handmaid.

In 1558 Knox intervened in the political struggle. He published a vehement little pamphlet entitled *The First Blast of the Trumpet against the Monstrous Regiment of Women.* Knox's point was simple: Mary should abstain from idolatry and convert to the true biblical religion. Those who wanted to read more than a simple exhortation could find something else in the tract: Knox asserted that a ruler who persecuted true religion (as did Mary) could not legitimately claim the loyalty of her subjects.

167

Confident of French support, the regent issued in February 1559, a proclamation which made any violation of ecclesiastical regulations— such as eating meat during Lent—punishable by death; Protestant clerics were outlawed. She was forcing a showdown. Again religion and politics intertwined. The Peace of Cateau-Cambrésis of April 1559 freed France to intensify its preoccupation with Scotland.

Scotland was soon at the brink of civil war. The Protestant nobility occupied Edinburgh and took hold of most of the country. Still, the outcome of their confrontation with the queen regent depended upon the success of either side to get reinforcements from England or France. In July the Protestant lords appealed to Elizabeth for help. The English queen realized the dangers of a French-dominated Scotland, though she also sensed the risk of a break with France. After some hesitation, England provided financial assistance to the Protestants. Then French troops arrived in Scotland whereupon the Protestant lords demanded that the regent send them back. She refused and the Protestant lords formally deposed her in October.

The new year brought England's naval intervention, and in February a treaty was concluded between England and the Protestant lords. Afterward English troops crossed the border and, together with the Protestants, began a siege of Leith. France, the only hope of the Regent, was beset by internal difficulties and was, moreover, threatened by Spain who was unwilling to condone French imperialism in Scotland.

On 10 June the queen regent died. Mary had tried valiantly to maintain order in the country and to thwart the advance of Protestantism. Her qualifications had been impressive and admirable, but her pro-French policies had alienated the nobles. In July both England and France agreed to withdraw their troops from Scotland. Parliament was to meet in August. Governmental authority was exercised by a council in which the nobility had a majority. The sentiment in the land and the withdrawal of French troops raised Protestant hopes.

When Parliament met in August, a petition was drafted in which the Protestant divines were asked "to draw, in playne and severall heidis, the summe of that Doctrine, quilk they wald menteyne, and wald desyre that present Parliament to establische, as hailsome, trew, and onlie necessari to be believit, and to be resavit [received] within that Realme." On 17 August Parliament adopted a confession drawn up by Knox and his ministerial colleagues; a few days later several statutes were passed against the mass and papal jurisdiction. The celebration of the mass was prohibited, but the political situation did not lend itself to the imposition of ecclesiastical uniformity. The

Scottish Reformation showed that even prudent political circumstances needed formidable popular sentiment.

The chronicler must not overemphasize the import of the events of 1560. Parliament had not been authorized to deal with the religious question, and not until 1567 did the crown finally give legal sanction to the new church. For seven years there was, as one of the Protestant leaders remarked, "nothing of our religion established, neither by law nor parliament." To say that the decision of Parliament in 1560 made Scotland Protestant begs the question of precisely how this occurred. In 1560 a new church was simply recognized, while the structure of the old church was left intact. While 1558 and 1559 had been a rather tumultuous time—Archbishop Parker remarked in England, "God keep us from such a visitation as Knox hath attempted in Scotland, the people to be orderers of things"—the establishment of Protestantism took place quietly. Continuity and gradual change characterized the atmosphere in Scotland in a setting of civil strife.

One final distinction must be duly recorded. The legalization of the Calvinist faith in Scotland marked the first (and last) instance of a formal establishment of Calvinism anywhere in Europe. The movement was formidable in many places—the Netherlands, France, Hungary—but only in Scotland did it score success.

Poland

AN ATMOSPHERE OF RELATIVE TOLERATION prevailed in Poland, making the resulting religious spectrum far more checkered than anywhere else. Whereas in Germany or France one faith dominated and fenced off its competitors, greater diversity prevailed in Poland. This made Lutherans, Calvinists, Anabaptists, Bohemian Brethren, and even Antitrinitarians more or less equal partners in their attempts to proselytize. Poland was a religiously pluralistic society where the arm of government was not used to establish a normative religious tradition. The consequences were twofold. One was the existence of an atmosphere of mutual affinity, what we might well call ecumenical temperament. The Consensus of Sandomiersz (1570) was a most eloquent expression of this. The other was that the absence of a strong, single, Protestant church made the country an obvious target for the Counter-Reformation. The varieties of Protestantism were a major argument in the Catholic polemic, which insisted that truth was one and Protestantism, variously divided, could not be truth. In the end the Catholic efforts were successful, and Poland reaffirmed its ties with Catholicism. Thus the story ended about where it had begun, and since success is for most historians the criterion of selection, the history of the Reformation in Poland seems to offer little excitement.

Still, in Poland the Reformation failed only after almost succeeding. The early spread of Protestant ideas, unsupported by governmental edict, was as successful as anywhere else in Europe. Then came the collapse, not quickly, but irretrievably. Since there was no determined persecution, such collapse of Protestantism is doubly noteworthy. It attests that neither the religious commitment of the Protestants nor their political strength was formidable enough to force the lasting recognition of their religion. Had the Protestants been able to entice the king to their side, the story would have been a different one. Nor were the Protestant nobility, the *szlachta* (lower nobility) and the higher magnates, willing to oppose the king. They possessed the power they wanted and had little political reason to support the cause of religion.

The initial form of Protestantism reaching Poland was Lutheranism. From the 1540s on, Calvinism made its appearance, and subsequently it emerged as the principal form of Protestantism in the country. Such Calvinist prominence is not surprising, and one need not consider such explanations as the Polish antipathy toward Germany, the Germanic character of Luther's message, or the congeniality of the more democratic form of the Calvinist church government for the temper of the Polish nobility. The simple fact is that Calvinism was the aggressive form of Protestantism at the time, and Calvin the shining star on the Reformation firmament. The impact of Calvinism was natural.

When King Sigismund I died in 1548, the presence of Protestant ideas in Poland had reached the point where the political authorities had to make a decision as to how to deal with them. The new king, Sigismund August, leaned toward Protestantism. He was devout, concerned about reform, and enlightened about ecclesiastical dogma. He had followed the theological controversy with unusual interest, and even corresponded with Melanchthon and Calvin, who twice challenged him to introduce the gospel in Poland. But Sigismund remained a faithful son of the Catholic church. He may have realized that Protestantism was not strong enough in the land to allow him to become a Protestant.

Important was the Protestant orientation of the *szlachta*. At diets in 1547 and 1548 they demanded that the Word of God be preached freely. While they were unsuccessful in their effort, the vigor of their demand was indicative of the atmosphere in Poland. Indeed, even the Catholic hierarchy lent support, albeit indirectly, to the Protestant cause by advocating ecclesiastical reform in ways hardly compatible with Catholic principles. Some demanded that the clergy might marry and others sought the Communion cup for the laity.

During the next years the Protestants continued to exert political pressure to secure legal recognition, hoping to achieve it at a diet in 1555. At that time negotiations were taking place at Augsburg, that were to give religious freedom to the German Protestants; the Polish Protestants were determined to attain the same. They demanded religious liberty. The bishops voiced their opposition, but negotiations brought an agreement to convene a national synod.

The king set out to obtain papal approval for such a synod, at the same time requesting a married clergy, the vernacular mass, and Communion under both species. The response of the Curia was negative. This response, together with the dispatch of a papal legate to Poland, may have caused the king to have second thoughts about the Protestant demands: in 1557 he prohibited any further expansion of Protestant worship. At diets in 1562 and 1563 the *szlachta* demanded a permanent end to ecclesiastical jurisdiction. Most of the ecclesiastical litigation came to a standstill, but there was no formal statement, a fact which allowed the king in 1564 to announce that the traditional rights of the clergy should never have been curtailed. That same year he accepted the decrees and canons of the Council of Trent, but in 1565 the Diet of Piotrków declared all decisions of ecclesiastical courts null and void. This meant a victory for Protestantism, but the situation continued to be ambiguous, since religious freedom was restricted to the nobility.

The decision of 1565 allowed an unmolested life for Protestantism for several years. Firmly established, its Lutheran, Calvinist, and Antitrinitarian branches took on distinct organizational forms, and printing presses poured out Protestant propaganda.

Only guesses are possible about the strength of Protestantism. In 1569 almost half of the upper house of the Polish Diet (comprised of the higher nobility), excluding the bishops, was Protestant. No comparable figures are available for the lower house, the Chamber of Representatives, though one may assume on the basis of the action taken at several diets that the majority was strongly Protestant.

The death of Sigismund August in July 1572 confronted Poland with the problem of its dynastic future, since the king had been the last of the Jagiellon dynasty. From then on the Polish kingship became an elective office, dominated and manipulated by a nobility unwilling to burden itself with the luxury of a strong monarch. During the deliberations following the king's death the diet agreed to legalize Protestantism. The Confederation of Warsaw of January 1573 granted religious freedom to Protestants but used nomenclature that was so vague as to raise doubts whether the Antitrinitarians were included in the provision. The confederation also failed to state expressly if the Protestants were assured only personal religious freedom, or if legal recognition was given to their public worship.

The successful candidate for the Polish throne was Henry of Valois, whose willingness to accept the confederation had a great deal to do with his election. His reign in Poland was short-lived, however, and after a brief interregnum Stefan Batory was elected king and ruled until 1586. His religious policy was ambivalent but generally favored Catholicism. His successor, Sigismund III, whose rule extended until 1632, pursued a determinedly Catholic policy. When he died, Poland was a Catholic country.

This revitalization of Catholicism took place without any aggressively active involvement of the king. Batory had been fond of the Jesuits and favored them in a variety of ways; Sigismund III was a devout Catholic. Yet neither Batory nor Sigismund openly persecuted the Protestants. Protestantism just faded away, sapped of its inner vitality and strength.

One reason for this was that Polish Protestantism was never a popular movement and always remained restricted to the nobility. Still, the absence of popular support alone was not fatal to the Protestant cause. There were other factors, and they proved to be decisive. The Catholic church was too strong, not so much religiously, but with respect to the power of the hierarchy which had political influence, the support of the king, and the ability to withstand the initial Protestant assault without noticeable defections from its ranks. Most importantly, the political base of Protestantism was not broad enough. The towns might have provided strength for the Reformation, but they possessed no political voice and, therefore, their religious sympathies could find no political expression. The Polish kings, finally, never wavered in their Catholic loyalty. Protestant sentiment remained restricted to the magnates and the *szlachta,* whose attitude thus became crucial for the cause of the Reformation. If either defected, Protestantism was lost. Such a defection did occur. In Poland, in other words, politics and the religious Reformation never coalesced.

Conclusion

THE ATTEMPT AT ECCLESIASTICAL TRANSFORmation was successful in two countries, while the outcome in the other two remained in doubt for a long time. The historian wonders if any generalizations emerge from this fact. The two countries that became Protestant were situated in northern Europe, and it is tempting to see some sort of pattern in this fact, especially since this corresponds to the situation in Europe at large. Nor is it helpful to consider the timing of ecclesiastical change: Sweden turned Protestant in the 1520s, while Scotland did so in 1560. One may only say that the two countries in which the outcome of the religious controversy was still undecided in 1560 eventually remained Catholic. This may be mere happenstance —or evidence for a significant turn of events.

The introductory paragraphs of this chapter suggested the eminent role of politics in ecclesiastical change. This concluding assessment must review the evidence. With one exception, each of the four countries was characterized by the presence of serious political problems. The issue of religious change did not confront a stable society, in other words, but one experiencing political turbulence quite independent of the challenge posed by the Reformation. The four societies experienced religious problems as well; but the relevance of these problems to the unfolding of ecclesiastical events was limited, contrary to what might be expected. The same holds true with regard to the social or economic conditions, where impact on the religious transformation was indirect.

In Sweden the political problem was posed by the recently won independence from Denmark and the financial needs of the crown. Gustavus Vasa found himself in dire financial distress, and the wealth of the church seemed likely to end his worries. Moreover, the church had been an active participant (and even partisan) in the struggle between Sweden and Denmark, and, unfortunately, had been on the losing side. The fact that no theological changes or liturgical modifications were undertaken on the heels of the confiscation of ecclesiastical property and the royal usurpation of ecclesiastical prerogatives would support the contention that the initial intent was by no means to cut the theological ties with Rome. Vasa's primary concern was to remedy his fiscal distress and, at the same time, make sure that the Swedish church was beyond the slightest suspicion of disloyalty. There was little theological agitation and the ecclesiastical transformation effected by the king was smooth and painless.

France and Scotland, in turn, experienced a different political problem. In these countries the attempts at ecclesiastical change had initially failed (because of the negative stance of the crown), but Protestant agitation continued for decades. Politically, in both countries competing factions strove for power. In Scotland the contest was between the nobility and the queen regent, though underneath lurked the resentment of Scotsmen against foreign (French) influence.

In France the controversy was between competing factions of the nobility. The king stood in the middle, without the ability (or the power) to prevent those factions from dragging the country into war and bloodshed.

These tensions existed independently of the religious turbulence and the efforts at ecclesiastical transformation. Indeed, they were earlier in time and weightier in substance. They had a bearing on the cause of the Reformation since a religious meaning could easily be attached to the existing political issues. The proponents of the political status quo generally favored the Catholic faith. This was true in the case of the queen regent in Scotland and the king in France, who felt prompted to suppress the manifestations of Protestantism. This, in turn, made it prudent for Protestants to support those in political opposition, since this political opposition seemed to assure the realization of their own religious and ecclesiastical goals.

If those concerned about religious change aligned themselves with a political faction because they saw religious advantages, those primarily concerned about politics could similarly discern the advantage of supporting the religious claims of the Protestants, inasmuch as this assured them additional political strength. Thus, there were advantages on both sides. Those interested in political change benefited from the support of those who desired change in religion, and vice versa. The Protestants did not introduce a political component into their quest for the gospel, for such a component had been present ever since the beginning. Given the intimate relationship of church and state, this had been an inescapable development.

In Poland, on the face of things, events did not differ in their outcome from those in France; both countries withstood the Protestant challenge and remained within the Catholic fold. An important difference existed with respect to the intensity of turmoil that accompanied the period of Protestant agitation. France suffered immense bloodshed and bitter civil war, while Poland escaped such a turn of events. The reason for this must not be sought in the areas of religious commitment or Protestant numerical strength. Rather, it lay with those indigenous political issues that were present in one country and absent in the other.

The Protestant nobility in Poland might have forced an issue at the death of Sigismund II, when the Jagiellon dynasty ended and the election of a Protestant king was a possibility. Apart from the desire of the Protestant nobility to have a Protestant king, there was no compelling reason to make such a move. Traditional prerogatives or constitutional liberties were not endangered, and the country would have been thrown, as was France, into a civil strife for no other obvious advantages.

The developments sketched and the comparisons drawn pertain only to external and empirical considerations. They say nothing about the profundity of the Protestant message or the persuasiveness of its claims, nor do they speak of the intensity of spirituality and piety that did (or did not) characterize the inner history of Protestantism (or Catholicism) in these countries. While the history of matters pertaining to legal recognition and political treaties is not the only one, it is the one that relates how inner conviction became embedded in the harsh realities of power politics.

That politics and religion should have been so intimately connected in the Reformation so that man's spiritual aspirations were seldom free of entanglement in utterly mundane matters was the legacy of medieval civilization to the sixteenth century. Whatever its shortcomings, and there were many, it also enabled the Reformation to exert its influence upon the history of Western civilization.

This map depicts in rough outline the ecclesiastical division of Europe in 1610. The reader is warned of two points. First, the territorial complexity of the empire in the heart of Europe in actual fact meant a far more divided situation than this simplified map is able to convey. Secondly, it shows only the official governmental recognition of a particular form of religion, not the extent of the actual religious beliefs held by the people.

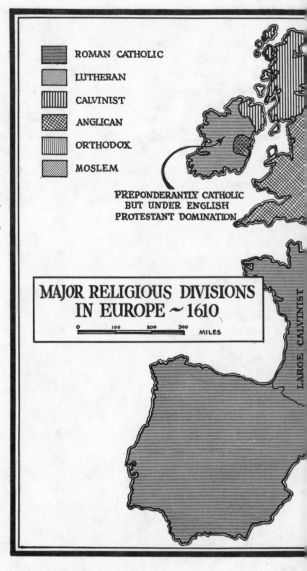

ROMAN CATHOLIC
LUTHERAN
CALVINIST
ANGLICAN
ORTHODOX
MOSLEM

PREPONDERANTLY CATHOLIC
BUT UNDER ENGLISH
PROTESTANT DOMINATION

MAJOR RELIGIOUS DIVISIONS
IN EUROPE ~ 1610

0   100   200   300   MILES

LARGE CALVINIST

LUTHERAN AND CALVINIST MINORITIES

MOSLEM DOMINATION OF LARGE
ORTHODOX AND ROMAN CATHOLIC
POPULATIONS

9 The Catholic Reaction

FOR CATHOLIC CHRISTENDOM THE TURBULENT sixteenth century was no less important than for the emerging Protestant churches. It was at once the hour of its greatest crisis and of its greatest triumph; perhaps the latter would not have been possible without the former.

About the depth and profundity of the crisis there can be little doubt. Never before had the Catholic church been confronted with such a formidable desertion, never before with such flagrant disregard of her principles. The seamless robe of the church was torn apart, and the one church became a wistful dream. Man after man, priest after priest, and even several countries renounced the Catholic faith which they had pledged to uphold; statues and shrines, revered for centuries, were removed from churches; spiritual endowments that had comforted men's souls were abolished; monasteries, in which men strove to live piously, were deserted. Some of the losses were countered, to be sure, and when the Reformation era had passed, the Catholic church—what was left of it—was assuredly stronger, more vital, and more aggressive than it had been when it all started. Even as the

178

destroyed shrines could not be restored, however, so were heresy, apostasy, and the rejection of papal authority irreparable.

Though there were varied Catholic efforts at spiritual renewal quite independent of the challenge of the Protestant Reformation, the fact remains that the Reformation intensified the sense of urgency with which new efforts at deepened spirituality (often copied from Protestants) were undertaken. There is no telling what might have been had there been no Reformation, for history does not reveal its alternatives. As matters stand, the impact of the Reformation upon Catholicism, directly and indirectly, was strong and formidable indeed.

Historical parlance has used the term "Counter-Reformation" to describe Catholic history in the sixteenth century, thus stressing the reaction against the Protestant Reformation as its dominant theme. This term overlooks, however, all those developments in the course of the sixteenth century which had little, if anything, to do with the Protestant challenge. Accordingly, some scholars have preferred as an alternate term "Catholic Reform and Counter-Reformation," to emphasize the dual characteristic of sixteenth century Catholic life, its indigenous self-renewal, and its reaction against the Protestant Reformation. While it is a bit clumsy and raises the question of chronological priority, it is useful and deserves acceptance.

The purpose of this discussion is not to unfold the full panorama of Catholic history in the sixteenth century; this would be an assignment of major proportions and should not be relegated to a few incidental remarks in one chapter. Those facets that have to do with the relation between Catholicism and the emerging Protestant tradition, with the way the Reformation became a part of Catholic history, and the Catholic church reacted to the Protestant challenge will be examined. Neither the label "Catholic Reform" nor that of "Counter-Reformation" is fully adequate to describe the intent of these pages.

The Reformation was a spontaneous movement of elementary religious forces that sought to replace a sophisticated church and religion with a handful of simple affirmations. Its cause was not the state of the church but the thought of Martin Luther. It was characterized, from the beginning, by the intrusion of nontheological factors into what might have been a purely academic debate. Thus an unexpectedly sharp tone characterized the ensuing controversy, which was incisively influenced, within a matter of three years, by the formal ecclesiastical verdict against Luther.

From the vantage point of the Catholic church, and especially the Curia, the situation was difficult. Neither the nature of the information about Luther reaching Rome nor the disposition of the officials entrusted with the examination of his teaching (such as Sylvester Prierias) allowed a comprehensive assessment. Considerations of European politics (the election of a new German emperor) preoccupied the Curia for almost a year and afterwards made it difficult to make up this deficiency.

In short, the course of Curial action was hardly surprising, and, given the situation, it could hardly have been otherwise. Yet a different and very perceptive comment had come from none other than Pope Leo X. It was a squabble among monks, he remarked. Probably this was not meant as a positive statement but it expressed, however unwittingly, the observation that events required as little Curial action as did a thousand other "monkish squabbles." With all his congeniality, his preoccupation with art and learning in Rome, even his view of the papacy as a temporal monarchy, Leo's initial remark was more astute than most that were made afterward.

In the great debate that followed, largely after rather than before Luther's excommunication, the Catholic church found itself at a decided disadvantage, if for no other reason than the disadvantage of being on the defensive. It is the dissenter who propounds novel and startling ideas, requiring the defender of the status quo to reiterate what has been said and written a thousand times before. Henry VIII's *Assertio Septem Sacramentorum*, a spirited defense of the sacramental teaching of the Catholic church, is a good case in point. If it was a mediocre work, as most commentators seem to think, then the explanation is that it was well-nigh impossible for Henry to say anything strikingly new on a subject that had already been discussed *ad infinitum*.

The stress of controversy has a way of calling forth extreme statements which, in a more relaxed and circumspect atmosphere, would probably not be made. Not surprisingly, the Catholic protagonists were driven to all sorts of dubious pronouncements. Perhaps they themselves did not fully fathom the authentic Catholic position, as has been suggested. More likely, however, the tensions of the polemical atmosphere misled them. They were inclined to degrade Scripture, denounce its use in the vernacular, reject the need for reform, precisely because their Protestant antagonists so emphatically affirmed all that. In so doing, they unduly narrowed the Catholic position, lost many friends, and influenced few people. The matter of ecclesiastical reform accentuated graphically the two horns of the dilemma. If the need for reform was conceded, it was a concession to the Lutherans, who could boast, as they did after Pope Adrian VI's famous confession of 1523, that this proved what they had been saying all along. If, on the other hand, Catholics denied the need for reform, they were likely to be chided for being dishonest in the face of indisputable evidence. The Catholic dilemma was obvious.

Of even greater importance was the lingering uncertainty, strangely enough, over the nature of the controversy. There was no end to persuasive or even prophetic pronouncements, and the multitude of suggestions was bewildering. Some thought that at issue were certain ecclesiastical abuses that needed only to be corrected to restore blessed tranquility. Others pointed to theological disagreements, but precisely what these were remained astoundingly enigmatic and uncertain. The bull *Exsurge Domine* seemed to suggest that Luther's errors pertained mainly to the doctrines of indulgences and penance; Erasmus singled out questions of anthropology as the crucial point; Melanchthon was persuaded at Augsburg in 1530 that conciliation would be possible if the Communion cup were offered to the laity and priests be allowed to marry. Luther declared that the controversy was about the proper understanding of Christ; and somewhere along the line the concept of justification crept into the picture. The number of suggestions increased the confusion.

It is hardly surprising, therefore, that the controversy remained inconclusive; not, of course, in terms of the official posture of the Catholic church, which was clear ever since the bull *Exsurge Domine,* but in terms of the nature of the controversy. It was a grandiose free-for-all, and subsequent generations of scholars assuredly have known the issues better than did the contemporaries.

Such was the burden (or curse) of all Catholic apologetics in the early years of the Reformation, theologians like Johann Eck, Thomas Murner, Johannes Cochlaeus, Thomas More, and others. These men differed in theological insight, religious acumen, and literary gifts, some arguing more incisively, some enjoying greater popularity than others. Above all, they all shared the formidable disadvantage of having to defend the status quo, reiterating the position that had been known for years and hardly allowed room for creative restatement. They had to counter bold and sweeping generalizations, for the reformers were the kind of *simplificateurs terribles* whose imprint on the course of history the famous nineteenth century historian Jakob Burckhardt so resoundingly bewailed. In short, the handicap was real and the obstacles virtually insurmountable.

The situation changed only after the mood of desperation (and righteous indignation) had given way to a calmer reflection on the nature of the controversy. Then, and only then, did Catholic writers—Peter Canisius is one of the eminent illustrations—adapt their ways. They supported the vernacular Scriptures, wrote popular catechisms, and denounced the life and thought of the new churches,

181

having enough empirical evidence before their own eyes to garner a most devastating polemic.

Two recurrent themes were heard again and again from the lips of Catholics: the call for reform and for a council. In both matters, as in all other Catholic affairs in the sixteenth century, the key lay in the papal office. The popes of the time of the Reformation labored under the handicap of the immediate past. The Renaissance popes, from Nicholas V to Julius II, had been concerned (successfully, as it turned out) to transform Rome, the center of religion, into a center of art and culture. They had also engaged in Italian power politics, seeking to preserve the integrity of the Papal States against the aggressive encroachment from other Italian states. When, in the course of the sixteenth century, the character of the popes changed, it was difficult to turn over a new leaf. Only slowly did they become concerned with more distinctly ecclesiastical matters. Even then they were caught in the fierce struggle between France and Spain as though between two millstones. Since ecclesiastical pronouncements and policies invariably entailed political ramifications, there was no easy way to proceed. Thus the relatively simple matter of Henry VIII's "divorce" from Catherine of Aragon became at once involved in European power politics, and Pope Clement VII, called upon to rule on the canonical regularity of the marriage, was faced with an impossible task. The proposal for a general council was as vehemently rejected by Francis I as it was advocated by Charles V, both guided greatly by political considerations: the situation was indeed difficult for the papacy.

The seven popes in the half-century between 1513 and 1565, from Leo X to Pius IV, were upright men; indeed, some, such as Adrian VI, were deeply spiritual. The tragedy was that each had his own view of the crisis besetting the church, and each prescribed different remedies. The brevity of papal reigns was undoubtedly a factor of importance. The seven popes ruled, on the average, for about seven years, all too brief a time to initiate, undertake, and carry out policies. If we omit the two lengthy papal rules, those of Clement VII (1523–1534) and of Paul III (1534–1549), the tenure of predecessors and successors shrinks even more. At the same time, Charles V ruled for almost half a century, and England had only four sovereigns during the entire century.

The rule of Leo X, during which the Reformation erupted, may have been handicapped by the pope's easygoing and somewhat secular disposition. Far more consequential, however, were other factors: the inadequate awareness of the true nature of the controversy across the Alps, and the feeling of accomplishment after the adjournment of the Fifth Lateran Council which had promulgated a great number of reform measures. It seems futile to ask whether the reform decrees of

182

the Lateran Council lacked seriousness of purpose or were haphazard; this legislation never had a chance. No sooner had the council adjourned than the Lutheran affair began to excite people with different issues and challenges. The council was rather like a fruit that ripened out of season: it sought to achieve its goals in terms of one epoch, but it was judged by another.

The election of Adrian VI in January 1522, was a compromise, the last effort before the cardinals agreed not to agree. Adrian was a devout and spiritually minded man who saw the reform of the church and especially of the Curia, as the eminent goal of his pontifical rule. He was alien to the workings of the Curia, however, and suspicious of his advisors. Above all, his rule was breathtakingly short; he died less than two years after his election. He had not had sufficient time to undertake his policies. Thus neither success nor failure was to be his.

The eleven years of the pontificate of Clement VII brought little change, prompting the great nineteenth century historian Leopold von Ranke, who was not easily given to dramatic pronouncements, to call Clement "the most catastrophic pope ever to occupy the throne of St. Peter." In part this verdict was prompted by Clement's temperamental inability to make decisions, though it might be more appropriate to say that he sought to postpone decisions he knew were bound to be catastrophic. Far more importantly, however, Clement faced virtually insurmountable political complications. The struggle between France and Spain reached the Holy City in 1527, with the spectacular Sack of Rome, and made Clement temporarily a prisoner of the emperor. The divorce of Henry VIII put him in a position where any decision was bound to have fateful political as well as ecclesiastical consequences. No wonder Clement sought to postpone the showdown. That he allowed the decision to be against Henry (it surely was the more catastrophic choice, the greater of two evils) speaks for his integrity. If all these were not sufficient problems, the persistent resistance of Francis I to a general council made such a council an impossibility.

So little happened during Clement's pontificate: no general council, no officially sponsored reform. England deserted the Catholic ranks, as did Sweden and a great part of Germany. But these facts tend to be misleading. England and Sweden could have been halted neither by a council nor by ecclesiastical reform. Only in Germany might this have been different, though even there the number of those who cited theological disagreements rather than practical abuse as the issues at stake (which made conciliation almost impossible) was increasing.

Under Paul III, who succeeded Clement in 1534, the various streams of Catholic vitality burst out into the open. The years of Paul's pontificate marked the turning point of Catholic history in the sixteenth century. Under him the Catholic church made a comprehensive effort to regain both its vitality and its self-confidence.

This last facet was particularly important. During Paul's pontificate the notion of "reform" was officially accepted by the papacy; at the same time, the vision of the triumphant church was recaptured, and self-confidence regained.

There was vitality in the Catholic church before Pope Paul: the work of individual bishops, the Oratory of the Divine Love together with its monastic offspring, the Theatines. Under Paul the little springs became a river. In 1535 the Regulars of St. Paul, or Barnabites, were approved and one year later, the Capuchins. In 1540 came the approval of the Society of Jesus. Although the Jesuits and their founder, St. Ignatius of Loyola, were to overshadow most other expressions of the resurging Catholic spirituality in the sixteenth century, they were but a small part of a much larger picture. Indeed, their real impact was not felt until many decades later. At midcentury the Jesuits were only a handful of men.

Initially, Ignatius and his companions had to endure a good deal of opposition and persecution from high and low places, an indication that not all were ready for new ways to foster spirituality and serve the Catholic church. Ignatius, rather like Luther, had experienced a spiritual crisis, but in contrast to the German reformer he had found the answer in the church. Thus, he indicates that the Catholic church did possess the vitality and spirituality needed in the early sixteenth century: the story of Martin Luther will always need to be juxtaposed with that of Ignatius of Loyola.

The story of Ignatius was the story of a man committed to serving his church. The existence and spread of the Protestant "heresy" played only a minor role in this resolve. Undoubtedly, he was made aware of it during his Parisian student days, but by that time his spiritual commitment was already made. Ignatius of Loyola would have walked his path even if the world had never heard of Martin Luther and the other reformers. He symbolizes indigenous Catholic reform in the sixteenth century and illustrates how reform could be turned to combat the Protestant Reformation. The Jesuits turned their attention to the suppression of heresy and became the most formidable expression of the Counter-Reformation.

184

10 Concluding Observations

AT THE END OF THE STORY THE HISTORIAN needs to offer some explanation of the nature of the events he has described. To do so is especially pertinent in the case of the Reformation in the sixteenth century because of the dramatic claims made on all sides, when men purported to have discerned the will of God or the perfect society. Claims of this sort have become an irritation or embarrassment for historians inclined to discern the rationality or irrationality of a historical epoch according to categories immanent in the historical process.

The very first question with regard to the Reformation is whether it was a religious or nonreligious event, whether the primary forces were theological or ideological. The Reformation may be viewed in nonreligious terms as an expression of political power politics, economic greed, and social change in Western society at the beginning of the sixteenth century. The argument is persuasive because the evidence seems all too obvious. The consolidation of political power and authority was a ubiquitous phenomenon throughout Europe in the early sixteenth century; the very fact that Germany perpetuated its own tradition of divisive particularism offers at once a plausible

185

suggestion for why the Reformation proved so successful there. Political aggrandizement conveniently led to economic gain. Whatever is said about the authenticity of the religious conviction of such rulers as Gustavus Vasa, Henry VIII, or Philip of Hesse—probably not much, since the historian is hardly privy to man's innermost feelings and convictions—the fact remains that all of them, without exception, were wealthier as the result of the ecclesiastical changes they undertook in their respective commonwealths. Of course, skeptics will find such harmony between spiritual truth and pecuniary gain a telling counterargument against religious conviction; it may well have been that for the Protestant ruler, even as for the capitalist entrepreneur, success was the mother of all things. Economic and social forces may have played an analogous role. In Germany the conflicts between peasants and their lords, between artisans and patricians, are an integral part of the early sixteenth century scene, just as is the emergence of new modes of production in silver and copper mining or textile manufacturing. In short, we may speak of a "crisis" of German (or even European) society in the early part of the sixteenth century—a crisis with several foci or only a single one—and suggest that the Reformation constituted but a consequence of this crisis.

A second major option is to see the Reformation as an authentically religious phenomenon, related perhaps to other, basically autonomous, societal forces. This, of course, has been the traditional perspective through the centuries. It has not been unanimous, all the same, for a kind of "cowboy" perspective has prevailed, with the "good guys" on the one side and the "bad guys" on the other. The specific designations of who was on which side differed, of course, according to the commitment of the observer.

To label the Reformation a "religious" phenomenon is to leave unanswered precisely how such religious orientation is to be understood. There are several possibilities. The Reformation can be seen as a phase of that quest for reform that accompanied the Catholic church from the eleventh century onward. Understood thus, the reformers echoed the cry for a reform of the church "in head and members" that was propounded from the councils of Constance and Basel to Nicholas of Cusa and Erasmus of Rotterdam, an illustrious line of progenitors for which the nomenclature "prereformers" constitutes an interesting description. Luther becomes a sort of sixteenth century Hus or Wycliffe, the only distinction being the brilliance of his theological insight or the ripeness of the time.

A variant of this view is to see the Reformation as a reaction—as a "counterreformation"—to the theological climate of the fifteenth century, particularly to the nominalism of such theologians as Gabriel Biel with the choice of viewing this nominalism as a consistent development of earlier trends or as an extraordinary theological confusion, alien to the authentic spirit of medieval theology. In either case, the Reformation becomes a "counter" movement, an understandable, though in light of its "heretical" deviation doubly ironic, phenomenon.

There is yet another interpretation, and these pages have sought to convey it. The Reformation, seen as a religious event (the "second phase" according to this book's definition), was eminently concerned with a revival of spirituality. The early "Reformation" was little concerned about explicit theological affirmations and hardly worried about ecclesiastical abuse. The reformer's call was simply for a deepened spirituality, for a religion of inward commitment rather than external observance, for reliance upon God rather than man-made rules. Luther and the other reformers did not mind stepping on the toes of the ecclesiastical establishment, or reminding it, sometimes angrily and sometimes sarcastically, that lately it had been moving in the wrong direction. The quarrel was within the family, so to speak, and the reformers' protestations of autonomy were rather akin to those of a child announcing that he will leave home forever.

Precisely for such reasons it was possible for many faithful and loyal Catholics to concur readily with this new message and to walk what increasingly turned into a precarious balancing act: support of this message on the one hand, and loyalty to the Catholic church on the other. The reformers did not see their proclamation as inescapably provoking a confrontation; nor did they deliberately break 'with the Catholic church, stubbornly and arrogantly confident that they were on the side of the angels. While their denunciations left little doubt about their conviction that the true gospel was not properly proclaimed in the Catholic church, they said nothing about irreconcilable opposition. The reformers thought that their specific theological affirmations could be subsumed, somehow or other, under the broad mantle of the larger church. After all, the one issue subsequently so important, the doctrine of justification by faith, was undefined by the Catholic church at the time the controversy broke out. For decades men of theological insight thought it was possible to engage in conciliatory conversations with an eye toward healing the breach. Of course, nobody seemed to know where that breach was in the first place, even though the scene was crowded with well-meaning and self-styled diagnosticians.

In the end, the reformers failed to obey; in the moment of truth, they rejected the notion that the church was infallible. The profundity of their own religious experiences probably goes a long way toward explaining such obstinacy. The course of events seemed to demonstrate that their concerns had been rejected out of hand and were never given a hearing. Luther, for one, outdid himself with subservient expressions of obedience and loyalty to the Roman church during the first years of the controversy.

The irony is that an intriguing constellation of factors catapulted the whole matter far beyond its expected dimension. What should have been a "squabble among monks" became embedded in the financial wizardry of the Curia and the internecine struggle between imperial and territorial power in Germany. In the sense that the latter forces elevated an otherwise innocuous matter to dramatic importance, they do deserve priority of place. Had religious (or theological) issues been the sole ingredient in the picture, a different and less dramatic course of events would clearly have ensued.

If the foregoing is reasonably accurate, it throws light on the nature of the impact made by Luther on his contemporaries. Most of those who thronged to him and supported his cause did not consider themselves in opposition to the Roman church, even if they opposed the clergy or ecclesiastical prerogatives. The resolute mood of separation came much later. The Reformation was a filial revolt; in other words, a prodding to get the church to undertake certain changes. Dissent and loyalty, defiance and obedience, combined to explain the popularity of Luther's cause, even as they explain the subsequent disintegration of Luther's movement, which occurred when the church demanded submission.

This brings us to a final reason for the schism. There were those who risked disobedience rather than give up what they had come to call the gospel. It is beside the point, therefore, to cull from the multitude of medieval theologians those whose views were akin to Luther's and the other reformers', label them "prereformers," and conclude that there was nothing new in the sixteenth century. Undoubtedly, similarities existed. Thus, Jacques Lefèvre's views on justification were virtually identical with those of Luther. But why did the one remain a faithful Catholic whereas the other was considered a heretic? More must have been at stake than theology.

By the same token, however, defiance and subjectivism alone do not account fully for the impact of the Reformation. If anything, they militated against it, for disposition to martyrdom is hardly a generic human characteristic, and the reformers surely were no exception. An exuberant disregard of possible consequences on the part of the reformers, characterized the early years of the Reformation, but during that time these consequences were not at all obvious. Still, something more than youthful rashness must have been present.

The conclusion is as simple as it is profound. No single factor was responsible for the Reformation: neither theological profundity nor the personalities of the controversialists; neither the state of the church nor that of society. The schism occurred because all these (and other) forces meshed in a striking way; a slight difference along the way would have precipitated (if a conjecture is in order) a different course of events. No single factor or party or person deserves eminent credit or blatant blame.

The Consequences of the Reformation

"AND ALL THE KING'S HORSES AND ALL THE king's men. . . ." One thinks of this trivial rhyme when reflecting on the Reformation, for its most spectacular consequence undoubtedly was the division of Western Christendom. There had been schisms before: the eminent one between East and West, the modest one between the Bohemian and the Roman church, the pathetic one between the rival factions of Rome and Avignon in the fourteenth century; but these divisions (not to speak of those created by the heretical splinter groups of the Middle Ages) hardly entered the consciousness of Western man. At the dawn of the sixteenth century the church was one, bedazzling in its complexity and confusing in its structure, yet one in faith. There was no doubt about allegiance to this church, holy, catholic, and apostolic. Even those who were uneasy about it, such as the humanists, remained loyal. At the twilight of the century everything was different: the unity of Western Christendom had vanished and become a wistful dream. Christendom in the West was divided—indeed not only into two factions, but into four or five: Catholics on the one hand, and Lutherans, Calvinists, Anglicans, and Anabaptists on the other. The coexistence of these rival churches was an uneasy one, since each claimed stubbornly the sole possession of truth and denounced its rivals with vehemence and self-confidence.

To what extent this diversity of the Christian church was a nagging problem for sixteenth century man is difficult to say. Within the borders of a country only one church was officially recognized and, accordingly, a kind of pragmatic, if artificial, uniformity of truth existed. Only France, the Low Countries, Poland, Germany, and England experienced religious diversity, though often of a most bitter kind, and thus evidenced the division of Christian truth in blunt and spectacular fashion. We must keep in mind that ecclesiastical uniformity was maintained by an external force, namely, the political authorities. Once this factor was removed (by the self-limitation of the authorities), the full impact of the religious diversity was bound to be felt in a dramatic way. In the sixteenth century the empirical division of Christendom clearly lessened the Christian claims for truth.

The division in the West entailed a weakening of the Catholic church, since the new Protestant churches grew on soil vacated by Catholicism. A glance at the map of Europe in 1600 might convey the conclusion that the Catholic losses were tolerable. In the end the desertion from Catholic ranks was less than some had hoped and others had feared. Germany, at one time on the verge of embracing the new faith completely, retained a Catholic majority, especially in the south and northwest; Poland, Hungary, and France, at one time likewise on the way toward Protestantism, eventually declared for the Catholic faith; Italy, Spain, and Ireland escaped the religious turmoil altogether.

If, as has been noted, the signal consequence of the Reformation was the division of Western Christendom, the significance of the division in Protestant ranks requires further comment. Neither historically nor theologically was there ever a single Reformation; there were several, certainly no less than five, and perhaps even more. The Protestant Reformation was never a monolithic phenomenon, but always a house divided against itself.

When Bishop Jacques Bossuet wrote his famous history of Protestantism, he gave it the telling title *Histoire des variations des églises protestantes* (1688). His argument was that the divisions within Protestantism, the lack of unity in doctrine, were persuasive proof of its falsehood. The hopeless and apparently insoluble divisions called into question the basic Protestant affirmation that Scripture was clear and self-evident, and that men of goodwill could readily agree on its meaning. Luther, who had first voiced such sentiment, was to learn its weakness in his controversy with Zwingli over the interpretation of Communion. His increasingly rigid view of Scriptural interpretation may well have been influenced by his dismay over the inability of men, even of men of goodwill, to agree on the interpretation of Sacred Writ.

The Reformation shows that external authority was not completely absent; indeed, where it was present little diversity prevailed. England under Elizabeth and German Lutheranism toward the end of the century are good cases in point. In both places theological agitation existed, creeds were formulated and revised, but the authority of government kept matters in check and retained uniformity.

None of the new Protestant bodies, once they had established themselves, was truly "catholic" in the sense that diverse or heterogeneous points of view were subsumed within them. Catholicism, on the other hand, possessed the ability to do that. Moreover, it had the "escape valve" of monasticism, which allowed those dissatisfied with ecclesiastical practices to go their own way and yet remain within the church. Such possibility did not exist in any of the Protestant churches, where a break was necessary to assert a different religious or theological position.

Once a new church had been created, Protestants found themselves confronted with the need to undertake a pedagogical effort of major proportions. This must be seen in proper perspective, guarding against two false impressions. The sixteenth century was not preoccupied with religion to the point that every man and woman (and perhaps even child) were obsessed with religion. Obviously, it is risky to generalize about Europe at large, both major religious factions, or developments extending over several decades, but the evidence suggests that after an initial period the preoccupation with religion declined in most countries. Many people were only little concerned about the things of the spirit. There are some indirect empirical clues, such as the persistent governmental mandates exhorting church attendance, the appalling religious illiteracy, or the pathetic self-indictments of the reformers. All these indicate that in Protestant lands the Kingdom had not come with the Reformation. The quasi-official homily *The Place and Time of Prayer*, issued in England in 1574, may be considered a bit of indirect evidence, for it said this about the way some people observed Sunday: "They rest in ungodliness and filthiness, prancing in their pride, pranking and pricking, pointing and painting themselves, to be gorgeous and gay; they rest in excess and superfluity, in gluttony and drunkenness, like rats and swine; they rest in brawling and railing in quarreling and fighting."

The hallmark of those unconcerned with religion was that they simply ignored the church. They pursued their business ventures, circumventing its moral teaching, and lived their lives unencumbered by ecclesiastical pronouncements. As long as governmental authority continued to enforce ecclesiastical standards, overt violations of these standards were rare; but wherever the atmosphere was lenient, as for example in England, a different situation prevailed. At issue was not so much outright opposition, for such was rare indeed and came, as matter of fact, mainly from a few religious zealots, such as the Anabaptists or the Puritans, rather than from the indifferent unbeliever. The anatomical posture where the head nodded and the heart remained uninvolved surely was not infrequent, and undoubtedly increased as the level of theological sophistication among the Protestants rose.

A second erroneous impression about religion in the sixteenth century concerns the level of religious literacy among the people. There may have been a few laymen who, with nothing at their disposal but a good portion of native intelligence, were able to confound the academic theologians, but these were the exceptions.

The masses of the people were illiterate and even good will could rarely overcome this handicap. After all, the ability to read generally is a prerequisite for theological competence.

If such widespread religious illiteracy were not enough of a problem, there was also a good deal of superstition, belief in magic, and astrology, which was hardly congenial to an informed understanding of religion. The tolling of bells during thunderstorms, for example, supposedly kept lightning from striking in the hearing range of the bells. Religious ignorance was universal, though more so in the rural areas than in the cities. Of this the church visitation records offer ample evidence. The records in Lüneberg in 1568 indicated that the people almost without exception were unwilling to come to the midweek catechetical instruction. There were blatant misunderstandings about the Decalogue, which in one village version was rendered as, "The first shall have no other goal; the second shall not use the name of God in vain; the third shall keep the sabbath holy." In a village near Magdeburg only three people of fifty-two families knew the Lord's Prayer.

The people were by and large religiously ignorant, a fact explained by the ubiquitous presence of illiteracy rather than any conspiratorial attempt on the part of the Catholic (or Protestant) church to keep the common people in darkness. This situation presented formidable problems for the Protestant churches in their educational efforts. Competent teachers were necessary, indeed, not just a few but one for every parish. Educational literature had to be written. Luther's *Small Catechism*, printed on cardboard to be hung on the walls of living rooms, was one of the earliest attempts to supply this need. Some 200 editions of such catechisms were published in the sixteenth century.

As matters turned out, the people often were neither willing to go through the rigid intellectual exercise nor able to devote the necessary time. In the first few years of the Reformation considerable exuberance had prevailed for religious matters; but this had faded, rather like the evening sun. The Lord's Prayer, the Apostles' Creed, and the Decalogue were the mainstays of the instruction, hardly sufficient to express the fullness of the Protestant faith. The visitation records indicate that the Decalogue was as much a mystery as the Trinity for the common people and that the simple recitation of the Apostles' Creed was unsurpassably difficult. The clergy was not much better. The famous visitation of the clergy of Gloucester by Bishop Hooper in 1551 revealed appalling clerical ignorance. The men of the cloth hardly knew the basic affirmations of the faith, not to speak of the specific Protestant affirmations. Obviously, a causal relationship existed between clerical incompetence and popular ignorance. Only as ministerial standards rose in the second half of the sixteenth century did the situation improve. More and more Protestant ministers received a university education and attained the formal competence to function as teachers. The lower clergy, such as the village vicar or pastor, continued to find themselves in a difficult economic position with few, if any, financial attractions. Such had been the case before the Reformation, though the married Protestant clergy had significantly larger economic needs.

Both Catholics and Protestants thus emerged from the Reformation era with a gigantic educational task: to dispel religious ignorance and to further spirituality. The former task enjoyed an advantage, because of the increasing stress on public education and widespread literacy; but also labored under a handicap, because of the religious apathy that followed the preoccupation with religion during the Reformation.

The Reformation and Women

WOMEN, GENERALLY CONDEMNED TO BE THE silent partners in the unfolding of the course of events, played an intriguing role in the Reformation. In some instances they became involved as partisans of the new faith. Some did so through their personal activism, exhibiting qualities uncommon for women in that male-oriented age. Tellingly, the majority of Anabaptist martyrs were women. Others, such as Argula von Grumbach or Ursala von Münsterberg, became literary spokesmen for the movement. For the proponents of the old faith such was truly the abomination of abominations. Their reaction, no matter how biased, shows that the place of women in the Reformation movement was of the sort that gained attention—or notoriety.

There may be several explanations for this phenomenon. It might be argued that religion always tends to be a highly feminine matter and so what happened in the early sixteenth century should not come as a surprise. One might also see a particular feminine empathy for the tenets of the Reformation, or one might perceive fundamental societal qualities or changes that had direct bearing on women.

Alongside such active involvement must be placed a secondary noteworthy characteristic pertaining to women in the Reformation: the formulation of striking new ideas concerning women by the reformers. The reformers propounded various ideas concerning womanhood and, in line with its implications, marriage. We need to

193

ascertain not only what these ideas were, but also how they came about and what impact they had upon society. In any case, to speak about women and the Reformation is to speak once more about the interrelationship of ideas and events, about how ideas are formulated and what role they play in societal affairs.

The traditional Western view of woman was ambiguous. It spoke appreciatively as well as skeptically of woman; this attitude was strikingly expressed by one early seventeenth century writer who remarked that "Woman is a stinking rose, a pleasing wound, a sweete poyson, a bitter sweete, a delightful disease, a pleasant punishment, a flattering death." Christianity shared and intensified this precarious paradox and for obvious reasons. The biblical story of Eve seemed to afford ever new possibilities for establishing woman's dubious character: she had been formed from the side of man; she had been created last; she had yielded to the serpent. The Apostle Paul advised women to be subject to their husbands and commanded them to be silent in churches. The biblical record thus seemed clear. The theological issue behind the biblical stories was the notion of original sin, which forced the theologians to account for the transmission of sinfulness from one generation to the next; the sexual act was the obvious instrument. That, somehow or other, seemed to implicate woman, who was viewed as more promiscuous than man.

The theologians of the Christian church increasingly came to espouse the ideal of virginity and permanent chastity, denying the sexual and reproductive role of woman, and thereby accepting a particular definition of the meaning of femininity. They distinguished the physical, sexual side on the one hand from the spiritual, intellectual side on the other, denouncing the former with stereotyped vehemence, while giving the latter cautious words of commendation. The disparagement of the physical element and of sexuality entailed a profound and far-reaching ramification. A specific definition of "woman" was provided, stressing that the "good" in woman was her intellectuality. Needless to say, this intellectuality was religious: it found expression in devotion, meditation, and reflection on spiritual things. Attention paid to beauty and appearance, even to motherhood or to being a housewife, was taken to be unbecoming to woman's true destiny. The ideal of virginity, while applicable to men and women alike, came to be more significantly identified with women. Possible explanations point to the biblical record and the fact that the theologians were without exception male and that lapses from the ideal of chastity could be more easily established for women.

The Protestant reformers' initial deviation from the traditional view was their vehement indictment of clerical celibacy. Martin Luther's treatise of 1522, entitled *Concerning Married Life,* expounded, in

194

classic fashion, the Reformation position: marriage is ordained by God, and thus a good. The disparagement of woman and marriage— for Luther the two went hand in hand—was a pagan principle which should be rejected: "There are many pagan books which treat of nothing but the depravity of womankind and the unhappiness of the estate of marriage, such that some have thought that even if Wisdom itself were a woman one should not marry." The polemic was specifically directed against the traditional notion of clerical celibacy; in order to counter it, a broad picture of the values of marriage and womanhood was necessary. The implications went beyond the restricted issue of the marriage of clerics. Tyndale put it rather pointedly: "Why hath God geven us these membres? Why these Pryckes and provocations? Why hath he added the power of begettynge, if bachelorshyp be taken for a praise?"

The affirmation of marriage entailed the acknowledgment of the physical side of man and woman. Sex was seen as a divine gift, no more, though also no less, under the curse of man's fall than the rest of creation. Thus, the "physical" and the "natural" received a striking affirmation. Yet sex was seen as a theological rather than a physiological problem: while writers reflected on its significance at the time of creation or the implications of the fall, when it came to the present their voices became remarkably muted.

The reformers' affirmation of the "natural" and "physical" dimension of existence was reinforced by their insistence that *all* human endeavors, no matter how lowly, have, if performed in the proper spirit, a positive good. Indeed, their two facets were but the two sides of the same fundamental purview. While the affirmation of sexuality pertained, needless to say, to men and women alike, the Protestant notion of "vocation" had a unique applicability to woman: her daily round of endeavor received uncommon appreciation. Luther summed it up by saying, "If the wife is honorable, virtuous, and pious, she shares in all the cares, endeavors, duties, and functions of her husband. With this end in view, she was created in the beginning; and for this reason she is called woman, or a 'she-man.'" Expounding on the creation narrative of the Book of Genesis, Luther observed that "in the household the wife is a partner in the management and has a common interest in the children and the property." Luther asserted the sanctity of the body and the spirituality of the common life.

The English reformer Miles Coverdale, in a tract entitled *The Christian State of Matrimony*, echoed these themes. The superiority of man was for him beyond question; the proof text was the Genesis account of Eve's creation: "Yet was she not made of the head; for the husband is the head and Maister of the wyfe . . . but even out of thy side, as one that is set next unto man, to be his helpe and companion."

195

In effect, this superiority evolved into a division of functions: there was to be a mutuality of respect: "The one ought to be an eye, eare, mouth, hand and foote to the other. In trouble the one must be the comfort of the other." Woman is submissive to man, though she occupies her own sphere of responsibility. "Whatsoever is to be done without the home, that belongeth to the man, and the woman to study for things within to be done."

The view of the reformers is a far cry from any notion of equality between man and woman. Compared with the medieval tradition, however, two striking modifications have occurred. For one, the new religious emphasis propounded by the reformers entailed a positive view of sexuality. Secondly, a new and positive emphasis was placed upon the home as the sphere of woman's activity and endeavor. In a sense, woman was equal to man in that she possessed her own particular responsibility.

The innovation by the sixteenth century reformers was that they no longer saw woman as separate and unequal, but as separate and "equal." To be sure, the reformers echoed the traditional notions that woman was weaker, more fickle, less cool-headed than man. In that sense, she was not equal. At the same time, the reformers stressed woman's positive significance. She was not an ethereal being, but a person of flesh and blood. The reformers acknowledged woman's contribution, her virtues, her strengths. These lay in the domestic realm of managing the household and rearing children—menial chores in the same sense that the man's chores were menial. They were "vocations," that is, the exercise of God-given responsibilities.

How the ideals of the reformers were translated into practice is quite another question, however. Their beautiful words about the virtuous woman or woman's positive role did not mean that such words were routinely translated into actions. What happened in the homes, marketplaces—and bedrooms—was a different matter. We are thus left with the problem as to how effective were the noble ideals, how much practical change did occur in the self-understanding and role of women.

The evidence for actual change is hard to come by. Even where changes occurred, their real source is in doubt. Indeed, in the early sixteenth century, there were other forces in the air, developments that antedated the changes in the realm of religion and may well be a more fundamental cause. The artistic evidence which strikingly harmonizes with the thrust of the Reformation is a perfect case in point.

In the sixteenth century artists discovered woman. To speak more precisely, they discovered the female figure, for woman, needless to say, had been known to artists all along. Heretofore she had been ethereal and spiritual; hers was a mystic and otherworldly beauty, evoking no human (or all-too-human) emotions, but lifting the mind heavenward. The Virgin Mary epitomized the spiritual qualities of true womanhood.

Unclad female figures were not absent in art before the sixteenth century, but in a sense they lacked reality. There is an air of innocence about Botticelli's *Birth of Venus* and *Primavera,* an evident unwillingness to depict the female body in all anatomic detail. Moreover, the figures are taken from the world of classical mythology. Not surprisingly, Marsilio Ficino, Botticelli's patron, found that Venus's "eyes [are] Dignity and Magnanimity, her hands Liberality and Magnificence, her feet Comeliness and Modesty. The whole, then, is Temperance and Honesty, Charm and Splendor." Such words clad an esthetic notion of woman, a philosophic understanding of beauty that harmonized splendidly with the theologians' perspective.

In the sixteenth century this artistic perception of woman underwent a change. Even a novice with regard to the finer points of sixteenth century art will note that the paintings of such artists as Caesare da Sesto, Giorgione, or Titian depicting women conveyed noticeable differences from the "asceticism" of the medieval period: not only was the subject matter frequently no longer religious, but secular and even pagan; and the women were depicted nude.

Thus, Caesare da Sesto's *Leda,* while still a figure from classical mythology is a woman of flesh and blood. Geometric harmony disappeared and voluptuousness took its place. Titian's nudes, notably his *Danae* and *Venus and the Organ Player,* intimate the same. Even Lucas Cranach's *Judgment of Paris* conveyed a new touch. In short, these painters, and many others, depicted a new kind of woman in whom ethereal or spiritual beauty gave way to the earthiness and even sensuousness.

In passing we must note that the evidence is similar in the realm of literature in that the very quantity of publications of the time intimates the lure of the subject. Beyond doubt, the proper understanding and appreciation of woman must have been prominent on many minds, as such names as Vives (*A Very Fruitful and Pleasant Booke Called the Instruction of Christian Woman*) or John Aylmer (*An Harborough for Faithful Subjects*), or such titles as *Of the Beauty of Women, The Prayse of All Women, A Woman's Worth,* and *A Lytel Treatyse of the Beaute of Women* signify.

In short, there was intellectual ferment in the sixteenth century, at once theological, artistic, and literary: a new concept of womanhood was being formulated. Whether there were also changes in the role played by women in home and society is difficult to say. Probably not, apart from the general changes occurring in society (such as greater literacy, for example). If women were happier or more frustrated, more frequently beaten by their husbands or less, more aware of their femininity or humanity or less, cannot be ascertained at this distance. Cursory evidence indicates that wife-beating may have been more than an isolated exercise of male prerogatives, that childbirth was thought to make women "unclean," even as the widespread witch craze in early modern Europe epitomized an antifeminist sentiment of ruthless cruelty. Such could not have prevailed without the concomitant continuation of the traditional notions concerning woman.

That God had ordained the inferiority of woman, that woman was particularly susceptible to the temptations of the flesh, that her virtues were few and her faults many, that her destiny lay in contemplation—all this we can read in the literature of the sixteenth century no less than before. A new view had made its appearance for which Sigmund Freud's slogan "anatomy is destiny" serves as apt description. The contribution of the Protestant Reformation to this new vision of woman was substantial. The reformers asserted that inferiority meant a difference in function: the man outside the home, the woman within. Alongside such difference in function stood a different definition of the meaning of womanhood. It was related to marriage, to woman's reproductive and physiological function, indeed, to sex. Woman was pulled down to earth, so to speak. She was told that she should be proud of her contribution in the kitchen, in the nursery; she should be proud of being a woman who could love with warmth and commitment. Subsequent decades and centuries would show that even this positive view was not without its serious problems, especially once social and economic mobility increasingly affected the male segment of society. Still, such was the contribution of the Reformation.

11 Reformation and Society

WHATEVER IS SAID ABOUT THE REFORMATION, there can be no doubt that it went beyond the realm of ecclesiastical affairs and, in a variety of ways affected society at large. To say this is not to suggest that the Reformation was the alpha and omega of the sixteenth century, that nothing of significance happened outside its confines, or even that whatever happened within them was meaningful. Much took place during the course of the century that was in no way related to the Reformation movement. The geographic discoveries, for example, would have occurred and in due time and season exerted their forceful impact on the European continent even if ecclesiastical affairs had been conducted as usual.

The argument that the effects of the Reformation encompassed society does not mean that the relationship between the two resembled a one-way street, though most scholarship has been disposed to argue that way, attributing to the Reformation all the blessings (or curses) of subsequent European history, from capitalism to indoor plumbing, or by insisting that the Reformation as a religious phenomenon was the direct result of societal changes. Rather, interaction between religion and society was mutual; while the Reformation exerted a variety of forceful stimuli upon society, causing change, realignment, innovation, society exerted its influence upon religion, and the religious turbulence of the Reformation, in a way, only reflected the society's prior turbulence. Thus no priority can be established. Rather like the chicken and the egg, both were present, somehow related, and dependent upon each other. After all, both breathed the same air, so to speak; a churchman was at once a citizen or a businessman or a teacher.

A complex cluster of political, economic, cultural, and religious factors characterized the sixteenth century like any other period. Short of a rigidly determinist view of history, of whatever variety, it seems most plausible to assume that these factors differed in importance at different times. Surely, at certain times religion was influenced by political or cultural factors, while at other times it may have exerted its own influence.

Moreover, it was one thing for the Protestant reformers to pontificate on the social or economic issues of their day; it was quite another to be able to effect actual change. In most instances the reformers were far removed from the centers of action and power. What they thought, felt, or wrote must not automatically be viewed as having had impact upon their society just by virtue of their thinking, feeling, and writing. The exploration of the impact of the reformers upon society must do more than list their programmatic pronouncements.

Politics

WITHOUT THE STRONG ARM OF THE POLITICAL authorities of the day, the Reformation could not have succeeded. This does not reflect negatively on the truth or profundity of the ideas of the Reformation, for ideas have their own persuasiveness and their own rationale, and are, once generated, little affected by external forces. Nor do ideas need a formal organizational backdrop for their effectiveness; the Enlightenment of the eighteenth century serves as a good case in point. Yet if the ideas of the Reformation went their own unfettered way the external consolidation of the Reformation was something else. Here the support of governmental authorities was both indispensable and crucial. In a way, this fact is explained by the medieval notion of society for which church and state were but two sides of the same reality. Any change in the one, therefore, had to be supported, or at least condoned, by the other.

The positive decision of those holding political power formalized the success of the Reformation, even as, conversely, the negative word, in countries such as France and Poland, led to failure. More was at stake than the decision of a whimsical ruler, as epitomized, for example, in Henry VIII of England. There were always other factors at work and they converged to provide a unique context for the quest for ecclesiastical change. The political factor, however, remained the prominent one in this phase of the Reformation.

None other than Emperor Charles V may be cited as an example. However much he was influenced by Erasmus, Charles was a loyal Catholic, determined to achieve a resolution of the Lutheran conflict in a way that would safeguard the honor of the Catholic church. By background, conviction, and temperament he was destined to be a guardian of the Catholic truth. By the same token, he aided more than most other individuals the spread of the Reformation in Germany, and thereby in the rest of Europe as well. The explanation for this intriguing paradox lies in Charles's dynastic and imperial interests which, in mind or deed, frequently assumed priority over matters of religion. During the thirty-five years of his rule, he spent less than a decade in Germany; of the first twenty years, less than three. Earlier in this volume Charles's peripatetic sojourns in Austria, Italy, and Spain are traced. Charles had good reasons for these absences; the time was anything but tranquil and sundry matters required his attention. To be sure, even as emperor, Charles lacked direct influence and power in the empire, which had already begun the trend to what two centuries later would be neither holy nor Roman nor an empire. At the same time, in view of his Catholic stance, Charles personified the efforts to resolve the controversy along lines congenial to the Catholic religion. Even if his presence, in the end, would not have altered the course of events, his absence assuredly worsened it.

Luther's territorial ruler, Elector Frederick of Saxony, must be mentioned in the same breath with Charles, for here, too, formidable political considerations were at work—with one difference. If Charles supported Luther's cause inadvertently, Frederick did so deliberately. Had it not been for Frederick's initial support, Luther clearly would not have survived the first years of controversy, and the movement would never have come about. Frederick held his protecting hand over the Wittenberg professor by insisting, in 1518, that Luther be examined in Germany rather than in Rome; by not recognizing, in 1520, the authenticity of the bull *Exsurge Domine;* by demanding, in 1521, that Luther be given a hearing before the German Diet; and afterward by protecting Luther in hiding at Wartburg. To this day scholars disagree about Frederick's motivation, for the evidence seems overwhelming that he was anything but avant-garde in his religious thinking. Aside from the question of religious conviction, Frederick had influence because he was a powerful political force in the empire.

Charles and Frederick epitomized the complex administrative structure of the empire, with its built-in conflict between imperial and territorial interests. Its administrative confusion was a decisive factor in the unfolding success of the Lutheran movement. The role of the *Reichsregiment,* which functioned as central authority in the emperor's absence from Germany, is an excellent case in point. Between 1522 and 1524 its members talked long and fast about the Lutheran controversy, but it was a case of much smoke and little fire. A myriad of cross-purposes compounded the lack of real power, and no forceful action, indeed no action of any kind, came forth.

The Ottoman Empire must be mentioned as an additional element of political importance, another indication of the complex interweaving of forces. From the early 1520s onward, the specter of a Turkish attack upon central Europe was real indeed. The number of pamphlets on the topic published at the time indicates that there was no little concern in Europe about the matter. The question was how to meet the Turkish threat. The obvious answer was to strengthen the armed defenses, but precisely that created a problem at once. Since the threat was to all of Europe, the defense called for a common effort of all Christendom. Only Austria and Germany were within immediate reach of the Turkish forces, and the other countries, understandably, perceived little urgency. In Germany, the issue clashed headlong with the dual problem of the tension between emperor and territorial rulers and the religious controversy. Any defense required the financial cooperation of the rulers. Precisely at this point the estates with Lutheran sympathies discovered a perfect opportunity for blackmail. At the diet at Speyer, in 1529, they announced that they would provide no financial assistance against the Turks unless the religious controversy were satisfactorily solved. What they meant, of course, was "solved to their particular satisfaction." Understandably, the Catholics balked. On that particular occasion the Lutheran position of "no aid without religious concessions" was modified, for in the end they agreed to render support despite the lack of a satisfactory religious settlement. But the basic approach had been enunciated and it proved to be the stereotyped ingredient in the years that followed. As matters turned out, the Protestants scored their greatest legal achievements in the context of an acute Turkish threat: in 1532, in the late 1530s, and finally the early 1550s. In each instance they were able to consolidate their ecclesiastical achievements because they shrewdly took advantage of a political predicament.

Needless to say, the Protestants had not manufactured the Turkish threat. It was preexistent; but if they did not manufacture it, they certainly exploited it to the fullest. The Catholic estates, which monotonously insisted that the Turkish and the religious problem had no connection, inadvertently contributed to the perpetuation of the precarious situation by refusing to supply enough financial and military aid against the Turks to render Protestant assistance superfluous. Had they been willing to reach deeper into their own pockets, the bluff would have been called on the Protestants. Money was as much of an issue as religion, however; and thus the Protestant contribution was all the more necessary. No matter how strong their religious commitment, the Catholics clearly drew the line when it came to finances.

Religion and politics converged in the Reformation yet another way, and once more incisive benefit accrued to the Protestants. From the mid-1520s onward, the cause of the Reformation in Germany became tied to a military alliance. Landgrave Philip of Hesse first made the suggestion that the new faith should be protected by an alliance, and his suggestion (as well as his persistence) eventually culminated in the formation of the League of Schmalkald. There can be little doubt that the league grew out of the awareness that military force threatened the Reformation with suppression; its survival, therefore, also had to be secured that way.

The alliance to safeguard the Protestant faith constituted a striking parallel to the role of the Turks. Religious concessions were to be effected on political grounds. The difficulties attending the formation of the league, discussed earlier in another connection, indicated that some Protestants were disposed to see the situation quite differently. Saxon officials openly expressed the suspicion that those who urged the formation of an alliance had rather more vital reasons on their mind: they were interested in political advantages rather than religious commitment. Such doubts were justified in regard to Philip of Hesse. As he saw it, any Protestant league would be anti-Hapsburg (because of the staunch Catholic attitude of the Hapsburgs) and his own greatest political troubles related to the Hapsburgs. His involvement in the Pack affair in 1528 demonstrated that an ostensibly religious reason was in actual fact a ploy to get himself out of hot water. The League of Schmalkald was clearly directed against the emperor; it could be justified not only on the grounds of religion, but also of the emperor's encroachment upon territorial prerogatives.

The ruler made the decision. It is difficult to perceive the reasons underlying individual decisions, though probably different reasons prevailed at different times and in different places. Considerations involving such matters as personal commitment and religious conviction are unfortunately beyond the historian's reach. The decision in favor of the Reformation made in Germany in the late 1530s had a different context from the one made ten years earlier, and was thus made for different reasons. Not only did the meaning of the change differ (in the 1520s the general ecclesiastical situation was still very much in a state of flux), but so did the political setting within which the change occurred. From 1531 onward, the League of Schmalkald provided a protective mantle (despite the uncertain legal situation) over most Protestants.

In the early years of ecclesiastical turbulence the political advantages of supporting the new faith were not immediately obvious. This observation is underscored by the reluctance of those in political control to support the Lutheran movement during its initial phase. If it had been clear that the prize of subjecting the church to secular control could have been had for the asking, there surely would have been little hesitancy to render this support.

One may observe that at some places forceful opposition against the Lutheran movement existed, as in England for example, and yet the momentum of the movement remained undiminished. The point is well taken. External forces could hardly suppress the Reformation as an ideological movement. Still, we must distinguish between a failure to effect suppression and tacit ineffectiveness. Moreover, the events in the various European countries must not be divorced from the German precedent; that is, the cause (and course) of the Reformation in the various European countries would not have had great impetus had not the movement already been firmly established on German soil. There was, in short, an unspoken alliance between "religion" and "regime" in the sense that the latter supported, either by way of active policies or by latent neutrality, the cause of ecclesiastical change. In so doing, the reformers were able to view them as properly "ordained" by God for the support of true religion.

There were also other situations; those government authorities that were outrightly hostile or, at best, reluctant to endorse precarious schemes of ecclesiastical change. The reformers' attitude then turned to a mood of defiance. Thomas Müntzer's fiery pronouncements left little doubt that true religion was to be established even against the rulers. In the heat of the Peasants' War Müntzer told the Count of Mansfeld: "The living and eternal God has ordered us to remove you from your place by force, for you are of no benefit to Christendom, you are nothing but a miserable dustbroom of the friends of God." Initially, Müntzer's dualism between the "elect" and the "godless" did not assume any sociological or political differentiation. The rulers were challenged to join the "elect" and carry out the divine will. By the time Müntzer printed his last tract in the fall of 1524, however, the tone had changed: the label was *"gotlose regenten"* ("godless rulers"). Müntzer's challenge of established authority was taken up by other reformers, somewhat gingerly by John Calvin, more confidently by John Knox, whose *Godly Letter of Warning and Admonition to the Faithful* (1554) included the significant phrase "for all those that would draw us from God (be they kings or queens), being of the devil's nature, are enemies unto God, and therefore will God that we declare ourselves enemies unto them."

The development of a right of resistance and, by implication, one of revolution, was a logical extension. Government support for ecclesiastical change was desirable in the sixteenth century, and the Protestant spokesmen spared no effort to be eloquent and persuasive; but when support turned into hostility, a problem existed. Calvinists in France and the Low Countries developed a full-fledged theory of resistance, precipitated by the concrete circumstances they faced. Bitter persecution and an ambiguous constitutional situation made this development almost inevitable. The French Monarchomachs Languet, Hotman, Duplessis-Mornay argued the case in an interesting juxtaposition of biblical and secular argumentation: the "tyrant" who violated both the law of God and of the land was to be resisted. The argument received theological respectability with the *Confessio Scotica* of 1560, which included "the repudiation of tyranny" among the good works of the faithful. Such was the sentiment of the "outsider," regardless of ecclesiastical label. It is noteworthy that during Elizabeth's reign Cardinal Allen spearheaded the attempts of the émigré English Catholics on the Continent to develop a theory of resistance and rebellion. Both sides propounded the same political theory when circumstances required it.

In the beginning Luther himself was reluctant to concede anything other than passive suffering by the faithful in the face of adversity. He argued that resistance against authority could pertain only to "worldly" matters in which one party had violated his obligations. One did not rebel on behalf of religious grievances; after all, in the Sermon on the Mount Jesus exhorted the believer to be long suffering. By 1531 Luther was willing to support resistance against the emperor on political grounds, but since the emperor was both a political and a religious opponent, Luther's notion was not as clear in practice as it was in theory.

Politically, the eminent significance of the Reformation was the comprehensive repudiation of ecclesiastical control over government. The perennial struggle between political and ecclesiastical authority, so graphically evidenced by Pope Boniface VIII's bull *Unam Sanctam,* was resolved in favor of the former. One might see this as the culmination of a trend appearing in the later Middle Ages. Indeed, some of the Protestant political theorists, such as Stephen Gardiner in England, insisted that the authority of the ruler embraced ecclesiastical matters as well. The most dramatic reversal of the relationship between church and state occurred in England, where the king's new title "Supreme Head of the Church" was a spectacular symbol for the change. Later in the century Thomas Erastus wrote his *Explicatio gravissimae quaestionis* to argue for the complete submission of ecclesiastical affairs to political authority. Even Catholic practice often conformed to Protestant theory. Little difference existed between Catholic and Protestant countries in this respect, a fact partially explained by the importance of the ruler in rejecting or introducing the new faith.

The acquisition of ecclesiastical authority on the part of government was only one of several developments that grew out of the religious turbulence of the sixteenth century. The state was autonomous, not under the jurisdiction of the church, and at the same time it exercised educational and charitable functions. This meant that the state assumed a direct moral stature it had theretofore lacked. In a way, it was a matter of taking over responsibilities previously carried out by the church.

The Reformation's theoretical justification for this may have been either an ex post facto *pièce justificative* or a revolutionary innovation. The fact itself proved to be of immense significance. A new kind of state made its appearance. No longer did it wrestle with the church, for it had acquired the power and prerogatives desired. While the state was still far from secular—religious affairs were important and in all countries an "established" church existed—religion was only one facet of many, not unlike trade and commerce.

Even as the proper care of ecclesiastical affairs was seen as the responsibility of the ruler, so loyalty and obedience on the part of the subjects were thought to be an expression of piety. Religion was seen as an immensely cohesive factor in society, its moral handmaid (with the cost to the state very modest). All this can be viewed as the continuation of principles long established.

Otherwise, the changes in the political realm were few. Religious dissent, if publicly expressed, continued to be unthinkable and was suppressed with varying degrees of sternness. Neither tolerance nor religious freedom was an entry in the vocabulary of sixteenth century man, though generally only the Anabaptists experienced fire and sword, and they suffered the double liability of being suspected revolutionaries and blasphemers. Otherwise, confiscation of property, compulsory emigration, or imprisonment was the normal legal procedure. All countries, Catholic and Protestant alike, clung to the notion that religious uniformity was indispensable to the tranquility of a political commonwealth, and the notion of the "Christian commonwealth" continued. Even the secularized functions assumed by the state, such as education, did not lose their religious ornamentation.

Society

THERE CAN BE LITTLE DOUBT THAT EUROPEAN society was undergoing social and economic change in the early sixteenth century. Evidence of grievances is not hard to find. In the German towns, these grievances were eminently political in character and concerned the attempt of some citizens to attain greater participation in civic affairs. The goal was constitutional change, the alteration of existing structures of governance. Occasionally, tensions erupted into outright confrontations with a modicum of subsequent change. Such was the case in the town of Mühlhausen, for example, where there were tensions, turbulence, and finally the adoption of a "recess" that provided for the establishment of a new government.

In the very beginning the cause of religion intertwined with societal matters. Even Luther's Ninety-five Theses touched, no matter how peripherally, on the financial implications of the sale of indulgences, and that peripheral involvement of social issues continued. Luther's *Open Letter to the Christian Nobility* of 1520 was largely a reiteration of traditional German grievances pertaining to religion and society: the import of costly spices, the restriction of luxury, the problem of university reform. Luther also wrote tracts on usury and the establishment of schools. Other writers likewise combined religious and societal concerns. Ulrich von Hutten, for example, added a goodly portion of hostility against things Roman and foreign by writing about social issues. Johann Eberlin von Günzburg, in turn, combined enthusiasm for Luther's religious message with a concern for the economic condition of German society. He wrote about high prices, juridical procedures, and (in his *Bundtgenossen*) even sketched a picture of a model society, called "Wolfaria."

The juxtaposition of religious and societal problems found graphic expression in the *Twelve Articles* of the south German peasants, of 1525. These *Articles* were hardly unique. Many of the "Lutheran" pamphlets of the years preceding had ventured to do the same: to show concern for the renewal of religion and of society, insisting that both went hand in hand, the former, indeed, providing the momentum for the latter. The *Twelve Articles* thus epitomized concerns already variously expressed. The peasants' use of the "flowing waters," the restriction of service to the lords, the reduction of the "death tax," etc., were

207

advocated, and, at the same time, directly and explicitly related to religious affirmations.

The catastrophe of the Peasants' War, together with Luther's emotional denunciation of the peasants, cast gloomy disparagement over the concern for relating religion to society. In fact, after 1525 the Lutheran reformers tended to be cautious about doing so. Luther's categorical pronouncement that the "gospel" and "politics" (in the Aristotelian sense) do not mix proved to be the leitmotiv for all reformers influenced by him. The impact of the Lutheran ethos upon society was indirect at best.

This turn of events in Germany did not, however, deprive the Reformation movement of its direct societal thrust elsewhere in Europe. Other reformers, notably Huldreich Zwingli in Zurich, Martin Bucer in Strassburg, and John Calvin in Geneva, propounded a notion of religious reform that explicitly encompassed societal concerns as well.

Among the many social pronouncements of the Protestant reformers, two topics appeared more frequently than any other; the alleviation of the plight of the poor and the improvement of education. One English writer put the two problems under one umbrella by noting that the "suppressinge of Abbeyes, Cloysters, Colleges, and Chauntries" would bring about a "better releve of the pore, the maintenaunce of learning, and settinge forth of goddes worde."

The first generation of reformers were visionaries, men and women who had caught a glimpse of what they took to be the true gospel, and set out to translate that glimpse into practice. In so doing, they were unperturbed by burdensome past experiences, unbothered by the complexity of practical problems, unaware of the sloth and nonchalance of people. Once the true gospel had been recognized, so they thought, people would joyfully and determinedly cling to it. Once poverty had been recognized as a Christian problem, its alleviation would follow as a matter of course.

The reformers' statements were numerous, but there was a kind of stereotyped monotony to them: they were all against poverty, hardly a revolutionary or startling fact. Intriguingly, Luther's comment, in his *Sermon on Usury*, that there should be no begging in Christendom was included among the condemned propositions in the papal censure of 1520. The other reformers echoed the sentiment, precipitating a kind of first "war on poverty." The legal introduction of the Reformation was ubiquitously accompanied by formal expression of concern for the problem. The reformers sought to outdo one another with appropriate and idealistic schemes.

As early as 1522, Luther and Carlstadt lent a hand in drawing up an "order of the common chest" for the town of Wittenberg, the first of many such Protestant "orders." Students who begged were to be expelled from town, and needy burghers were to be given loans from the "common chest." This was a term to be taken quite literally: it was a chest with two locks and two separate keepers of keys. The necessary funds were to be derived from property confiscated from the Catholic church.

These "orders for the poor" may be seen as vigorous expression of the reformers' social spirit. All the same, the reformers' involvement reflected but a general concern permeating society at the time. Toward the end of the fifteenth century changing social and economic conditions intensified the problem of the poor, and when the sixteenth century brought an upsurge of poverty, frustrated civic authorities sought solutions of their own. The orders for the poor promulgated in such cities as Nuremberg, Regensburg, and Ypres in the early 1520s, at a time when the impact of the Reformation could hardly have been of much consequence, illustrate that there was deep concern for the alleviation of poverty quite independent of the religious controversy. The foremost theoretician of poor relief in the early sixteenth century, the Spanish humanist Luis Vives, was anything but a Protestant reformer!

The real contribution of the reformers lay in the emphasis on the laity. Repudiation of the Catholic church prompted a comprehensive reconsideration of the methods of dealing with poverty. Traditionally, the church had handled the problem on its own: it had the moral precepts and, in a way, the resources. By the early sixteenth century it was obvious, however, that the church had failed to provide a satisfactory solution. Now new solutions were possible. The vast properties of the church, destined for purposes no longer considered spiritually legitimate (such as the endowment of masses), could be used for the alleviation of social ills. Although in the end, the greedy hand of the powerful appeared and caused a good many theoretical schemes to be like words spoken into the wind, the Reformation "baptized" the various lay efforts by acknowledging that the civic community could perform a function in this regard. The emphasis on lay activity with regard to relief for the poor must be seen both as the outgrowth of trends already discernible in the late fifteenth century and as a consequence of the repudiation of existing ecclesiastical structures that reinforced the role of the laity as a viable alternative. With the rejection of the Catholic ecclesiastical structure only the laity was able to formulate the necessary policies and undertake changes. The Reformation's emphasis on the laity—what Luther called the "priesthood of all believers"—meshed superbly with the exigencies of the practical situation.

What the reformers propounded hardly deserves a label of

unusual. These notions fitted harmoniously with certain trends in the air, notably the increased involvement of the secular authorities. Nuremberg might have issued an order for the poor in the 1520s even if the world had never heard of Martin Luther. The Reformation influence pertained less to the practical measures than to a new ethos or ideology.

In any case, with respect to the economic and social dimensions of society, the Protestant Reformation was indirectly revolutionary and directly conservative. Luther's concept of "vocation," which held that all professions and endeavors had a spiritual blessing, was of immense significance. It made all work, no matter how lowly and mundane, if performed in the proper spirit, pleasing to God and thereby undoubtedly released creative and stimulating forces. The significance (if any) lies in the fact that this secularization of man's "vocation" redirected some of the talent that previously had wound up in the ministerial profession and made some men become teachers, lawyers, or doctors who might have turned to the church in an earlier age. In the early eighteenth century the English physico-theologian William Derham was to calculate how much manpower had been lost to European society through the monasteries. His point was naïve, but well taken. Instead of disappearing behind the walls of the monasteries, men in Protestant lands strove to live their religious faith in the classroom or the court chamber. To use a modern term, they "secularized" the gospel. The impact, while beyond verification, must have been substantial.

On the more explicit level of economic and social considerations, however, the reformers were conservative. Though they differed over the mandates of the gospel for the economic and social realms, they hoped to explicate these mandates and, moreover, basically express their distrust of the marketplace. Rather like their scholastic predecessors, the reformers pondered endlessly such problems as the just price, the legitimacy of taking interest, or poverty. They propounded new notions (Calvin, for example, rejected the economic dogma of the Middle Ages that money was sterile), but they sought to influence society by hammering in the rigorous ethical concepts of the gospel rather than by offering innovations in economic theory. If Luther and Calvin had had their way, economic life would have continued as before.

The plain fact was that commerce and trade were not any more receptive to Protestant ethical counsel than they had been to Catholic. Indeed, new empirical developments, such as the supplies of silver and spices from the New World, the rise of the chartered trading companies, the geographic discoveries, and increased population, cast their spell over the economic activities of the sixteenth century.

210

Moreover, real economic innovation did not come until the seventeenth century, and by that time Protestantism, including Calvinism, played a lesser role in the affairs of society.

There may have been some men, even groups of men, whose economic endeavors were influenced, as Max Weber suggested, by their religious ethos, by such virtues, at once religious and economic, as thrift, self-denial, and self-discipline. One surely cannot dismiss Weber's thesis altogether, but many other men pursued their economic endeavors with technical competence rather than religious faith, and the course of the economic development in western Europe was influenced by facts rather than ethos. The Augustinian theologian Peter of Aragon provided an apt commentary on the whole matter toward the end of the century when he confessed that "the market place has its own laws."

The reformers inveighed against sundry social abuses, such as prostitution, excessive drinking, or luxury in dress, as Catholics had done all along. Their vehemence raises the suspicion that they realized the colossus against which they were struggling. Luther (witness his *Open Letter to the Christian Nobility*) had strong opinions concerning these matters, but argued that the secular authorities (the "Christian" nobility) should formulate and execute the proper policies in this respect, with the church providing the ethos to inspire such action. Accordingly, there were few formal ecclesiastical pronouncements from Lutheran bodies, only individual proposals or governmental edicts. The number of those was legion. It is hard to say, however, if they were always issued (or received) with the religious ethos Luther desired; certainly they were not always successful.

Among the Calvinists the story was different, for here the moral mandates of the gospel were seen to be more directly applicable in society. Certain activities, such as dancing or playing cards, were prohibited in Geneva, and in place of the usual tavern Calvin sought to institute (unsuccessfully, as it turned out) a new version in which beverages were weak and theology was strong. Calvinists elsewhere sought to do the same. They relied on governmental mandates; whenever issued, these were, in contrast to those in Lutheran lands, transparently religious.

With respect to the cultural consequences of the Reformation, the conclusions come more easily since the evidence is more clear-cut. Still, a caveat is necessary: whatever consequences can be discerned were indirect, not direct, ramifications of religious emphases. They were derived from the nature of the Protestant message, which was as demanding as it was simple. Thus, people had to be able to read in order to comprehend for themselves the meaning of Scripture. If the church was to be a dynamic community of all the faithful, literate men and women were necessary. The consequences were many. The Scriptures and pamphlets in the vernacular were emphasized, a fact that aided the emergence of vernacular literature in the various countries.

Education was likewise changed. The intent was not so much to further secular education or the liberal arts, but to train informed Christians. Religion and education worked harmoniously together. At the beginning of the religious controversy the Reformation had seemed hostile to education. Had not Luther's proclamation been a blunt and comprehensive repudiation of traditional learning? Had not the reformers charged that the universities were teaching abominable error, and that the study of Aristotle was despicable? Luther had asserted that the learned theologians and academicians were in error and that it was given to simple and unlearned men to understand the gospel.

Education before the Reformation was characterized not so much by quantity as quality; it was, moreover, undertaken by the church. The reformers argued that the responsibility should be in the hands of the secular authorities. Luther argued the case in his 1524 tract *To the Councillors of All German Cities That They Establish and Maintain Christian Schools*, and this was the way it worked out practically. The confiscated property of the Catholic church provided the financial basis for the educational effort.

The contribution of the Reformation to the notion of public education was thus twofold. It consisted of the demand, perpetually put forward, that schools be established, and, secondly, in the transfer of educational responsibility from the church to the state. This did not mean, however, that the church abdicated its educational involvement. The ties between church and school remained strong and the Peace of Westphalia of 1648 explicitly stated that schools were *"annexum religionis."* Often the Protestant parson took care of the heavenly alphabet and the worldly one as well.

The reformers echoed the goals of the humanists concerning the content of education. They stressed the study of languages (Latin for clarity of thought, Greek and Hebrew for understanding Scripture) and advocated textual criticism and literary analysis. At the same time they emphasized the value of historical studies. The primary motivation was to provide the basis for theological understanding (along lines congenial to Protestant thought), with the training of teachers, lawyers, and doctors as a corollary concern.

Protestant learning enjoyed the advantage of not being unduly restricted by the weight of tradition. It was able to explore new avenues. That the Nuremberg reformer Andreas Osiander contributed a preface to Copernicus's famous work on *The Revolutions of the Heavenly*

Bodies, in which he defended the scientist's right to offer hypotheses, is worthy of note in this connection. In part this attitude finds its explanation in the self-confidence of Protestantism, in part by the Protestant conviction that any pursuit of truth would confirm rather than deny religious truth. More important, however, may have been a kind of pragmatic self-limitation. Protestantism, after all, was a divided house, and nowhere possessed the universal stature of Catholicism. The condemnation of Galileo by the Saxon consistory would have looked rather foolish and would have been ineffectual besides. In other words, the very division of Protestantism made for its relative congeniality to scientific endeavor.

In the arts Calvinist austerity cast a shadow over whatever artistic exuberance the new faith generated. Artistic endeavor must be directly related to the liturgical life of the church to assume an immediate religious dimension; but Calvinist churches were white-washed and plain, devoid of ornamentation and decorations, the outgrowth of a literal application of the Old Testament proscription of graven images. Wherever this rigid temperament made its appearance—in Zurich, Geneva, or England—treasured works of art were destroyed, while no new creative forces were released. The visitor to English cathedrals encounters with painful monotony the destruction wrought by the Edwardian Reformation—from the shrine of St. Thomas à Becket at Canterbury to the decapitated statues of saints at Ely. One must acknowledge these iconoclastic tendencies of the Reformation, remembering that the men with paintbrush and hammer did not look at objects of art, but at idolatry, not at treasures to be esteemed, but at blasphemy to be removed. In the Lutheran and Anglican traditions no such austere rigidity existed, but even they had little opportunity to demonstrate artistic propensity. Since the Middle Ages had bequeathed magnificent churches to the sixteenth century, no need existed to build new ones and in so doing express the new faith in artistic form.

In the realm of music the Reformation found a splendid expression. This is not surprising, for here the liturgical life of the church allowed a direct application. To be sure, there again were exceptions: in Zurich, for example, church music was considered an abomination and worship without congregational singing prevailed until the end of the century. On the whole, however, the Reformation was a singing movement. The Protestant hymn was the expression of the entire congregation (and thereby was related to the musical tradition of St. Ambrose of Milan). Its lyrics were in the vernacular, which enabled the people to understand what they were singing.

Luther's musical inclinations were influential. He arranged the publication of a modest German hymnal in 1524, and contributed twenty-four of the thirty-two hymns. Other reformers also wrote and composed hymns, at times using popular tunes of the day, at times translating ancient Latin hymns, frequently rendering psalms into German. The latter form was found particularly attractive since it symbolized the biblical orientation of the Reformation. Calvin insisted that only biblical words could be used in the divine service and the first French Protestant hymnal, of 1539, contained only vernacular "paraphrases" of the psalms from the pens of Calvin and Clement Marot. Subsequent hymnals were characterized by the same literal use of the psalms, by their earthy language, and by melodies derived from the ancient Gregorian chant and from contemporary melodies.

Strictly speaking, these developments pertained to the life within the church and cannot really be viewed as cultural consequences of the Reformation. In the secular realm, composers continued to be preoccupied with religious music. The trend toward secular music may have been temporarily halted in the sixteenth century, a result of the religious orientation of the age. But there was nothing peculiarly confessional in the religious music of the time, except in the formal sense that Catholic composers, such as Palestrina, used for their works the liturgical frame of reference provided by the mass.

That there were cultural consequences of the Reformation would seem to need little verification. The difficult question pertains to their extent and significance. What can be said is that the Reformation instilled a new ethos into society: the notion of direct, personal responsibility; the concept of personal (and corporate) election; the postulates of discipline, of autonomy of the secular powers. To say this, however, is neither to suggest that such notions were absent before the Reformation nor to argue that the fact of their propagation alone proves their practical influence.

The question of the cultural consequences of the Reformation, in the final analysis, raises the question of the role of ideas in the affairs of men. Religious ideas were present in the sixteenth century, forceful, daring, revolutionary ideas, though not all that had the label was really religious; nor did authentic religious ideas always appear in pristine form. But they made their impact within the Protestant churches, probably also within society, and thereby did their share to help transform Western civilization.

Bibliography

General

A GOOD AND CONCISE INTRODUCTION INTO THE major historiographical strands of Reformation scholarship is offered by H. J. Grimm, *The Reformation in Recent Historical Thought* (American Historical Association Center for Teachers of History, No. 54). B. Moeller, "Problems of Reformation Research," in *Imperial Cities and the Reformation** (paperback) (Philadelphia, 1972), discusses the main directions of Reformation scholarship and offers suggestions for needed work. The new edition of the textbook by J. J. Grimm, *The Reformation Era* (New York, 1973), contains an extensive bibliography. Another important bibliographical aid for anyone studying the Reformation is the *Archive for Reformation History*, published biannually.

The best brief introduction to the question of the "causes" of the Reformation is J. Lortz, *How the Reformation Came** (New York, 1964). Its main thesis that on the eve of the Reformation Catholicism had lost some of its authentic self-understanding has been questioned, notably by H. A. Oberman (see below). S. Ozment, ed., *The Reformation in Medieval Perspective* (Chicago, 1971), contains a useful collection of essays by various authors on the connection between the Middle Ages and the Reformation. Otherwise, the best idea is to look into the opening chapters of the general Reformation surveys, such as the first volume of P. Hughes, *The Reformation in England* (New York, 1950–54). H. Oberman, ed., *The Forerunners of the Reformation: The Shape of Late Medieval Thought* (New York, 1965), offers a collection of documents as well as a concise overview of the various streams of thought. J. R. Hale, *Renaissance Europe, 1480–1520* * (London, 1971), is splendid in surveying the general pre-Reformation scene.

The World of the Reformation

Among the standard introductions the following deserve to be singled out: G. R. Elton, ed., *The Reformation*, New Cambridge Modern History, vol. 2 (Cambridge, 1958), is comprehensive; L. Spitz, *The Renaissance and Reformation Movements** (Chicago, 1971); G. R. Elton, *Reformation Europe, 1517–1559** (Cleveland, 1964); E. G. Leonard, *The Reformation*, A History of Protestantism, vol. 1 (London, 1965), is strong on ecclesiastical history, almost exclusively Protestant. R. H. Bainton, *The Reformation of the Sixteenth Century** (Boston, 1953), offers a useful summary of the major theological foci of the various Reformation streams. The new irenic Catholic interpretation is exemplified by J. P. Dolan, *History of the Reformation** (London, 1967).

The Reformation in Germany

A GREAT DEAL OF SCHOLARLY ATTENTION HAS BEEN paid to the German Reformation, a natural matter since that was where it all began. The work most accessible in English is J. Lortz, *The Reformation in Germany* (London, 1968), a reasonably sympathetic account by an irenic Catholic author. The book by F. Lau and E. Bizer, *The German Reformation* (London, 1969), is rather general in its first part, and altogether esoteric in its second. G. Ritter, in "Why the Reformation Occurred in Germany," *Church History* 27 (1958), addresses the specific "causes."

And then Martin Luther! His works fill almost one hundred folio volumes, and scholarly contributions are added at the rate of over three hundred a year. L. Spitz, "Current Accents in Luther Study: 1960–1967," *Theological Studies* 28 (1967), is the best account of recent scholarly efforts. An extensive translation of Luther's writings is found in the fifty-five volumes of *Luther's Works* (St. Louis and Philadelphia, 1955). A brief selection of sources is in E. G. Rupp and B. Drewery, *Martin Luther** (New York, 1970). Among the many biographies R. H. Bainton, *Here I Stand: A Life of Martin Luther** (New York, 1950), is the liveliest; R. H. Fife, *The Revolt of Martin Luther* (New York, 1957), offers the greatest detail; while A. G. Dickens, *Martin Luther and the Reformation** (London, 1967), has the best general summary of Luther and his times. E. Erikson, *Young Man Luther** (New York, 1957) is frequently cited as the seminal psychoanalytical study of Luther.

Theological studies of Luther tend to be demanding and presuppose considerable expertise in the field. P. Althaus, *The Theology of Martin Luther* (Philadelphia, 1965), is routine; G. Ebeling, in *Luther: An Introduction to His Thought* (Philadelphia, 1970), uses categories germane to his own theology to circumscribe the categories of Luther's thought.

E. Iserloh, *The Theses Were Not Posted* (Boston, 1968), is an interesting monograph arguing that Luther never posted the Ninety-five Theses. The lengthy essay of H. Baron, "Religion and Politics in the German Imperial Cities during the Reformation," *English Historical Review* 52 (1937), should be placed alongside the more recent study by B. Moeller, *Imperial Cities and the*

Reformation* (Philadelphia, 1972), which deals with acceptance of the Reformation by the imperial free cities in Germany. K. Brandi's biography *Emperor Charles V: The Growth and Destiny of a Man and of a World Empire* (London, 1938), while lacking conciseness in places, is written by a true expert.

K. C. Session has gathered an interesting collection of materials on the German Peasants' War, *Reformation and Authority: The Meaning of the Peasants' Revolt** (New York, 1965). Otherwise, we must use (with caution!) the older work by J. S. Shapiro, *Social Reform and the Reformation* (New York, 1909). H. Mackensen, "Historical Interpretation and Luther's Role in the Peasants' Revolt," *Concordia Theological Monthly* 34 (1964), offers a concise statement. The classic Marxist interpretation is now available in a convenient English translation: F. Engels, *The Peasant War in Germany** (Chicago, 1967). The convergence of religion and politics in the German Reformation is exemplified in the career of Landgrave Philip of Hesse in H. J. Hillerbrand, *Landgrave Philip of Hesse: Religion and Politics in the Reformation** (St. Louis, 1967). S. Fischer-Galati, *Ottoman Imperialism and German Protestantism* (Cambridge, 1959), examines the same problem vis-à-vis the role of the Turks. Various strands of the social involvement of the Reformation are discussed in essays by several authors in L. Buck and J. Zophy, *The Social History of the Reformation* (Columbus, Ohio, 1972).

The Radical Reformers

AMONG THE RADICALS OF THE REFORMATION THE Anabaptists occupy the most spectacular post. Recent literature is summarized in G. H. Williams, "Studies in the Radical Reformation (1517–1618): A Bibliographical Survey since 1939," *Church History* 27 (1958). The same author has written a formidable monograph with the title *The Radical Reformation* (Philadelphia, 1962), which vividly conveys the range of the heterogeneous spectrum of radical sentiment. The *Mennonite Encyclopedia* (4 vols., Scottsdale, Pa., 1955–59), constitutes a useful reference work regarding the Anabaptists. The volume edited by G. H. Williams, entitled *Spiritual and Anabaptist Writers* (Philadelphia, 1957), contains a judicious collection of primary sources. A good biography of one of the outstanding Anabaptist leaders is by H. S. Bender, *Conrad Grebel* (Goshen, Ind., 1950).

Much of the recent literature views the Anabaptists of the sixteenth century positively and, moreover, from a theological perspective. A different approach is taken by C. P. Clasen, *Anabaptism: A Social History* (Ithaca, 1972), a work that utilizes the methodology of social science; its findings, accordingly, are more restrained and less theological.

The Münster episode has received extensive treatment, none of which, however, is in English; this means that we must utilize the fictional treatment of the work by P. Vansittart entitled *The Siege* (New York, 1962). N. Cohn's

The Pursuit of the Millennium* (Fairlawn, N.J., 1957) includes chapters on the Anabaptists and Münster. While provocative, it is history written in the optative mood and therefore should be used with a good deal of caution. E. W. Gritsch, *Reformer without a Church: The Life and Thought of Thomas Müntzer* (Philadelphia, 1967), and E. G. Rupp, *Patterns of Reformation* (Philadelphia, 1969), offer vivid biographical sketches of some leading radicals.

Less has been written on the Spiritualists. After all, as noted in the text, they founded no church, and we are saved, therefore, from institutionalized hagiography. R. H. Bainton's *The Travail of Religious Liberty* (Philadelphia, 1951) deals with a limited aspect and goes chronologically beyond the sixteenth century, but it is altogether useful for conveying something of the mood of these men. The larger work by J. Lecler, *Toleration and the Reformation* (London, 1960), is not confined to the Spiritualists, but devotes, by virtue of its topic, a good deal of attention to them. It is well written and documented.

The standard work on Socinianism, in addition to the work of G. H. Williams, continues to be the encyclopedic work by E. M. Wilbur, *A History of Unitarianism* (Cambridge, 1945). It goes beyond the sixteenth century and tends to confuse the reader with an abundance of names and dates. A succinct introduction is J. C. Godbey, "Faustus Socinus in the Light of Modern Scholarship," *Proceedings of the Unitarian Historical Society* 15 (1964).

The Reformation in England

THE ENGLISH REFORMATION HAS RECEIVED COMPEtent treatment by P. H. Hughes, whose three volumes of *The Reformation in England* (New York, 1950–54) embody a restrained Catholic bias and an abundance of useful material. A. G. Dickens, *The English Reformation** (New York, 1964), is both more concise and more balanced. The state of affairs before the Reformation is treated by M. Bowker, *The Secular Clergy in the Diocese of Lincoln, 1495–1520* (Cambridge, 1968), with findings that run counter to the traditional notion of perversion and ignorance as the hallmark of the pre-Reformation period. The same "revisionist" character holds true for the splendid work by P. Heath, *The English Parish Clergy on the Eve of the Reformation* (London, 1969).

Useful bibliographies are found in C. Read, *Bibliography of British History: Tudor Period*, 2nd ed. (Oxford, 1959), and M. Levine, *Tudor England, 1485–1603* (Cambridge, 1968). A good, succinct bibliography, together with splendidly chosen documents, is in C. H. Williams, *English Historical Documents, 1485–1558* (London, 1967). A sprightly-written general history of sixteenth century England is G. R. Elton's *England under the Tudors* (Cambridge, 1955).

The overtowering figure of Henry VIII has been the subject of surprisingly few literary attempts. We have the older work by A. F. Pollard, *Henry VIII** (London, 1905), and the more recent (and splendid) work by J. J. Scarisbrick, *Henry VIII** (London, 1968). The scholarly erudition of the latter is impressive. A provocative book, though not a biography in the traditional sense, is L. B. Smith, *Henry VIII: The Mask of Royalty* (New York, 1972). G. R. Elton, whose researches have endeavored to portray the dimension of the revolution, administrative and other, accomplished under the leadership of Thomas Cromwell, has recently published a book that may be said to epitomize his earlier findings: *Policy and Police* (New York, 1972). J. Youings, *The Dissolution of the Monasteries** (London, 1971), is excellent.

The theological and religious components of the changes and ideas in England are ably discussed by W. A. Clebsch, *England's Earliest Protestants, 1520–1535* (New Haven, 1964), and in the earlier work by E. Rupp, *The Making of the English Protestant Tradition** (Cambridge, 1947). P. E. Hughes, *The Theology of the English Reformers* (London, 1965), serves as a good introduction for the thinking of the English reformers on the standard theological issues, while C. George, *The Protestant Mind of the English Reformation* (Princeton, 1961), encompasses broader intellectual aspects. J. K. McConica, *English Humanists and Reformation Politics under Henry VIII and Edward VI* (Oxford, 1965), examines the influence of humanism and particularly Erasmus upon the English religious scene, while the broader matter of interaction between statecraft and religion is discussed by L. B. Smith, *Tudor Prelates and Politics, 1536–58* (Princeton, 1953). W. K. Jordan, *Edward VI, the Young King: The Protectorship of the Duke of Somerset* (Cambridge, Mass., 1968), and *Edward VI, the Threshold of Power: The Dominance of the Duke of Northumberland, 1549–1553* (Cambridge, Mass., 1970), deal, by virtue of the passivity of their "hero," extensively with the character of the reign of the youthful king.

The Puritans have received, needless to say, extensive treatment. The standard work is M. M. Knappen, *Tudor Puritanism** (Chicago, 1949). The more recent book, P. Collinson, *The Elizabethan Puritan Movement* (Berkeley, 1967), offers what might be called a "social history" of the movement and is indispensable. W. P. Haugaard, *Elizabeth and the English Reformation* (New York, 1968), deals with the Elizabethan settlement, for which the work of J. Neale, *The Elizabethan House of Commons* (London, 1949), is essential. Puritan sources are found in L. Trinterud, ed., *Elizabethan Puritanism* (Oxford, 1971).

The Reformation on the Continent

HULDREICH ZWINGLI HAS HAD ONLY MODEST SCHOLarly attention in the Anglo-Saxon world. A translation of a useful introduction to the researches is G. W. Locher, "The Change in the Understanding of Zwingli," *Church History* 34 (1965). J. Courvoisier, *Zwingli: A Reformed Theologian** (London, 1964), offers a concise biography, while the book by R. Walton, *Zwingli's Theocracy* (Toronto, 1968), splendidly discusses the actual situation in Zurich under the ecclesiastical leadership of Zwingli.

R. M. Kingdon, *Geneva and the Consolidation of the French Protestant Movement, 1564–1572* (Geneva, 1967), shows the interaction between Geneva and

France. J. T. McNeill, *The History and Character of Calvinism** (New York, 1954), goes far beyond the sixteenth century, but serves as a concise and well-written introduction. F. Wendel, *Origin and Development of Calvin's Religious Thought* (New York, 1964), combines a brief biography with an excellent exposition of Calvin's thought. W. Niesel, *The Theology of Calvin* (Philadelphia, 1956), is more traditional in its orientation, but useful. Of the several works that have sought to gauge the relationship between Calvin's thought and capitalism, we note K. Samuelson, *Religion and Economic Action* (New York, 1961). E. W. Monter, *Calvin's Geneva** (New York, 1967), summarizes the inner workings of Geneva during Calvin's activity. M. Walzer, *The Revolution of the Saints: A Study in Origins of Radical Politics** (Cambridge, Mass., 1965), explores the rise of the seventeenth century revolutionary ideology in England and has provocative comments on the sixteenth century scene as well.

J. Ridley, *John Knox* (Oxford, 1968), and the older work by E. Percy, *John Knox* (London, 1937), are good introductions to the life of the Scottish reformers, while G. Donaldson, *The Scottish Reformation* (New York, 1960), deals with the historical narrative.

There is not much on the course of the Reformation in the northern and eastern countries though the following may be noted: *The Cambridge History of Poland*, vol. 1 (New York, 1950); M. Roberts, *The Early Vasas: A History of Sweden* (Cambridge, 1968); C. Bergendoff, *Olavus Petri and the Ecclesiastical Transformation in Sweden* (Philadelphia, 1965); O. Garstein, *Rome and the Counter-Reformation in Scandinavia*, vol. 1 (Oslo, 1946).

The Catholic Reaction

THE LITERATURE ON THE COUNTER-REFORMATION or Catholic reform is extensive. Of the works available in English, we note the following: G. H. Tavard, "The Catholic Reform in the Sixteenth Century," *Church History* 26 (1957), is a good but by now somewhat outdated bibliographical survey; B. J. Kidd, *The Counter-Reformation* (London, 1953), is a bit pedestrian with its extensive marshaling of facts, dates, and names; E. M. Burns, *The Counter-Reformation* (Princeton, 1964); A. G. Dickens, *The Counter-Reformation** (New York, 1969), deals less with the Catholic side of things than with the entire age dominated by the Catholic resurgence; H. O. Evennett, *The Spirit of the Counter-Reformation** (Cambridge, 1968), is a superbly analytical work that explores the main themes and forces in the Catholic resurgence; P. Janelle, *The Catholic Reformation* (Milwaukee, 1949); H. Jedin, *History of the Council of Trent* (2 vols., London, 1953–58), covers, in masterly exposition and detail, the first two periods of the council; J. Brodrick, *St. Ignatius Loyola: The Pilgrim Years* (New York, 1956), is a good biography of the founder of the Jesuits.

Index

Acts, in England: Act for the Advancement of True Religion, 126; Act for the Dissolution of the Lesser Monasteries, 122; Act of Submission of the Clergy, 120; Act of Uniformity, 129, 130–31, 140; Dispensation Act, 120; Ecclesiastical Appointment Act, 120; First Act of Succession, 120; Restraint of Annates, 122; Six Articles Act, 125, 128; Supremacy Act, 120, 134, 139–40; Treasons Act, 120, 128, 140

Admonition to the Parliament, An (Field and Wilcox), 144

Adrian VI (pope), 49, 180, 183; and Sweden, 164

Albert of Hohenzollern (archbishop of Mainz), 14–16; and sale of indulgences, 5

Aleander (papal nuncio), 23, 25, 32, 38

Allen, William Cardinal, 205

Amboise, Peace of, 159

Ambrose of Milan, Saint, 213

Anabaptism, 61, 62–67, 69–70, 148, 169, 191, 193, 206; expansion of, 62–67; at Münster, 65

Andreae, Laurentius, 164

Angoulême, Marguerite d', 153

Anne of Cleves, 126

Anticlericalism, 49; in England, 116–17

Antitrinitarianism, 59, 61, 69–71, 169; in Poland, 172

Aquinas, Saint Thomas, 7; *Summa Theologica*, 18

Art, 196–97, 213

Astrology, 192

Augsburg, Confession of, 88, 138, 160; Decree of, 91; Diet of (1518), 17; (1530), 88–89, 171 181; (1547) 105–6; (1550) 106–7; (1555) 107

Austria, 202

Aylmer, John, *Harborough for Faithful Subjects, An*, 197

Barlow, William, *Dyaloge Descrybyng the Orygynall Ground of These Lutheran Faceyons, A*, 113

Barnabites, 184

Barnes, Robert, 112, 114, 126, 150

Basel, 76; and acceptance of Protestantism, 38, 93; Council of, 186

Batory, Stefan, 172

Beaton, David Cardinal, 166–67

Becket, Thomas à, 213

Believer's baptism, 61–62

Berne, 78; and acceptance of Protestantism, 38, 93

Beza, Theodore, 80; *Du droits des Magistrats sur les sujets*, 160

Bible, 62; and influence on radicals, 58; in the vernacular, 44, 112–13, 124, 126, 142

Biel, Gabriel, 186

Bilney, Thomas, 150

Biros, Matthias, 150

Bishop Cranmer's Recantacyons, 136

Bishop's Book, 120

Black Rubric, 131, 140

Blauer, Ambrosius, 106

Bohemian Brethren, 169

Boleyn, Anne, 115, 119, 137

Boniface VIII (pope), *Unam Sanctam*, 205

Book of Common Prayer, 129, 130

Bossuet, Jacques (bishop), *Histoire des variations des églises protestantes*, 190

Botticelli, *Birth of Venus*, 197; *Primavera*, 197

Bourbon family, 156–57

Brandi, Karl, 108

Brandon, Frances, 131

Bremen, and acceptance of Protestantism, 97

Brenz, Johann, 41, 106

Brethren of the Common Life, 7

Briçonnet, Bishop, 148

Briefe Discourse against the Outwarde Apparell and Ministring Garments of the Popishe Church, A, 143

Browne, Robert, *Treatise of Reformation without Tarying for Anie, A*, 145

Bucer, Martin, 32, 41, 98–99, 102, 106, 131, 144, 208

Bugenhagen, Johann, 41

Bullinger, Heinrich, 32, 137

Burckhardt, Jakob, 43, 181

Cajetan, Cardinal (papal legate), 17, 47; and examination of Luther at Augsburg, 18

Calvin, John, 46, 71–80, 155, 158, 167, 170, 205, 208, 210, 211, 214; and acceptance of Regensburg agreement, 99; birth, youth, and education of,